THE WORLD
AT WAR
— 1939-45 —

FOREWORD

To celebrate the turn of the century and the new millennium, **THE EVENTFUL CENTURY** series presents the vast panorama of the last hundred years – a century which has witnessed the transition from horse-drawn transport to space travel, and from the first telephones to the information superhighway.

THE EVENTFUL CENTURY chronicles epoch-making events like the outbreak of the two world wars, the Russian Revolution and the rise and fall of communism. But major events are only part of this glittering kaleidoscope. It also describes the everyday background – the way people lived, how they worked, what they ate and drank, how much they earned, the way they spent their leisure time, the books they read, and the crimes, scandals and unsolved mysteries that set them talking. Here are fads and crazes like the Hula-Hoop and Rubik's Cube . . . fashions like the New Look and the miniskirt . . . breakthroughs in entertainment, such as the birth of the movies . . . medical milestones such as the discovery of penicillin . . . and marvels of modern architecture and engineering.

THE WORLD AT WAR brings alive the drama of the Second World War. It was a war that saw the valour of 'the few', the pilots of RAF Fighter Command, as they fought off Hitler's Luftwaffe during the Battle of Britain. It also saw the unspeakable evil of the Holocaust, the Nazis' so-called Final Solution to the 'Jewish problem'. In clashes on a mammoth scale, armadas of tanks, Soviet and German, battled on the steppes around Kursk. In the chill waters of the North Atlantic, convoys of merchant ships ran the gauntlet of the U-boat menace. **THE WORLD AT WAR** tells the extraordinary story of how a former corporal gained control of Germany and pulled Europe into the abyss. France fell, and Britain stood alone, led by the indomitable Churchill. The war spread. Hitler invaded Russia; Japan attacked Pearl Harbor. Across the globe, the Axis powers (Germany, Italy and Japan) were pitted against the Allies (Britain and its Commonwealth and Empire, the USA and the Soviet Union). On D-Day, the Allies reinvaded north-western Europe; the Soviet juggernaut advanced from the east. In the Pacific, the Americans fought inch by bloody inch against the Japanese. Amid the ruins of Berlin, Hitler eventually committed suicide. It took the atomic bombing of Hiroshima and Nagasaki to bring Japan's resistance to an end.

THE WORLD
AT WAR

—— 1939-45 ——

Reader's
Digest

PUBLISHED BY
THE READER'S DIGEST ASSOCIATION LIMITED
LONDON NEW YORK SYDNEY MONTREAL

THE WORLD AT WAR
Edited and designed by Toucan Books Limited
Written by Duncan Anderson
Edited by Andrew Kerr-Jarrett
Designed by Bradbury and Williams
Picture research by Julie McMahon

FOR READER'S DIGEST
Series Editor Christine Noble
Editorial Assistant Caroline Boucher
Production Controller Byron Johnson

READER'S DIGEST GENERAL BOOKS
Editorial Director Cortina Butler
Art Director Nick Clark

First English Edition Copyright © 1998
The Reader's Digest Association Limited,
11 Westferry Circus, Canary Wharf,
London E14 4HE

Reprinted with amendments 1999

Copyright © 1998
Reader's Digest Association Far East Limited
Philippines copyright © 1998
Reader's Digest Association Far East Limited
All rights reserved

Printing and binding: Printer Industria Gráfica S.A.,
Barcelona
Separations: Litho Origination, London
Paper: Perigord-Condat, France

ISBN 0 276 42379 8

FRONT COVER
Background picture: US paras drop in to France,
June 1944, top; German panzers on their way to
France, May 1940, bottom.
From left to right: American commemorative postage
stamp; Adolf Hitler; a box of Spitfire matches; British
soldier with his son.

BACK COVER
Clockwise from top left: Afrika Korps soldier with
periscope binoculars; US battleship *Arizona* is hit at
Pearl Harbor; US soldier in the Ardennes, December
1944; British girls dancing with US airmen.
Page 3 (from left to right): Soviet Order of Victory
medal; newspaper vendor, September 3, 1939;
German aircraft spotter's handbook; British land
army girls.

Background pictures:
Page 15: Rescue workers at a bombed hospital,
London, October 1940
Page 37: US air attack on Japanese ships,
September 1942
Page 81: Ration books issued in Britain, May 1943
Page 105: Allied reconnaissance planes during the
invasion of France, June 1944.

CONTENTS

THE ROOTS OF WAR

NATIONALISM, ECONOMIC CRISIS AND A RUTHLESS GAMBLER IN CHARGE IN GERMANY MADE A FATAL BREW AS EUROPE LURCHED TOWARDS WAR

Why was the world at war again? In the early months of the conflict, German and British magazines both tried to answer the question. *Signal*, the Wehrmacht's fortnightly paper, explained that the present hostilities stemmed from the 'betrayal' of Germany in the aftermath of the 1914-18 war. At the Versailles peace negotiations the German delegation had been dominated by 'disloyal' Jews. Instead of standing up for the Fatherland they had capitulated to terms set by Anglo-French capitalist imperialists – also heavily Jewish, according to *Signal* – including crippling reparations, the loss of 25 per cent of German territory and other humiliations.

Since then the Germans had endured two nightmare periods. Between 1921 and 1924 attempts to pay the war reparations resulted in rampant inflation which ruined millions; savings were wiped out and the middle class was pauperised. Tens of thousands, especially children, died of malnutrition and related diseases, and thousands more, despairing, committed suicide. Most German businessmen were badly hit, but a minority – many, though not all, of them Jewish, with links to the City of London and Wall Street – prospered. Then, after a period of recovery, came the Great Depression of the 1930s. By 1932 a staggering 6 million Germans were out of work. Disciplined Communist militias – many of which were commanded, as it happened, by Jews – marched in the streets, intimidating the people *Signal* would have described as 'decent' Germans.

The redeemer comes

At this point, when all seemed lost, the redeemer of the German *Volk* had arisen . . . or so the *Signal* story went. Adolf Hitler, a wounded veteran of the trenches, leading the National Socialist German Workers' Party (NSDAP), had been working since 1920 to save Germany from international capitalism, Communism and the Jews. Laughed at,

despised, imprisoned, he and his movement had survived; in 1933, when all seemed darkest, President Paul von Hindenburg asked the former corporal to accept the chancellorship. From that moment on, all was well – in the *Signal* view of things. Communists soon found themselves in concentration camps learning to become decent Germans; increasingly effective legislation prevented Jewish exploitation of German workers and prohibited sexual intercourse between Jew and German.

The new chancellor had also set about re-uniting the ethnic German peoples of Europe into a Greater Reich – not just a reclamation of the old German frontiers of 1914. In March 1936 the Rhineland, the area on the left bank of the Rhine where the 'Versailles *Diktat*' had forbidden Germany to station troops, had welcomed remilitarisation. In April 1938 cheering crowds in the streets of Vienna celebrated the *Anschluss*, Austria's incorporation

> ### PURGING GENIUS
> Nazi anti-Semitism drove from Germany its most distinguished intellectuals and artists, including Einstein, Freud, the novelist Thomas Mann, film director Ernst Lubitsch, conductor Bruno Walter, theatrical producer Max Reinhardt and physiologist Otto Warburg.

into the Reich; so did the 'oppressed' ethnic Germans of Czechoslovakia's Sudetenland six months later. The German people of western Poland and Danzig (Gdansk) – territory Germany had been forced to give up at Versailles – had suffered appallingly, *Signal* informed its readers. The Poles, it said, had beaten and raped German women and massacred entire German villages. When Germany had finally moved to protect its *Volk*, Britain and France had declared war.

Two key issues underpinned *Signal*'s Nazi version of history: Jewish guilt and Germany's need for *lebensraum* – room to grow and develop. Both were rooted in racial theory. The world's economic problems stemmed, *Signal* argued, from a pernicious combination of international capitalism and international Communism. Both systems were dominated, it contended, by Jews. The world could not be at peace until someone had dealt with the problem of the Jews, a race at once supremely cunning and yet parasitic, inferior, almost subhuman, who had to be prevented from interbreeding with Aryans – white, preferably

DISABLED BY WAR   Disillusioned veterans in all the First World War combatant nations were often no longer able to pursue their former occupations. In Germany many proved ready recruits for Nazism.

with plans for world domination. He had exploited the trauma of the Great Depression in order to force his ultra-nationalist anti-Semitic party of uniformed bullyboys into power. Hitler, a deranged rabble-rousing guttersnipe, was tearing the heart out of German culture. Obsessed by the Jewish threat, the Nazis had forbidden the music of Gustav Mahler and Felix Mendelssohn, the poetry of Heinrich Heine and the art of Max Liebermann. Loyalty to the Fatherland counted for nothing if one was Jewish: the physicist James Franck (Iron Cross First Class) and the chemist Richard Willstatter (holder of the *Pour la Mérite*, Germany's highest award for bravery) were expelled along with the rest.

The right-wing tide

The British interpretation of recent events, like the German, was only partly right. Hitler's persecution of the Jews was unquestionably a fact, but the phenomenon that had resulted in his rise to the chancellorship could be observed in other European countries, many of which in 1930 harboured extremist parties

similar to the NSDAP. These had been formed at the end of the First World War, usually around a core of ex-servicemen. Embittered at finding their bravery repaid with unemployment and by the perceived humiliations of their nations, they took direct action. In Italy – on the victorious side in the First World War, but disappointed at its pickings afterwards – Benito Mussolini, a former corporal in the 11th Bersaglieri regiment (a corps of sharpshooters), founded the Fascist Party and seized power in a coup in 1922. Parties elsewhere tried to emulate his success.

The NSDAP, despite the image of its brown-shirted ultraradical militia, the *Sturmabteilungen* (SA), had not 'coshed' its way into power. Much more important had been the dire economic situation in the wake of the New York stock exchange crash of October 1929 and the subsequent collapse of Germany's largest banks. This had transformed the political landscape. The German middle classes had already experienced the hyperinflation of the early 20s; now they were once again on their knees. Even this economic extremity need not have catapulted the NSDAP into power. NSDAP support
continued on page 10

OPPOSITE VIEWS A Nazi election poster of 1932 appeals to women with husbands out of work. An English parody of the children's story, *Struwwelpeter*, ridicules Nazi pretensions.

Nordic, non-Jews. At the same time, a dynamic, growing people like the Germans could not survive cooped up in central Europe: they needed *lebensraum* to the east. It was morally wrong that these vast territories should be occupied by inferior Slavic peoples like the Poles and the Russians who lacked the intelligence, discipline and dynamism to develop them properly.

In Britain, meanwhile, the weekly *Picture Post* supplied its readers with a very different version of history. Hitler was not the saviour of an oppressed nation but an evil opportunist

GET GERMANY WORKING Nazis campaigning in Berlin (below left). By 1934 the building of the *autobahnen* (below) and other public works were easing unemployment.

WHO WAS HITLER?

No single individual in the 20th century has had a more devastating impact on the lives of millions of people than Adolf Hitler, so it is tempting to see him as a monster on a superhuman scale. In fact, Hitler was very ordinary. Every society in every age has Hitlers. In our own time we can see him muttering in bus queues or holding forth in pubs. In a time of defeat and despair he represented a 20th-century Everyman. The frustrated, the humiliated and the oppressed could (and some still can) see in Hitler's struggle a reflection of their own.

Like Shakespeare's Coriolanus, Hitler was a 'mummy's boy'. He was born on April 20, 1889, in the Austrian border town of Braunau am Inn, to Klara Poelzl, a devoutly Catholic peasant girl, the wife of Austrian customs official Alois Hitler. His school reports described him as 'moody, lazy and of unstable temperament', though he could work hard at what interested him. He filled up notebooks with sketches of landscapes and buildings. He showed talent, though not enough to gain entry to the Viennese Academy of Fine Arts, which rejected him three times. The death of his mother from cancer in December 1908, followed by the frustration of his artistic ambitions, embittered the young Hitler. He was to spend five years of 'misery and woe' as a bohemian artist in Vienna. It was during this period, one of great turmoil in the Habsburg Empire, that he came under the influence of extreme pan-German and anti-Semitic movements. By the time he left Vienna for Munich in 1913 he was convinced that all his problems had been caused by the Jewish domination of Vienna's professions. He also believed that one day all Germans in Europe – the *Volk* – had to be united in a single nation.

In August 1914 Hitler joined the 16th Bavarian Reserve Infantry Regiment, serving as a dispatch runner. He was a brave soldier, won the Iron Cross (First Class) and was twice wounded. He found the rear echelons packed with Jews – 'nearly every clerk was a Jew and every Jew was a clerk'. His resentment and dislike had hardened into paranoia by 1919. Everywhere Hitler looked the Jewish conspiracy was taking concrete form in the shape of Communists and revolutionaries such as Rosa Luxemburg in Berlin, Bela Kun in Budapest, and Trotsky, Kamenev and Zinoviev in Moscow. Still serving as a corporal, he was selected for special duties because of his skill as an orator. He was ordered to join and investigate the German Workers' Party, founded earlier in the year by Munich toolmaker Anton Drexler. He liked what he saw, changed its name to the National Socialist German Workers' Party and by 1921 was its chairman. Two years later, convinced that the Weimar republic was tottering to collapse, Hitler and the NSDAP took part in an abortive putsch to overthrow the government of Bavaria. Hitler's reward was a spell in prison, which he put to good use writing his biography and political manifesto *Mein Kampf.*

Hitler was a brilliant speaker. Starting slowly, quietly and methodically, he would appear a model of reasonable restraint as he enumerated wrongs and provocations, gradually raising the emotional tension until he burst forth in full fury. At a time when the impact of radio and the newsreel film were still little understood, he was a master of both media.

SPECTACLE OF POWER Young men doing labour service carry their spades military-style at a review by the Führer in 1937. Top left: Hitler's gun licence (*Waffen-Schein*) and his NSDAP membership card. Left: A photo taken around 1928 shows Hitler wearing Nazi uniform and a suitably brooding expression.

was patchy – strong in southern Germany and provincial towns, but weak in the Ruhr and big cities like Berlin and Hamburg. In the Reichstag elections of July 1932, it was Germany's ultrafair electoral system of proportional representation which boosted the NSDAP's representation to 288, making it the largest single party. The NSDAP then entered into coalition with some of the smaller nationalist parties, gaining an overall majority, and on January 30, 1933, Hitler accepted President von Hindenburg's offer of the chancellorship.

He moved fast to consolidate power. On the night of February 27, 1933, flames engulfed the Reichstag. Hermann Goering, a First World War air ace, now Hitler's most trusted lieutenant, was minister of the interior for Prussia. He tried, unsuccessfully, to save the burning building. Luckily for him, he found a scapegoat inside – a Dutchman called Marinus van der Lubbe, in reality only a drifter, whom Goering accused of Communism and homosexuality, and subsequently had executed. The Reichstag fire had far-reaching consequences. At Hitler's insistence Hindenburg issued emergency decrees outlawing the Communist Party and suspending free speech and a free press. On March 23

NOT FOR JEWS Anti-Jewish measures took a huge variety of forms, from the petty to the grotesque. Jews were forbidden to use this park bench, and a man's nose is measured to see if it fits Aryan dimensions. Bottom left: Members of the Hitler Youth burn banned books in Salzburg in 1938.

Hitler used his majority in the Reichstag (meeting in the Kroll Opera House in Berlin) to give himself dictatorial powers.

Well on the way to controlling the country, Hitler was not yet fully in command of his own party. On June 30, 1934, members of his protection squad, the *Schutzstaffel* (SS) – commanded by another trusted lieutenant, the former chicken farmer Heinrich Himmler – systematically murdered the leadership of the SA. This incident, dubbed the 'Night of the Long Knives' by the world's press, neutralised the left wing of the NSDAP. Hitler was to spend the rest of his life fearing a revenge attack by survivors, but the advantages far outweighed this consideration. German business interests like Krupp and Siemens, which had been wary of the NSDAP, now became firm supporters. A month later Hindenburg died and Hitler proposed uniting the posts of president and chancellor into the new post of Führer – a proposal that won overwhelming endorsement from the electorate.

THE FUTURE WAR

A controversial film opened in British cinemas in April 1936. *Things to Come* showed a world war lasting from 1940 to 1970 in an 'Everytown' clearly recognisable as London. Its opening sequence depicted a sudden end to Christmas revels in Piccadilly. Klaxon horns sounded, loudspeaker vans called on people to take cover, then high explosive and gas bombs rained down. In a few short minutes Everytown was reduced to a wasteland.

A BROKEN WORLD *Things to Come* gave a hideous glimpse of what war might bring.

As early as 1926 the Italian Giulio Douhet had asserted that future wars would be won by bombers hitting enemy transport systems, power supplies, factories and cities. By the late 1930s, newsreels from Spain, torn apart by civil war, and China, invaded by Japan, were confirming that vision. When Chamberlain took off for Munich in September 1938, he looked down on the 'rows and rows of frail houses' and was oppressed by a sense of their vulnerability. The Air Ministry calculated that the first air attack on Britain could produce 2 million casualties.

DICTATOR TO DICTATOR *Il Duce* visits the Führer in 1934. Hitler had been in power for just one year; Mussolini had ruled Italy for 12.

In a referendum 38 million voted in favour; only 4 million against. There was intimidation, but not as much as was claimed at the time by the foreign press, or, after 1945, by the Germans themselves. The fact was that in 1934 Hitler was very popular.

Rearmament

Hitler was a supreme opportunist, probing constantly to see where the opposition was weak, a gambler used to playing long odds for very high stakes. His conquests were not the result of a blueprint, but evolved as he saw the opportunity. The first step had been the restoration of Germany's military power. In October 1933 he formally denounced the disarmament clauses of the Versailles Treaty and withdrew from the League of Nations. France and Britain, the most powerful guarantors of the treaty, did nothing. Hitler's reintroduction of conscription on March 16, 1935, was taken as an indication that German industry was surging ahead with military production; in fact, France and Britain were also rearming rapidly, and in some areas, such as the production of tanks, heavy guns and warships, massively outclassed Germany. In public, Hitler cleverly stressed one aspect

of rearmament that he knew would give him a psychological advantage over his adversaries – the Luftwaffe. By 1935 he was claiming that his air force was stronger than the RAF; it was not, but many believed him.

On March 7, 1936, Hitler ordered two battalions into the Rhineland. France, appealing in vain for British support, did nothing. Four months later German Ju52 transport aircraft carried Moroccan troops led by the rebel Spanish general, Francisco Franco, from Melilla to southern Spain. This was the start of an increasing involvement in the Spanish Civil War, with Germany and Italy supporting Franco and the USSR supporting the left-wing Republican government. Britain and France opted for non-intervention. Hitler, wanting to test out his new Luftwaffe, ordered the formation of a 'volunteer' air force, the Condor Legion. This provided Franco's forces with invaluable air support; it also allowed German pilots and aircrew unrivalled opportunities for testing out new techniques. The Condor Legion's activities in Spain included the destruction of the Basque town of Guernica on April 25, 1937.

On November 5, 1937, Hitler met in secret with the heads of his armed forces and his

CONDOR SPIES A seaplane from the German Condor Legion taking part in a reconnaissance mission to the Balearic Islands in 1939. Luftwaffe 'volunteers' used the Spanish Civil War as a training ground for the greater conflict that inevitably lay ahead.

foreign minister, and outlined a programme for the systematic incorporation into the Reich of Austria and the substantial German minorities in Czechoslovakia and Poland. He believed this could be done without war, but if needs be he was prepared to risk conflict. The eventual objective – expansion into the western parts of the USSR – would definitely mean war, but he reckoned that this was at least five to six years distant.

The expanding Reich

In the second week of March 1938 columns of new panzer divisions wound through Bavaria towards the Austrian border. The advance almost degenerated into farce, and taught the Wehrmacht many hard lessons about armoured forces and logistics, which it would put to good effect 18 months later.

Austria was thus incorporated; next on Hitler's list were the ethnic Germans of Czechoslovakia's mountainous Sudetenland bordering Austria and Bavaria. Here, a home-grown Nazi movement under Konrad Henlein had been agitating to join the Reich since 1933. During the summer of 1938 tension grew steadily as German forces massed against its borders. The French premier, Edouard Daladier, was convinced that the time had come to confront Hitler, but not without British support. His British counterpart, Neville Chamberlain, was unwilling to expose the British people to the terrors of modern warfare, notably aerial bombardment, 'because of a quarrel in a faraway country between people of whom we know nothing'.

Chamberlain flew to Germany three times for meetings with Hitler and other European leaders, during which it was decided to cede the Sudetenland to Germany. He flew back to London after the third meeting at Munich with an agreement that both he and Hitler had signed, expressing their determination 'to continue our efforts to remove possible sources of difference and thus to contribute to assure the peace of Europe'. This was the paper that Chamberlain waved to the Press at Heston airport. Later that night, addressing a huge crowd from a window in 10 Downing Street, Chamberlain said: 'I believe it is peace for our time.'

The Munich agreement was popular throughout Europe, and Chamberlain was hailed as a peacemaker. But within Britain, criticism came from a small group of radical Conservatives who looked to Winston Churchill for leadership. On October 3, 1938, in a debate on Munich, Churchill addressed the House of Commons: 'We have sustained a great defeat without a war, the consequences of which will travel far with us . . .

PROUD TO BE GERMAN Swastikas and Nazi banners bedeck the streets of a Sudeten town. Local ethnic Germans welcomed incorporation into the Reich.

And do not suppose that this is the end. This is only the beginning of the reckoning.' But Churchill was still a voice crying in the wilderness. Since losing office when Labour won the 1929 election, he had seemed ever more 'yesterday's man', irresponsibly endangering the peace of Europe with provocative speeches denouncing the dictators. During the winter of 1938-9 Conservative Central Office resolved to be rid of him. At a meeting of his constituency association, a leading figure denounced him as a '65-year-old "has-been" who should be put out to pasture'. This was the prelude to two very nearly successful attempts to secure his deselection as a sitting Conservative MP.

By early 1939 Chamberlain was looking forward to a new era of peace in Europe. He would now consolidate and build on his achievement with Germany. The German *Kristallnacht* of November 9-11, 1938 (a pogrom sparked when a German embassy official in Paris was assassinated by Herschel Grynszpan, a young Polish Jew) outraged the Anglo-French and American press, but governments chose to regard it as an internal matter. They also turned a deaf ear to Hitler's outrageously anti-Semitic Reichstag speech of January 30, 1939, in which he implicitly threatened 'the annihilation of the Jewish race in Europe!' This speech was, they reasoned, intended for domestic consumption; it beggared belief that the leader of the third largest industrial economy on the planet could seriously entertain such views.

The nice old gentleman

But while Chamberlain and Daladier continued to view Hitler as a populist, vulgar version of Germany's 19th-century 'Iron Chancellor', Bismarck, Hitler viewed them with contempt. To Hitler, Chamberlain was 'that nice old gentleman', not the leader of the greatest empire the world had yet seen. Hitler was convinced that the French and British leaders were so supine that they would no longer interfere with his plans. In February 1939, trouble broke out between Czechs and Slovaks in the rump of Czechoslovakia. When the Czech president declared martial law Hitler saw yet another opportunity for expansion. On March 15, declaring that Germany could not sit by and watch Czechs ill-treat their Slovak neighbours, Hitler ordered his divisions into what was left of Czechoslovakia. The German troops met no

THE GUILTY MEN OF MUNICH

Were Chamberlain and Daladier justified in abandoning Czechoslovakia? The British public certainly thought so. In the three weeks after Munich, Chamberlain and his wife received more than 52 000 letters of congratulation. To defend the Munich agreement, Chamberlain's supporters have argued that Britain and France were not ready, that they had neither the armaments nor the national will. This is questionable: by sacrificing Czechoslovakia, Chamberlain and Daladier handed over substantial military assets to Hitler – for example, the Skoda works – making Germany much stronger than it would otherwise have been. The argument about national will is more substantial. The majority of British and French in September 1938 did not want to go to war, no more than the majority of Germans. But if Britain and France had backed Czechoslovakia in 1938, the USSR, too, would almost certainly have intervened on Prague's behalf. Had this happened Germany would have found itself from the outset in a war on two fronts. Perhaps Britain would not have been driven from the Continent and France would not have fallen. With Hitler in charge in Germany, war was inevitable. By delaying the inevitable Chamberlain and Daladier may have been guilty of making it more terrible for their peoples than it might otherwise have been.

VAIN HOPE **Chamberlain speaks to the Press at Heston airport on his return from Munich, and reads from his agreement with Hitler (above).**

resistance; in Bratislava, capital of Slovakia, they were greeted as liberators.

Chamberlain reacted much as Hitler had predicted; he initially thought that Hitler had cleared up a mess in central Europe. But for growing numbers of Conservative supporters this was the last straw. The foreign secretary, Lord Halifax, and Geoffrey Dawson, editor of *The Times*, warned Chamberlain that the national mood had changed and that the rank and file of the party might try to unseat him. That evening, Hitler listened in disbelief to a translation of Chamberlain's speech to the Commons. The 'nice old man' claimed that Hitler had betrayed him, and this was not going to happen again. Within days Britain and France had offered to guarantee the territorial integrity of Poland, Romania, Yugoslavia, Greece and Turkey, though it was far from clear how either country could ever honour these commitments.

Britain and France had thrown down the gauntlet. On April 1, 1939, Hitler responded, telling the Reichstag: 'The German Reich is in no sense prepared to tolerate intimidation permanently, or even a policy of encirclement.' For several weeks Ribbentrop, the German foreign minister, had been conducting negotiations with the Polish foreign minister, Colonel Josef Beck, on the status of Danzig and the Polish corridor – which Versailles had cut out of East Prussia and Pomerania in order to give Poland access to the sea. Beck, who had been charmingly evasive, eagerly seized on the Anglo-French offer and became obdurate. Summoning the German ambassador, Beck told him that any attempt to change the status quo of Danzig would be regarded as an act of aggression against Poland.

On April 3 Hitler issued a directive to his senior commanders in which he stated that

HORSES AGAINST PANZERS Polish cavalry manoeuvre near the German border in April 1939. They made an impressive spectacle, but would be no match for Hitler's mechanised forces in September that year.

the intolerable situation on Germany's eastern frontier necessitated force. Plan White, an attack on Poland, was scheduled for September 1. Hitler was sceptical that Chamberlain and Daladier would ever honour their pledges, but if they did he had to avoid a war on two fronts. In the following weeks his diplomats did the unthinkable; they entered into negotiations with the Soviet Union.

Chamberlain's policy, while now publicly opposed to appeasement, was designed to accommodate Germany at virtually any cost. There seemed to be no limit to the humiliation the British premier would accept in his desire for peace. Chamberlain made a secret offer of a 25 year defensive alliance with Germany which would include economic advantages for the Reich and the return by stages of Germany's colonies, lost at Versailles. Hitler soon decided the British were not genuine in their offer: it had clearly been thought out by little men, who saw it merely as a means to prevent him from reincorporating into the Reich the millions of Germans languishing in Polish-occupied territory. It was at this point that his diplomats in Moscow produced a coup; on August 23, Foreign Minister Joachim von Ribbentrop signed a Soviet-German non-aggression treaty with Soviet Foreign Minister Molotov. The way to the east was now open.

At 4.45 am on Friday, September 1, 1939, German forces in East Prussia and recently occupied Slovakia struck into the northern and southern flanks of Poland. While 2000 aircraft of the Luftwaffe reduced Polish airfields to rubble, 3000 German tanks supporting more than a million men, closed in an enormous pincer on Warsaw. The main Polish forces, deployed well to the west along their frontiers with Silesia and Pomerania, soon risked having their rear areas enveloped.

In London the next evening Chamberlain addressed a packed House of Commons. Members expected him to announce that he had issued an ultimatum; but incredibly he said that if the Germans would withdraw to their frontiers 'the way would be open to discussions between the German and Polish governments of the matters at issue between them, on the understanding that the settlement arrived at was one that safeguarded the

WAR – AT LAST The waiting is over. A paper seller shouts out the news on September 3, 1939.

vital interests of Poland and was secured by an international guarantee'.

As he sat down the House exploded in shocked surprise. The Labour deputy leader, Arthur Greenwood, was on his feet. 'Speak for Labour, Arthur', called his backbenchers. From the Conservative benches Churchill's friend, Leo Amery, shouted back: 'No. Speak for England, Arthur. Speak for England.' Greenwood rose to the occasion. 'I wonder,' he said, 'how long we are prepared to vacillate at a time when Britain and all that Britain stands for, and human civilisation, are in peril.'

When Chamberlain met his cabinet at 11 o'clock that evening, members left him in no doubt that the Commons would not accept a 'Polish Munich'. Hitler had pushed them too far. They all knew what would follow – devastating air attacks, millions of casualties, the destruction of the world they had known – but this was preferable to another deal with Hitler. At 9 o'clock the next morning the British ambassador in Berlin presented an ultimatum to Germany. When it expired at 11 am Chamberlain went on radio to announce that the British Empire and Germany were at war. Six hours later Daladier announced that France was also at war.

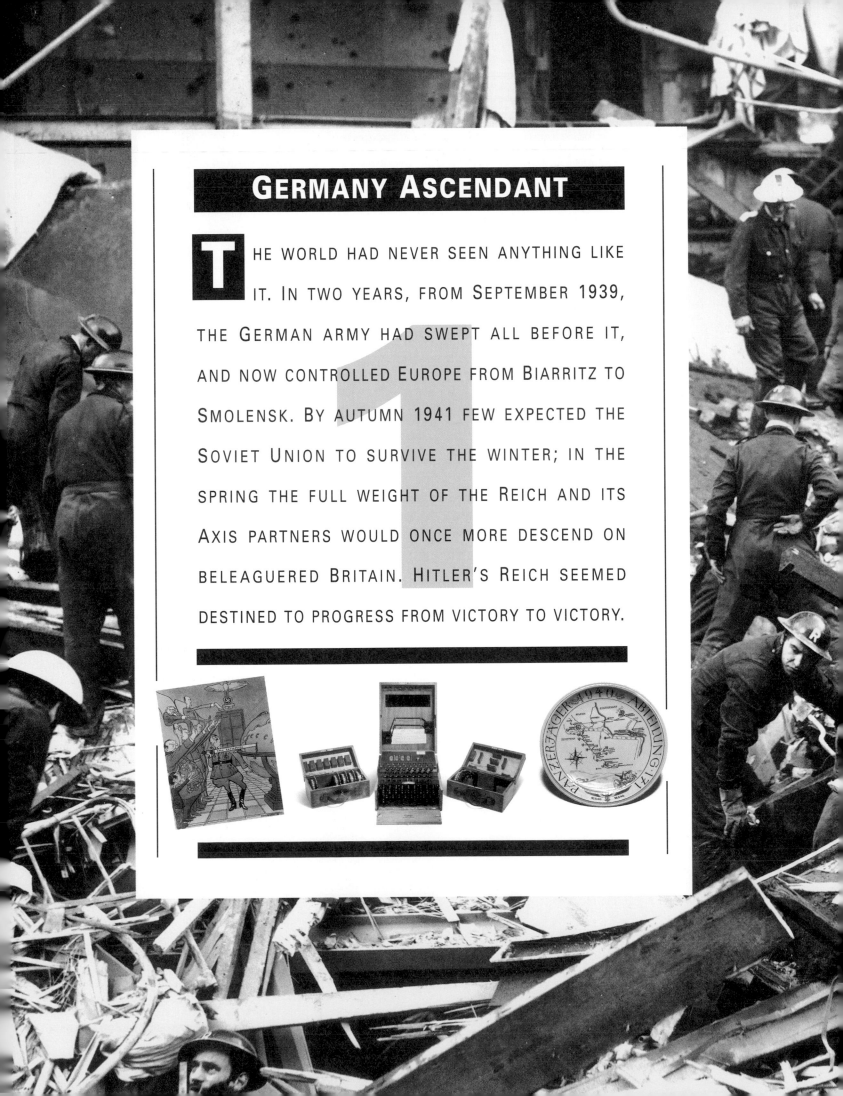

GERMANY ASCENDANT

THE WORLD HAD NEVER SEEN ANYTHING LIKE IT. IN TWO YEARS, FROM SEPTEMBER 1939, THE GERMAN ARMY HAD SWEPT ALL BEFORE IT, AND NOW CONTROLLED EUROPE FROM BIARRITZ TO SMOLENSK. BY AUTUMN 1941 FEW EXPECTED THE SOVIET UNION TO SURVIVE THE WINTER; IN THE SPRING THE FULL WEIGHT OF THE REICH AND ITS AXIS PARTNERS WOULD ONCE MORE DESCEND ON BELEAGUERED BRITAIN. HITLER'S REICH SEEMED DESTINED TO PROGRESS FROM VICTORY TO VICTORY.

THE FALL OF FRANCE

WAR CAME IN EARNEST FOR THE ALLIES IN MAY 1940, WHEN HITLER INVADED FRANCE, STRIKING HARDEST WHERE LEAST EXPECTED

General Maurice Gamelin, the 68-year-old French commander in chief, was a picture of satisfaction on May 10, 1940. He had just received a note from Prime Minister Paul Reynaud – a long-standing opponent of appeasement who had succeeded Daladier as premier in March that year – calling an end to a months-long feud. Reynaud had written: '*Mon général*, the battle is engaged, only one thing matters; to win it.' The Germans had at last attacked, and from exactly the direction Gamelin had predicted – through southern Holland and across the Flanders plain.

At 7 am Gamelin activated the French masterstroke. By midday, giant 27 ton Char B tanks of France's First Army Group, led by General Billotte, were crossing the Belgian frontier. Alongside the French moved the nine divisions of General Lord Gort's British Expeditionary Force (BEF), equipped with Matilda tanks, at that time the most heavily armoured tanks in the world. The Anglo-French armies advanced north through villages and towns filled with cheering Belgian civilians. Overhead circled squadrons of British and French fighters.

Neither the French nor the British had ever moved such large armoured forces at one time before. Some units had spent the eight months of the so-called 'Phoney War' in static positions along the French-Belgian border. When the order to move came, at least 40 per cent of British vehicles and even more French ones broke down, and large traffic jams developed. Nonetheless, the British entered Brussels that evening, while other units began to deploy along the River Dyle to the east to await the German thrust.

Gamelin was yet to realise it, but he had just advanced his most powerful formations into the greatest military trap ever devised. The German plan, nicknamed '*Sichelschnitt*' ('Sicklecut'), was audacious to the point of recklessness, the sort of scheme that a half-crazed corporal, used to gambling on long odds and winning, might come up with. Such a man was Adolf Hitler. His erratic flair coupled with the professional attention to detail of one of his staff officers, Erich von Manstein, shaped the plan in its final form.

The birth of Blitzkrieg

Hitler had turned his attention westward when the campaign in Poland ended in autumn 1939. The campaign in the east had ended much sooner than he or anyone else could have hoped; it was all over so quickly that American and British journalists referred to it as a '*Blitzkrieg*' ('lightning war'). Hitler

CHURCHILL BECOMES PRIME MINISTER

On May 7, 1940, the House of Commons debated the Norway campaign. Prime Minister Chamberlain was already ill with the still undiagnosed cancer which would kill him six months later, and did not perform well. The 77-year-old Lloyd George, in his last great speech, spoke against him; Churchill's friend, Leo Amery, used Cromwell's words when he dismissed the Long Parliament in 1653: 'Depart, I say, and let us have done with you. In the name of God go!' When the House divided Chamberlain had won, but more than 30 Conservatives had supported the Opposition. On May 9 Chamberlain offered the Labour leaders, Attlee and Greenwood, places in a coalition government, but they would not serve under him. Determined that the alternative should not be Churchill, Chamberlain chose the foreign secretary, Lord Halifax. He summoned Churchill and Halifax to Downing Street, pointed out that Halifax was the king's choice and asked Churchill if he would serve under him. Churchill was silent. The seconds dragged by until Halifax, a shy man, could stand it no longer. He stammered out that he was willing to serve under Churchill. It was not the result Chamberlain or the king had wanted. But so it was that Churchill became premier on May 10, 1940.

TOP BRASS In January 1940 Churchill, still only First Lord of the Admiralty, stands with (from left to right) Generals Ironside, Georges, Gamelin and Gort.

WARS IN THE SNOW: FINLAND AND NORWAY

THE FINNS BEAT OFF A SOVIET INVASION, BUT THE NORWEGIANS – FACING A BETTER EQUIPPED, MORE FORMIDABLE FOE IN THE GERMANS – COULD NOT HOLD OUT

Between November 1939 and March 1940 Finland, with a population of 3 million, inflicted a series of humiliating defeats on the 165-million-strong Soviet Union. In the end, it had to submit to Soviet demands, including the loss of large chunks of territory, but the rest of the country remained free. In a modern version of the David and Goliath story, the Finns gave Moscow a sufficiently bloody nose to make it think twice about outright occupation.

How did it happen? In October 1939, the USSR, convinced that war with Germany was inevitable, had extorted agreements from Latvia, Estonia and Lithuania to allow Soviet troops onto their soil. Finland refused and, under the command of its veteran soldier, Baron Carl Mannerheim, mobilised forces along its frontier. Stalin responded by mobilising 26 Soviet divisions. But the frontier, with its maze of forests and lakes, was less vulnerable than it seemed. The Soviets had banked on using frozen lakes as highways for men and tanks, but the lakes turned out to be death traps, swallowing masses of men and equipment. Those who made it to the far shores found only a handful of exit points where the Finns were waiting for them with machine guns. By February 1940 an infuriated Stalin had concentrated overwhelming forces in the Karelian Isthmus. By March 13, the exhausted Finns had suffered 68 000 casualties and finally agreed to the Soviet demands. Later in the war, in 1941, they tried to regain their lost territories by allying themselves with Germany. They failed and in 1944 Mannerheim, by now president, once more had to make peace with Moscow.

Germany's supplies of high-grade iron ore, nickel and chrome from northern Scandinavia lay at the heart of their Norwegian campaign of April and May 1940. France and Britain threatened to send an expeditionary force to the region; the commander of the German fleet, Grand Admiral Erich Raeder, noting this danger, planned a coup in Norway. On December 11, 1939, he took Vidkun Quisling, a pro-Nazi former Norwegian defence minister, to meet Hitler, and together they planned the German occupation of Denmark and Norway. Hitler gave the green light on April 5, 1940, in response to an announcement by Churchill, then First Lord of the Admiralty, that the Royal Navy was to begin mining Norwegian coastal waters.

Hitler and Raeder hoped that Denmark and Norway could be persuaded to capitulate without a fight. On Friday, April 5, the German legations in Oslo and Copenhagen showed members of the Norwegian and Danish governments a documentary film, *Baptism of Fire*, depicting the Luftwaffe's destruction of Warsaw. The message was clear: don't oppose Germany. In Denmark it worked. When German paratroopers landed at the Danish airbase of Ålborg on the morning of April 9 the garrison surrendered.

Norway was different. As five German naval task forces moved up the coast on the night of April 8/9, they collided with Royal Navy mine-laying patrols. In subsequent actions the Germans suffered heavy losses, but succeeded in most places in getting men ashore. Despite gale-force winds on April 9, their airborne operations were almost universally successful. The British and French response came too little and too late. Not until April 14 did the first 10 000 Anglo-French troops start landing in central Norway. They found themselves outflanked by the advancing Germans and were forced to withdraw. They achieved success only in the far north. Here a small force of German mountain troops held at bay 25 000 British, French, Polish and Norwegian soldiers, until sheer weight of numbers forced the Germans to withdraw. By this time, May 27, the situation in France was so desperate that the Allies themselves evacuated Narvik on June 8/9. Even this went wrong for the Allies: the German battle cruisers *Scharnhorst* and *Gneisenau* surprised the British aircraft carrier *Glorious*, sending her and her two escort destroyers to the bottom.

SNOW WARRIORS Despite the encumbrance of gas masks, ski-mounted Finnish soldiers manoeuvre nimbly in the snow during the 1939-40 war with the USSR. Their white garments made effective camouflage.

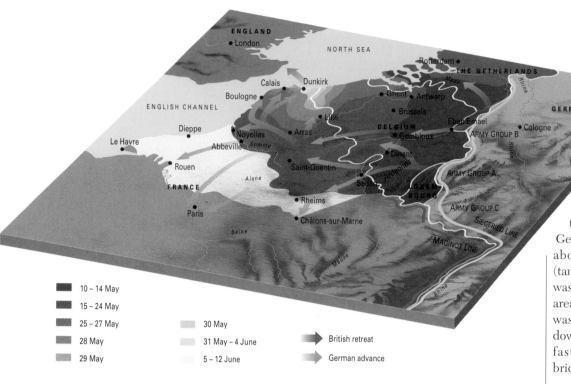

10 – 14 May	
15 – 24 May	
25 – 27 May	30 May
28 May	31 May – 4 June
29 May	5 – 12 June

→ British retreat

→ German advance

Line, a zone of underground forts which ran along the Franco-German border.

The main German thrust was aimed at a 70 mile (110 km) gap between Sedan in the south and the Flanders plain in the north. The troops given the task of passing through the gap – Army Group A, under General Gerd von Rundstedt – comprised about 90 per cent of Germany's panzer (tank) forces. In geographical terms the 'gap' was anything but a gap. The Ardennes, an area of heavily forested hills and mountains, was passable only by roads which twisted down river valleys, crossing and recrossing fast-flowing torrents on narrow stone bridges. Down these roads 3000 tanks had

UNSTOPPABLE ADVANCE Hitler's gamble in sending the bulk of his forces through the Ardennes paid off handsomely (map, above). German panzers emerging from the Ardennes in May 1940 (left). German troops in the Netherlands crossing the Maas on inflatable crafts following the destruction of a bridge (below). A plate (right) commemorates the German victory in France.

knew that an attack on France would be much more difficult and tried to avoid it. In early October 1939 he sent peace feelers to both France and Britain.

It was only when these were rejected that he determined to strike west, and the planning for *Case Gelb* (Plan Yellow) began. He was unhappy with earlier plans, which called for a massive thrust through Belgium and southern Holland – almost exactly the route the German armies had taken in 1914 when they failed to defeat France. In its final form the Hitler-Manstein plan turned the thrust through Belgium and Holland into a subsidiary attack, to be launched by a force designated Army Group B. This assault was designed to draw Billotte's First Army Group into Belgium. Well to the south another force, Army Group C, was to keep up pressure on French troops stationed on the Maginot

1939

| September 1939 Britain and France declare war on Germany | November 1939 USSR attacks Finland | April 1940 Germans invade Denmark and Norway | May 1940 Germans invade Low Countries and France | June 1940 Pétain signs an armistice with Germany |

FLATTENED The ruins of a church lend emphasis to the desolation of Rotterdam, razed by bombs and fire. People hurry along streets, like ants across an open wasteland.

just 48 hours to get to the River Meuse, and another 48 hours to cross it.

All depended on surprise – and surprise they achieved. On May 10, scores of Fiesler Storch light aircraft carried special forces of the *Grossdeutschland* Regiment down the valleys of the Ardennes to seize bridges and crossroads. Many lost their way, but enough landed to confuse Belgian and French cavalry posted there. Meanwhile, throughout May 10 and 11, Army Group A's panzers crawled undetected through the wooded hills.

In the Low Countries

Unaware of the danger closing on his right flank, Billotte concentrated on the situation to his front. The Dutch and Belgians were already in a poor state. German special forces, some disguised in Dutch uniforms, had seized many bridges across the Maas (the Dutch name for the Meuse) while paratroopers and airmobile forces had landed deep in the heart of 'Fortress Holland', the area between Amsterdam, Rotterdam and the Hague. In Belgium, a handful of gliderborne engineers landed on top of Eban Emael, the strongest fortress in Europe. Using shaped charges, which concentrated explosive power into a

white hot jet, they smashed through the reinforced concrete of the roof, and forced the surrender of 1200 surprised Belgian defenders. German troops were now flooding into Belgium, their spearheads moving towards the small city of Gembloux.

Around midday on May 12, French tanks smashed into the German spearhead, and for the next three days they clashed bloodily in the fields and woods north of Gembloux. Meanwhile, reports filtered through from the section of the Meuse adjacent to the Ardennes that forces there – mostly over-age reservists – were having difficulties. 'There seems to be a serious pinprick at Sedan', the French commander in chief in the northeast, General Georges, told Billotte.

On the morning of May 13, panzer assault forces reached the Meuse between Dinant and Sedan. The defenders poured a withering fire onto the river, killing hundreds of German assault troops as they tried to paddle across in rubber dinghies. At Sedan the battle was going well for the French when suddenly Stukas flew along the river. German mortar crews lobbed coloured flares across to mark the location of French positions; all day long Stukas screamed down, destroying position after position. The defenders' morale began to crack; by evening a rout was in progress.

During the night of May 13/14, German engineers worked furiously to erect pontoon bridges across the Meuse. By dawn tanks of

the panzer corps, led by Lt General Heinz Guderian, were streaming across. But the French commander in chief, General Gamelin, remained ignorant of the extent of the disaster. During the night of May 14/15 three powerful French armoured divisions moved towards the Meuse; these surely would remove the 'serious pinprick'. The problem was that they were moving on three separate axes. One division, on its way to attack a German bridgehead at Dinant, stopped at dawn on the 15th to refuel. The tanks were deployed over several acres of fields when the Germans arrived. Major General Erwin Rommel's 7th Panzer Division roared amongst them, shooting up the French tanks at point-blank range.

The other French formations fared no better. The tanks of the 2nd Armoured Division were moving by rail along the east bank of the Meuse when German panzers got between the trains. At Sedan the tanks of the third division had just begun detraining from flat-cars when Guderian's panzers arrived; it was not so much a battle as a walkover.

That evening Lt Colonel Guillaut, a staff officer Gamelin had sent to Sedan, reported

MARGARINE BLAZE

On May 14, 1940, Luftwaffe bombers hit central Rotterdam; the results exceeded their wildest expectations. A bomb hit a warehouse crammed with margarine and produced a fire that burned for days. The Dutch government claimed 30 000 dead, 30 times the real number, and capitulated.

back: 'The disorder of this Army is beyond description . . . The Army General Staff has lost its head. It no longer knows even where its divisions are.' At last the scales fell from Gamelin's eyes. He telephoned the French war minister, the former premier Daladier, who was dining with the US ambassador, William Bullitt. Bullitt heard Daladier exclaim: 'No! What you are telling me is not possible! You are mistaken! It's not possible!' As the full extent of the catastrophe sunk in, Daladier's shoulders sank and tears filled his eyes. He asked Gamelin: 'Then this means

GETTING OUT For the second time in the 20th century, families in northern France pile their belongings onto carts in a mad scramble to escape the invading *'Boche'*.

the destruction of the French Army?' 'Yes', replied the commander in chief.

Dawn on May 16 found Paris close to panic. The Germans had broken through at Sedan, and even now must be on their way to the capital. Churchill, who had been British prime minister for just six days, flew to Orly for a meeting with Reynaud and some members of his cabinet. This convinced him that nothing short of a miracle could save France. Back in London that night he ordered the drawing up of contingency plans for the evacuation of the BEF from the Continent.

Events moved with stunning rapidity. Breaking out from Sedan, Guderian's panzer

corps did not head for Paris, but instead swung north-west across the lines of communication of Billotte's First Army Group; it reached the Channel coast at Abbeville on May 20. French command and control disintegrated. General Georges suffered something like a nervous breakdown, as did many of his officers. Gamelin worked out a plan for a counterattack but just as he was about to implement it, he was sacked.

Now desperate, Reynaud turned to still-living symbols of France's heroic resistance in the Great War. The ambassador to Madrid, the 84-year-old hero of Verdun, Marshal

MASS EVACUATION British and French soldiers form a snaking line across the sands as they await evacuation at Dunkirk. Trawlers and pleasure craft (right) played a vital part in conveying soldiers across the Channel.

Pétain, was recalled to Paris to become vice-president of the council; 73-year-old General Maxime Weygand, now commander in chief in the Levant, was brought back to replace Gamelin. On May 21 Weygand flew to see Billotte. The two men agreed on a combined Anglo-French offensive. Unfortunately, Lord Gort was not present, as no one seemed to know the whereabouts of the BEF's headquarters. A confused situation degenerated into black farce when Billotte was killed later the same night in a car crash.

Dynamo from Dunkirk

Meanwhile, Guderian's panzers had captured Boulogne on May 24 and Calais on May 26. The Germans also struck at the Belgian army. King Leopold was not like Albert, the Belgian monarch of 1914; he had no intention of turning his country into a wasteland for France or Britain. The British Government learned on May 26 that he had decided to capitulate, and Churchill authorised Operation *Dynamo*, the evacuation of the BEF and other Allied forces through Dunkirk. Nobody remembered to tell the French about either decision.

THE GERMANS IN PARIS

The American William L. Shirer, Berlin correspondent for CBS, drove into Paris on June 17, 1940. It was a beautiful day, but nothing (thought Shirer, who knew Paris well) was as it should have been:

'First shock: the streets are utterly deserted, the shops closed, the shutters down tight over all the windows. It was the emptiness that got you... Now before us, the familiar view. The Place de la Concorde, the Seine, the Chambre des Députés, over which a giant Swastika flag flies ... Demaree [a friend] says the panic in Paris was indescribable. Everyone lost his head. The government gave no lead. People were told to scoot, and at least three million out of the five million in the city ran, ran without baggage, literally ran on their feet towards the south... The inhabitants are bitter at their government, which in the last days, from all I hear, completely collapsed. It even forgot to tell the people until too late that Paris would not be defended...'

June 18: 'Most of the German troops act like naive tourists, and this has proved a pleasant surprise to the Parisians. It seems funny, but every German soldier carries a camera. I saw them by the thousands to-day, photographing Notre-Dame, the Arc de Triomphe, the Invalides. Thousands of German soldiers congregate all day long at the Tomb of the Unknown Soldier, where the flame still burns under the Arc. They bare their blond heads and stand there gazing.'

On May 28 Paris was once again in shock. Leopold had announced the unconditional surrender of the Belgian Army. On the same day, Weygand realised that increased British shipping movements in and out of Dunkirk were, in fact, the evacuation of the BEF. The British press rubbed salt into the wound by creating the 'Miracle of Dunkirk', transforming the largest evacuation in history into something approaching a victory. In a purely logistic sense it was an impressive operation. In just eight days – May 28 to June 4 – 338 000 Allied soldiers were evacuated from the harbour and the open beaches. Most left in destroyers, but about 30 000 were carried across the Channel in hundreds of small boats, some of which had never before left the Thames.

But the British accounts left out the fact that the evacuation was possible only because of the sacrifice of the French rearguard, 40 000 of whom were taken prisoner. There was, too, some indirect help from the Germans. On May 26, Hitler had ordered a halt to the panzers' drive against the southern flank of the

Allied pocket so as to allow Goering's Luftwaffe to deliver the coup de grâce. A combination of bad weather and the operations of RAF fighters from bases in Kent meant that the Luftwaffe was unable to make good Goering's promises.

The British were going and would not be back for many months, certainly not before January 1941: Churchill made this clear on May 31, when he flew to Paris for another meeting with the French Government. Reynaud argued that the British could at least commit RAF Fighter Command to what he called the 'battle for France'. Churchill prevaricated. Four days later he addressed the House of Commons, concluding with the rousing lines: 'We shall fight them on the beaches . . . we shall never surrender.' To Reynaud's cabinet this seemed like hollow boasting. It was France that was fighting virtually alone.

The Germans resumed their offensive on June 5. Four days later panzers reached the Seine west of Paris. On June 10 Mussolini broadcast Italy's declaration of war on Britain and France. The next day Churchill again flew to meet the French Government, now based outside Orléans. The discussions verged on the poisonous. Weygand and Reynaud demanded

THE FÜHRER IN PARIS On June 28, 1940, Hitler made a three-hour visit to the French capital. According to Albert Speer, he was at heart like any other tourist. He told Speer: 'It was the dream of my life to be permitted to see Paris. I cannot say how happy I am to have that dream fulfilled today.'

the complete commitment of RAF Fighter Command to the battle for France. Churchill refused, and suggested instead that the French should prepare to conduct a guerrilla campaign within their country while carrying on the war from French North Africa. He was utterly sincere; within a few weeks he would be preparing to do much the same thing in London. But to the Frenchmen he was flying back to safety. Weygand and Pétain, convinced of the perfidy of all Anglo-Saxons, wanted an immediate armistice with the Germans, but Reynaud was against the idea.

On June 14, German forces entered Paris. Two days later, at the suggestion of General Charles de Gaulle in London, Churchill proposed the formation of an Anglo-French union. When this was not accepted by the French cabinet, Reynaud resigned. Pétain formed the new government and opened negotiations with Germany via the Spanish ambassador to France.

Newsreel film of Hitler waiting for the French to sign an armistice showed him stamping his left foot enthusiastically. British propagandists later looped the stills of the film to make it look as if Hitler was dancing a jig. He was not, but that was certainly the way he felt.

On June 21, shortly after Hitler had met the French delegation in the Forest of Compiègne in the same railway carriage in which the Armistice had been signed in 1918, Hitler ordered the carriage to be blown up.

BELEAGUERED ISLE

WITH THE ALLIES DRIVEN FROM THE CONTINENT, THE BATTLE SHIFTED TO THE AIR. BRITAIN'S SURVIVAL LAY WITH RAF FIGHTER COMMAND

On the evening of July 19, 1940, Hitler addressed the Reichstag: 'In this hour I feel it to be my duty . . . to appeal once more to reason and common sense in Great Britain . . . I consider myself in a position to make this appeal since I am not the vanquished begging favours, but the victor speaking in the name of reason.

NAZI REASON   In his 'Appeal to Reason' which was dropped over Britain, Hitler proclaimed that 'If the struggle continues it can only end in annihilation for one of us. Mr Churchill thinks it will be Germany. I know it will be Britain.'

I can see no reason why this war must go on.' On the night of August 1, the Luftwaffe flew over Britain dropping thousands of copies of the so-called 'Appeal to Reason'.

In Britain, some thought the government *should* enter into negotiations with Hitler. Lord Halifax, an ardent Chamberlain supporter, argued that Britain, now fighting against overwhelming odds, would not be dishonoured by an armistice. Most Britons, however, refused to acknowledge the hopelessness of the situation. The *Daily Mirror*, a left-wing paper, spat defiance: 'You need not worry about the men and women of Britain, Mr Churchill. The common people of the land have the courage. Give them arms and

give them leadership and they will not fail as they have been failed. But above all give them – LEADERSHIP.'

Leadership Britain now had. From the moment Churchill became prime minister there was not the slightest prospect of a compromise peace. To his enemies and critics the new leader was an unscrupulous opportunist and a drunken bully. But he was also a visionary romantic, a warrior-poet who wielded the English language like a sword. He believed in the special destiny of the English-speaking people with the same fervour that Hitler believed in the destiny of the Germanic *Volk*. But Churchill's concept of 'people' was inclusive – a club whose membership was based on shared cultural values rather than exclusive racial traits.

Hitler's propaganda chief, Dr Joseph Goebbels, declared that Churchill was an

DAD'S ARMY   In the face of possible invasion, the Local Defence Volunteers – later the Home Guard – were formed in Britain, chiefly to fight in the cities. Here, a unit lines up for an exercise. Right: A Home Guard sniper dressed in makeshift camouflage made from dyed sacking.

alcoholic who made his decisions roaring drunk. He was closer to the truth than he knew. Churchill was at times almost overwhelmed by 'black dog', the nickname he gave to his severe bouts of depression. He knew that Britain's survival – indeed, the survival of civilisation – was held by a slender thread. To keep himself going when 'rational and sensible' men would have thrown in the towel, he kept his bloodstream laced with a mixture of champagne and brandy.

Killing the invader

The British were in a mood of feisty defiance . . . but how could they put their words into actions? The army had been reduced to one trained division; there was also a Canadian

CONTROLLING AIR DEFENCES Women of the ATS (Auxiliary Territorial Service) track the progress of an attack in the control room of London's antiaircraft defences.

division and an Australian brigade. More help from the dominions was on the way and new armies were forming, but it would be the spring of 1941 before these could take the field. In the meantime, Germany could boast more than 100 divisions.

In the event of German landings in Britain, Churchill intended to draw the invading army into London and force it to fight street by street. He would command this battle from a bunker complex in Neasden, from where the entire city could be seen. They were brave plans, but the truth was that the Germans, had they landed, would almost certainly have crushed resistance very quickly.

Yet Britain did have some cards to play – just. In the face of intense political pressure during the battle for France, the head of RAF Fighter Command, Air Chief Marshal Hugh Dowding, had refused to commit more than a fraction of his slender resources to the conflict beyond the Channel. He had, in the process, made many enemies among Whitehall bureaucrats who were already plotting to retire him, but he had preserved Fighter Command. This now consisted of about 200 Spitfires and 400 Hurricanes, whose pilots were predominantly British, but by a bare majority. In addition to Canadians, New Zealanders, Australians, South Africans and Rhodesians, Dowding had Polish, Czech, Dutch, Belgian and French pilots. And there were enough American volunteers to form a special all-American unit, the Eagle Squadron.

The British had other cards, too. Fighter Command was too small to deal with the Luftwaffe, which now boasted more than 3000 aircraft, unless its squadrons knew when the enemy was coming and where. During the late 1930s mysterious masts had appeared all over southern and eastern England, the brainchild of a Scottish physicist, Robert Watson Watt. His Radio Detection and Ranging ('radar') would give British fighters an early warning of the direction and strength of an enemy attack. Members of an Observer Corps would confirm enemy numbers.

Other scientists had been at work in related fields. The physicist Professor Reginald Victor Jones had detected German navigational radio beams, which the Luftwaffe had codenamed *Knickebein* ('Crooked Leg') after a giant in German folk stories. Jones was now devising a way of using the world's first television transmitter, on top of the BBC building at Shepherd's Bush in London, to bend the beams and so misdirect German bombers. But Britain's greatest asset by far was the brilliant team at Bletchley Park in Buckinghamshire. Led by the Cambridge mathematician Alan Turing, some of the best brains in Britain – linguists, historians, philosophers – had reconstructed the German Enigma encoding machine. Aided by the world's first analog computer, a huge valve-powered apparatus nicknamed Colossus, they were reading some of Germany's top secret signals traffic.

Beating off Sea Lion

Bletchley Park knew Hitler was preparing to invade before most of his generals did. Turing's team decrypted signals ordering a concentration of barges from the Baltic, the Rhine and even the Danube on Calais, Boulogne and Dunkirk. This was the first indication that preparations for Operation *Sea Lion*, the projected invasion of Britain, were under way. By early September 1940 the Germans had more than 1200 craft in the Pas-de-Calais, with 20 divisions. But first the Luftwaffe had to win control of the air.

The first phase of this battle was fought from mid July to early August 1940 over the English Channel. It proved costly for Fighter Command's Spitfires and Hurricanes. The Me109 outclassed the Hurricane, and the Luftwaffe had four times as many of these fighters as the RAF had Spitfires. In addition, the RAF battle formation, a V-shape, proved to be inferior to the German 'Schwarm', a formation of two pairs. Fighter Command pilots soon appropriated the *Schwarm* – they called it the 'Finger Four' – and had some notable successes. On July 28, 1940, for example, the South African 'Sailor' Malan shot down Luftwaffe ace Werner Molders.

Dowding was thinking of letting the battle move inland, when the Germans did it for him. On August 12, 1940, *Schwarms* of Me110 fighter-bombers and

CODING MACHINE The German's Enigma machine had a typewriter-style keyboard connected to rotors, like those in the small boxes below. As the operator typed in the letters of the message, the rotors automatically converted them into code.

ANOTHER ONE DOWN Smoke trails from a Luftwaffe Heinkel bomber shot down over England by a Hurricane.

EAGLE SPIRITS Back from a mission in November 1940, US volunteers serving with RAF Fighter Command's Eagle Squadron report to a British intelligence officer.

Me109s struck at the south-east's radar network. They temporarily knocked out stations on the Isle of Wight and along the Kent coast. Over the next three weeks large formations of fighters and bombers swept in to attack the RAF's air bases. At RAF Manston in Kent, it was a massacre. An attack on August 24 reduced the airfield to a cratered moonscape. Officer and NCO casualties were heavy and the discipline and morale of some of the ground staff began to break down. Some were found up to three days later hiding in the wreckage.

Elsewhere, the story was more glorious. The heaviest fighting took place at RAF Biggin Hill in Kent, which covered the south-east approaches to London. Constant raids culminated in an all-out attack on August 30, which left 39 dead and 36 wounded. Even so, a single squadron of Spitfires managed to survive there until the Germans eventually turned their attention elsewhere. Throughout, officers and NCOs of the WAAF played key roles; a Military Medal went to Sergeant Joan Mortimer, for example, who identified and flagged unexploded bombs while the battle raged overhead.

Just before 4 o'clock on the afternoon of August 20 Churchill had risen in the House of Commons and paid tribute 'to the British airmen who, undaunted by odds, unwearied in their constant challenge and mortal danger, are turning the tide of world war by their prowess and by their devotion. Never in the field of human conflict was so much owed by so many to so few.' But despite the heroic sacrifices, it was clear by the end of the first week of September 1940 that the 'few' were becoming fewer. Over the period August 24 to September 6, Fighter Command lost 295 Hurricanes and Spitfires.

It was at this point that technology, in the form of Professor Jones' radio beams, intervened, albeit indirectly. On the night of August 24/25, German bombers flying along the *Knickebein* homing beam towards Shorts aircraft factory at Rochester became confused by British countermeasures of the kind devised by Jones. The bombers attempted to follow the Thames, missed Rochester, and dropped their bombs on central London and the West End. The following night 81 British bombers flew towards Berlin. Many lost their way and actual damage was slight, but bombs did fall in central Berlin. The psychological impact was enormous. Outraged, Hitler ordered the Luftwaffe to concentrate on all-out attacks on London.

London bombed

The Luftwaffe struck on the afternoon of Sunday, September 7, 1940. Squadron after squadron hit the East End. The warehouses of Surrey Docks, filled with rubber, paint and rum, were soon ablaze, as were 250 acres (100 ha) of timber stacked along the waterfront. The Luftwaffe came over again

AIMING FOR THE ENEMY The gunner in the nose of a Heinkel 111 bomber keeps his eyes open for enemy fighters. By 1940 the Heinkel, which had first seen service in the Spanish Civil War, was becoming outdated.

NIMBLE FIGHTERS: SPITFIRE VERSUS Me109

The development of the Luftwaffe's Me109 and the RAF's Spitfire was closely interrelated. Both traced their origins to 1934 as a response to Air Ministry and Luftwaffe calls for single-seat monoplane fighters. From then, teams in Germany (Willi Messerschmitt and Walter Rethel) and Britain (led by the Supermarine company's Reginald J. Mitchell) worked on their designs. The first production model of the Me, the Bf109, came off the production line in February 1937, a few weeks before the first production model of the Supermarine Spitfire Mk 1.

ACHTUNG! The Spitfire struck fear into Luftwaffe pilots.

They looked very different. The Spitfire's wings were longer, 36 ft 10 in (11.2 m) as opposed to 28 ft 4 in (8.7 m), and had a distinctive gull shape. Both, however, were of a similar length: 29 ft 11 in (9.1 m) for the Spitfire; 28 ft 4 in (8.7 m) for the Me109. The engines were of similar power and quality, each generating just over 1000 horsepower. The Spitfire, because of more effective streamlining, was marginally faster – 355 mph (570 km/h) against 342 mph (550 km/h). In armament, they differed markedly. The Spitfire carried eight machine guns; it was designed to close with the enemy and saw him to pieces. The Me109 carried two machine guns and two 20 mm cannon, which had a greater range than the Spitfire's machine guns, and were more effective in bringing down an enemy. In combat performance when flown by pilots equally well trained, there was little in it. But during the Battle of Britain the Me109 was usually at the extremity of its range, putting it at a disadvantage through the fear of running out of fuel.

during the night. By dawn of September 8, 448 Londoners were dead.

September 7 was the beginning of a sustained attack on London and other British cities, from Plymouth to Glasgow, Belfast to Hull, which was to continue almost unabated until May 16, 1941. There were certain benefits. The change in target away from the airfields gave Fighter Command time to recover and the predictability of the attacks allowed Dowding to concentrate his fighters in a way not possible before. For their part, the Germans were now convinced that they had whittled Fighter Command down to its last few squadrons. Accordingly, they made an all-out effort on Sunday, September 15.

They threw everything into the battle, which was fought mainly over south London. At the end of the day British papers were claiming 185 enemy aircraft downed for the loss of only 40 British fighters. The real totals – 56 Luftwaffe and 23 RAF – were much smaller, but it was still a great victory. By evening the morale of the Luftwaffe was beginning to break. Pilots had been told that the RAF was on its last legs; instead Britain seemed to have an inexhaustible supply of fighters. On September 17 Hitler ordered the indefinite postponement of *Sea Lion*.

No sooner was the battle won than Dowding's enemies in the Treasury and Air Ministry descended on him. Within weeks he was removed from Fighter Command and eventually forced into retirement.

The immediate danger of invasion was past, but for London and many other cities the worst period of the war was just beginning. Daylight bombing raids diminished as autumn approached, but large formations of German bombers now came over every night. Fortunately for the British, Goering made a major error in planning this campaign. Instead of delivering a limited number of devastating attacks on selected targets such as power stations, he ordered long processions of bombers to scatter bombs across wide areas of London during raids lasting ten hours or more. Such tactics meant that although people got little sleep, the ARP (Air Raid Precautions) personnel, firemen

A BED FOR DOLLY Mother, father, daughter and doll take shelter in Liverpool Street Underground station in November 1940. Most Londoners responded to the ordeal of the Blitz with defiant good humour.

BOMBS OVER LONDON Smoke rises from Docklands during an air raid, photographed from a German bomber. Right: A double-decker bus flipped over by a bomb. Right, below: A special tool devised for pulling down ceilings in bombed-out buildings.

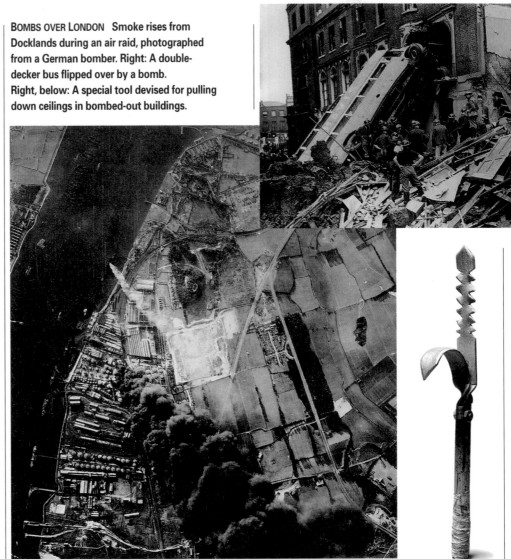

and ambulance services could usually deal with the damage and casualties.

During the Blitz – September 1940 to May 1941 – more than 40 000 British civilians were killed and about 46 000 seriously injured, about half in London. If Goering had hoped to bomb Britain into submission, however, he had miscalculated. The attacks caused enough death and damage to make people angry but not enough to cow them.

Churchill, meanwhile, had been oppressed throughout the winter by the thought that Hitler would resume preparations for invasion in the spring. Help from the Empire was making Britain stronger by the day, but it was almost impossible to imagine one day launching a major offensive without American assistance. The US ambassador in London, Joseph P. Kennedy, an Irish American who was violently anti-British, was doing his best to convince President Roosevelt that Britain was

finished. As it became clearer that the Battle of Britain had been won, Kennedy's influence waned. Roosevelt sent special advisors such as Harry Hopkins and Averell Harriman. In addition, during the Blitz, US newsmen like Quentin Reynolds and Ed Morrow produced live radio broadcasts from London which had the emotional quality of poetry.

Harriman and Morrow both fell in love with England and the English – literally so, for the prime minister's daughter-in-law, Pamela, made it her business to have affairs with both men. In March 1941 Roosevelt pushed through Congress a Lend Lease bill, which in effect underwrote the British war effort. Though the long-term effect was to make Britain an economic colony of the USA, it meant that the British had the resources to transform themselves into the most highly militarised warrior-state since Sparta. The beleaguered isles could now hit back.

COVENTRY BLITZED

ONE NIGHT OF INTENSIVE BOMBING BY THE LUFTWAFFE DEVASTATED THE MIDLANDS CITY, LEAVING MORE THAN 500 DEAD AND SOME 800 INJURED

BBC News, 1 pm, Friday, November 15, 1940: 'The City of Coventry was heavily attacked last night. Preliminary reports indicate that the number of casualties may be in the order of a thousand.' This is how the world learned of the destruction of Coventry. The previous evening 440 German bombers had dropped more than 1000 tons of high explosives on the Midlands cathedral city, killing 568 and seriously injuring 863. The British Ministry of Information made no attempt to hush up the disaster. By making all the details public they turned a German military victory into a potent piece of British propaganda.

The press campaign began on November 16. Across the front page of the *Birmingham Gazette* blazed the headline: 'COVENTRY OUR GUERNICA' – referring to the destruction during the Spanish Civil War of Guernica in the Basque country by German bombers. The

US press soon picked up the story with a poignant description of Coventry Cathedral's proud spire standing sentinel over a ruined city. As the campaign grew in intensity, so, too, did reports of the devastation. On November 30 the *Coventry Standard* claimed that at least 3000 had been killed, about five times the actual number.

The real devastation was bad enough. One report for the Home Secretary noted that the 'tremendous impact of the previous night had left people practically speechless in many cases'. The local authorities were unable to cope with the corpses, both their number and their condition. Instead mass funerals, the first ever held for air-raid victims, were organised. Mechanical diggers cut long trenches and on November 20 the first 172 were interred, followed three days later by another 250. It was only then that the work of rebuilding could begin. Coventry was a wasteland, without running water, gas or electricity. Field kitchens fed up to 20 000 people a day. Fortunately, the Germans did not return in strength until the spring of 1941. Had they done so earlier, observers believed, morale in the population might well have collapsed completely.

THE DUN COW STANDS Survivors go about their business in Coventry the day after the raid. Although the main part of the cathedral was smashed, its spire still probes skywards in the background.

DESERT RATS, DESERT FOX

SUCCESS SWUNG TO AND FRO IN NORTH AFRICA AS BRITISH EMPIRE TROOPS SLUGGED IT OUT WITH ROMMEL AND THE AFRIKA KORPS

Sir Francis Drake, who was reputed to be playing bowls when the Spanish Armada was sighted in the Channel, was not the last English officer to have his sport interrupted by bad news. On June 22, 1940, Britain's Commander in Chief Middle East, General Sir Archibald Wavell, was on the 15th tee of the Gezirah golf course in Cairo when an aide hurried up with a top secret telegram. Wavell read the announcement of the fall of France without flinching. He put the telegram in his pocket, said quietly, 'Well, I don't think I can do anything about it', and did the last two holes in a bogey.

Wavell's sang-froid was impressive given that his strategic position had suddenly become untenable. Britain and France had been at war with Italy for just 12 days; now the powerful French forces in North Africa, Lebanon and Syria were suddenly neutral, rather than allies. Wavell's forces numbered no more than 60 000 men. They faced two Italian armies, each with about 250 000 men, one on the Libyan-Egyptian border, the other in Ethiopia.

For Mussolini, by contrast, the collapse of France provided a stunning opportunity. Like Hitler in Germany, he had embarked on a programme of expansion in the mid 1930s; the Italians had invaded Ethiopia in 1935 and Albania in April 1939. Although *Il Duce* had entered into an offensive-defensive alliance with Hitler in May 1939 – the Axis agreement – he decided to remain neutral when war came in September 1939. By June 10, 1940, however, it seemed that France was finished and Britain would soon follow: he declared war on both countries.

Greek diversion

Events in Greece, which Mussolini invaded from Albania in late October 1940, overshadowed the first months of the North African campaign. On September 13, the Italians launched an attack from Libya into Egypt, advancing to Sidi Barrani before their supplies ran out. Then, on October 28, everything changed when Mussolini ordered the invasion of Greece. For the time being the Italians in Egypt would be on the defensive.

Wavell, too, was distracted by the Greek campaign. But by December 7, 1940, he was ready for a large-scale raid against the Italians at Sidi Barrani, having assembled the Army of the Nile – the 7th British Armoured Division, the 4th Indian Division and the 6th Australian Division – under General Richard O'Connor. Formed in 1938 as the Western Desert Force, the 7th Armoured Division – known as the Desert Rats after their symbol, a red jerboa – boasted unrivalled experience of desert conditions.

Moving across terrain the Italians considered impassable, the Desert Rats came up behind them on the night of December 9. Surprise was complete. Smashing their way into the southernmost camp, British tanks gunned down the Italian commander as he fired a machine gun from the mouth of his dugout still dressed in his pyjamas.

Over the next two months O'Connor's men pushed the Italians back and back. Then, early on the morning of February 4, Colonel Jock Campbell of the Royal Horse Artillery led a column of 2000 men in trucks and armoured vehicles deep into the Cyrenaican Desert. The going was bad, but speed all important. Shortly after dawn on February 5, Campbell reached the coast road just south of Beda Fomm. At 2.30 that afternoon the first retreating Italians appeared. A desperate 36 hour battle began as Campbell's column held the Italians, while the bulk of 7th Armoured Division moved through the desert to complete the

SPOILS OF VICTORY British soldiers pose astride captured Italian motorcycles in mid December 1940. The soldier in the centre is reading out a congratulatory telegram from Anthony Eden, secretary of state for war.

| June 1940 Italy declares war on Britain and France | July 1940 Sinking of French fleet at Mers El Kébir | September 1940 Italians invade Egypt | December 1940 Wavell counterattacks in North Africa | February 1941 Rommel and Afrika Korps arrive in North Africa | May 1941 Fall of Crete | July 1941 Operation *Battleaxe* | November 1941 British counterattack in North Africa |

SAND WARRIORS German soldiers advance across the Cyrenaican Desert. The arrival of the Afrika Korps in February 1941 dramatically shifted the balance of power in North Africa.

AT WAR WITH VICHY

On July 3, 1940, Britain effectively went to war with Vichy France – or the part of the French Empire (most of it) that adhered to Vichy. That evening shells screamed down onto the French fleet at Mers El Kébir, near Oran, France's main naval base in Algeria. By dusk three French battleships were on fire and sinking, and 1297 French sailors dead. The attack had been carried out by the Mediterranean Fleet in the best traditions of the Royal Navy: when threatened with invasion, Britain never allowed war-ships to remain in neutral hands, which might fall into enemy hands. The attack came only after the French had rejected ultimatums either to scuttle their ships or sail to British ports. On July 5 Vichy broke off diplomatic relations with Britain. At the same time, Vichy French warships stopped and then seized three British merchant ships, and on July 5 and 6 bombers made an ineffectual attack near Gibraltar.

DON'T FORGET
A Vichy poster sums up French resentment.

trap. It was the culminating point of an astonishing campaign in which 33 000 men advanced 1000 miles (1600 km), capturing 130 000 prisoners, 1300 guns and 400 tanks.

By now O'Connor's logistics were at breaking point, and it was the British who had to stay on the defensive. By February, Bletchley Park knew that Hitler had reluctantly decided to send troops to North Africa. The code-breakers also knew their commander's name: Lt General Erwin Rommel. He had been ordered to remain on the defensive, however, and the British position seemed secure.

Rommel confounded everyone. On March 31, 1941, he sent two Italian divisions against weak British and Indian forces around El Agheila, while he struck inland with his German battle groups to erupt onto the coast at Gazala. On April 6 General O'Connor and General Philip Neame drove out to recon-noitre. They became lost but, just before dusk, sighted and joined a column of trucks. It was only when they were in the midst of the convoy that they realised the trucks were German. In the dark the two British generals managed to keep up a pretence for some time, answering questions with 'ja' or 'nein' – but eventually they gave the wrong response.

In the aftermath of the disaster British intelligence was bitterly criticised, but they had read the signals correctly. What no one

yet realised was that Rommel did not necessarily obey orders. He was insubordinate, bloody-minded, erratic and, because no intelligence system could predict what he was going to do, he was successful. The British admiringly labelled him the 'Desert Fox'. Even the Führer realised he would need to offer suggestions rather than give orders.

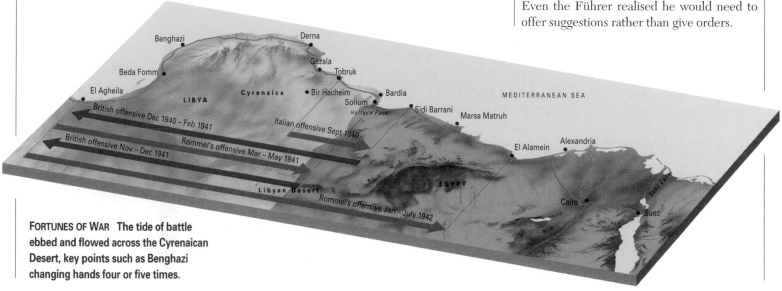

FORTUNES OF WAR The tide of battle ebbed and flowed across the Cyrenaican Desert, key points such as Benghazi changing hands four or five times.

SCREAMING INTO THE ATTACK An Italian illustration shows a scene of devastation as German Stukas dive-bomb British tanks in the Libyan Desert in November 1941.

In his haste to reach the Egyptian frontier Rommel had bypassed Tobruk. By April 10, however, an advance guard from the 15th Panzer Division had raced to the outskirts of the port, which they believed to be lightly defended. Instead, shells crashed down among them, killing the divisional commander, Major General Heinrich von Prittwitz und Gaffron. The Germans retired but attacked again on April 11, 12 and 13. On the last day 15th Panzer's tanks broke through the perimeter, only to find that enemy infantry emerged from dugouts after they had passed to shoot up German supporting infantry. Deep inside the enemy perimeter, the panzer commanders realised too late that they were in a trap.

The rats of Tobruk

The defenders were the fresh 9th Australian Division, commanded by Major General Leslie Morshead, a formidable First World War veteran. 'Australians, you are trapped like rats in Tobruk', sneered the turncoat broadcaster Lord Haw Haw. The Australians took the insult for a compliment and christened themselves 'The Rats of Tobruk'.

Rommel, now obsessed with Tobruk, tried to obliterate it. He concentrated the bulk of the Italian and German air force against the harbour, but at night convoys of destroyers and sloops continued to bring in supplies. The Australians supplemented the work of the 'Tobruk Ferry' by raiding Axis positions.

In mid May Wavell ordered the new commander of Western Desert Force, General Beresford-Pierse, to launch an attack towards Tobruk. The key to this lay on the Egyptian-Libyan border where the 600 ft (180 m) escarpment of the Libyan plateau comes close to the sea. Here, the coast road swings south up the escarpment, winding through Halfaya Pass; anyone who controls the pass controls movement between Libya and Egypt. The British captured it on May 15, but were pushed out again by a German counterattack. Wavell launched another attack, Operation *Battleaxe*, on July 15, but it ran slap into an ambush of German 88 mm batteries. The first salvo destroyed 12 Matildas, blowing their turrets into the air like corks popping from champagne bottles. By the end of the battle Halfaya had a new name – Hellfire Pass.

With the failure of Operation *Battleaxe*, Churchill removed Wavell to India. He had never liked the subtle and intelligent Wavell, who responded to the prime minister's bullying with withering irony. When Churchill hinted that Wavell's low casualty figures indicated that his army was not fighting, Wavell replied that 'a large butcher's bill' was not necessarily an indication of military success. From India came Claude Auchinleck, while General Alan Cunningham arrived to replace Beresford-Pierse.

TANK AND ANTITANK A British Crusader tank passes a burning German Mk IV Panzer during the advance to Tobruk in November 1941. Inset: German gunners wheel one of their 88 mm antitank guns into position.

THE WAR IN THE BALKANS

The Balkans spelled trouble for the Axis. In October 1940 Mussolini tried to invade Greece from Albania and got a trouncing; on November 4, the Greeks counterattacked, and within the month the Italians were in full retreat. Then came Yugoslavia: on March 25, 1941, Germany forced it into the Axis. Two days later, a coup in Belgrade replaced its pro-German government with a Serb-dominated body. This immediately denounced the Axis and began negotiations with Britain. Blind with fury, Hitler dispatched about a third of his armed forces to crush Yugoslavia and Greece, which had allowed British troops on its soil. On April 6 the Luftwaffe struck at Belgrade, destroying the small Yugoslav Air Force, while panzer columns swept across the Danube plain, encircling and annihilating the Yugoslav Army. An attack along Greece's mountainous roads should have been more difficult, but the Germans slipped through a gap between Greek forces in the west and British and Commonwealth troops in the east. Australian troops did hold them at Thermopylae for nearly a week in April 1941, but this merely covered the evacuation of the bulk of British forces.

Then, on April 29, 1941, Bletchley Park warned British high command that the Germans were preparing an air and sea assault on Crete. British, Greek and Commonwealth troops had almost three weeks to prepare, and Churchill was quietly confident. On land, where the defenders faced paratroopers and gliderborne forces on May 20, the Germans were easy targets and the defence was well dug in – yet within 48 hours it had crumbled. Poor morale explained much. Since Norway it seemed that the British Army had been involved in nothing but evacuations, and the troops no longer believed they could beat the Germans. For the Germans, Crete was a costly victory; 6200 paratroopers fell as casualties.

SOLDIERS OVER CRETE German parachutes in the sky above Heraklion on May 20, 1941. Though a success, the invasion was so costly that Hitler limited future airborne operations.

Throughout the autumn of 1941 reinforcements poured into Egypt. By November Auchinleck and Cunningham had seven divisions with 900 tanks, the largest force of armour Britain had yet assembled. This was formed into a new army, the Eighth. Cunningham's staff, meanwhile, had studied German methods and decided that the key to success was flexibility. The Germans achieved it by devolving command to the level of a *Kampfgruppe* or battle group; this encouraged junior officers to display initiative. Cunningham made the brigade group the main British fighting formation.

On November 18, 700 tanks of the Eighth Army began a long flanking movement around Axis positions at Sollum and headed towards Tobruk. By the next morning, however, the new devolved command style had allowed the brigades to spread out over a front of 50 miles (80 km). The Desert Fox could scarcely believe his luck. He destroyed first the isolated 7th Armoured Brigade, then the 5th South African Brigade. The battle fell to pieces in Cunningham's hands. He suffered a nervous breakdown and was evacuated to an Alexandria mental hospital.

Despite overwhelming British superiority it suddenly looked as though Rommel would win. On November 26, Auchinleck replaced Cunningham with General Neil Ritchie, at 44 the youngest general in the British Army. Auchinleck and Ritchie decided to fight a battle the British Army understood. The redoubtable 2nd New Zealand Division, led by Major General Bernard Freyberg VC and supported by massed artillery and air power, pushed up the coast towards Tobruk. Rommel was drawn into a battle of attrition which it was impossible for him to win. By early December his fuel situation was critical. On December 7, Rommel began a grudging withdrawal which was eventually to take Axis forces back to El Agheila.

STRIKING EAST

BARBAROSSA, HITLER'S ASSAULT TO THE EAST, LOOKED LIKE BEING A WALKOVER, BUT THE SOVIET UNION PROVED TO BE A RESILIENT FOE

German troops celebrated the fall of France with a triumphal march through Berlin on July 6, 1940; two weeks later staff officers at army high command (OKH) were poring over maps of eastern Europe. An invasion of the Soviet Union was the next move. Not only was France defeated and Britain

A SWORD TO THE HEART A Russian cartoon ridicules the Nazi top brass in their unanimous support of a dandified Hitler and his attack on the Soviet Union.

impotent, but the USSR's armed forces were in a sad state. Hitler's panzer supremo, Heinz Guderian, could hardly believe the contrast between the impressive Soviet manoeuvres he had witnessed in the mid 1930s at Kiev, and the ill-equipped troops he encountered in September 1939 at the demarcation line between German and Soviet-occupied Poland. The cowed, ignorant officers were, he said, 'incapable of going to the latrine without written permission from a political commissar'.

One man alone was responsible for the decline of the Soviet army: Joseph Stalin. In 1937-8, in a bloody purge, he had murdered more than 30 000 senior officers. The great tank armies that had so impressed Guderian were broken up, and the army reduced to a people's militia. However, the blitzkriegs in Poland and France produced panic among the Soviet leadership, and the winter of 1940-1 saw them desperately trying to put armoured formations back together again.

For his part, Stalin anticipated a German attack, but assumed that the driving force would be aristocratic Prussian generals rather than a radical man of the people like Adolf Hitler. By cooperating closely with Nazi Germany he hoped to delay any attack. Every day from October 1939 onwards, Soviet trains laden with grain, oil and metal ores helped to supply the German war effort. In September 1939 Stalin had ordered Soviet forces westwards into eastern Poland, and in June 1940 troops were sent to the newly occupied territories of the Baltic states and the Romanian province of Bessarabia (Moldovia). Surviving officers of the Soviet army knew that this policy was misguided; it meant abandoning long-prepared defensive positions on the Dnieper and Dvina rivers, but no one dared to tell Stalin he was wrong.

Directive 21

Führer Directive 21 of December 1940 – Operation *Barbarossa* – was the culmination of a summer and autumn of plans and war games. Reports from Abwehr (German military intelligence) showed the Soviets split into two more or less equal groupings by the Pripet (Poles'ye) Marshes, a swamp about the size of England, straddling eastern Poland and western Ukraine. The prognostications were almost too good to be true. Hitler decreed three thrusts: Army Group North, Army Group Centre and Army Group South. With the Soviets deployed so far forward and the Pripet Marshes making north-south communications difficult, OKH reckoned that it should take only six to eight weeks to destroy them. Germany deployed more than 3.3 million men, 3600 tanks and 2500 aircraft. It was the largest, most powerful army that, until then, had ever been assembled.

It caught the Soviets spectacularly unprepared. At 2.40 in the morning of June 21, 1941, Major General V.E. Klimovski, in eastern Poland, sent an urgent message to Moscow. He reported suspicious large-scale German movements. Back came the reply: 'Don't panic! The Boss knows all about it.'

A little over 24 hours later, at 3.15 am on June 22, the front from the Baltic to the Carpathians erupted. As dawn broke Stukas,

TRAIL OF DEVASTATION Soviet aircraft reduced to mangled wreckage by a German attack in 1941 (bottom), and a Soviet mortar crew in exhausted sleep after fighting all night (below).

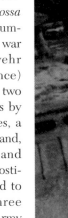

followed by Heinkels and Dorniers, swept over Soviet airfields. The Red Air Force had parked its machines wing tip to wing tip – there was no early warning system, no anti-air defence. By the end of the day the Germans had struck 66 Soviet airfields, and destroyed more than 2000 machines. Soviet ground forces fared no better; the advancing panzers overran vast parks of tanks, which the crews did not have time to bring into action.

The confusion went all the way to the top. The 'Boss' had received many warnings, particularly from British intelligence. But Stalin, deeply suspicious of the British, had chosen to ignore them. Faced with evidence that he had been wrong, he withdrew into denial. He drank himself into a stupor, from which he did not fully emerge until July 3.

Problems in the Ukraine

By this time the German offensive had developed in two different ways. To the north of the Pripet Marshes, Army Group North was making rapid progress and by July 18 would be only 80 miles (130 km) from Leningrad. Two large panzer groups attached to Army Group Centre – one commanded by General Hermann Hoth, the other by Guderian – closed in quick succession around Brest-Litovsk, Bialystok, Minsk and Smolensk.

Army Group South was doing less well. The problem was geographical: its attack was compressed into a relatively narrow gap

HESS: MYSTERY LANDING IN SCOTLAND

The news from Berlin on the evening of Monday, May 12, 1941, began with the startling announcement that the Deputy Führer, Rudolph Hess, had gone mad: he had vanished in an aircraft and was believed to have committed suicide. Then at 11.20 the same night came the news from Downing Street that Hess had landed by parachute in Scotland on Saturday night. He had broken his ankle and was now being interrogated. So began one of the most curious episodes of the Second World War, one that is still shrouded in secrecy.

Hess truly believed that as Deputy Führer he was uniquely placed to bring about peace between the British and Germans. He believed that the reins of government were in the hands of a warmongering clique, and that an appeal to the British Establishment, bypassing 'Churchill's gang', might yield results. On his first day in Scotland Hess persuaded his captors to bring the Duke of Hamilton, whom he had met briefly during the 1936 Berlin Olympics, to see him. Much to Churchill's displeasure, the duke subsequently held an interview with the king. It is still not known what was discussed, as this particular file in the Royal Archives at Windsor will remain closed until 2041.

Interviewed nine years later, Hess said: 'I couldn't stop this lunatic struggle between nations . . . but I'm glad that at least I tried.' At the time, however, he had less elevated motives. He needed to pull off a dramatic coup in order to secure his position as Hitler's heir, because rivals with more real power were closing in. These included Hermann Goering, commander in chief of the Luftwaffe as well as head of a gigantic industrial empire, the Hermann Goering Works; Heinrich Himmler, who since 1929 had headed Hitler's bodyguard, the *Schutzstaffel* (SS), which now amounted to a state within the state, controlling a huge security apparatus, its own industry, its own army (the Waffen SS) and a network of concentration camps; and the propaganda minister, Dr Joseph Goebbels, the most intelligent and highly educated of the senior Nazis (he had a doctorate from Heidelberg). In the end, it was Goebbels who became more and more important to Hitler. From the summer of 1944 onwards he was de facto Deputy Führer, and he was the only one of the senior Nazis to remain loyal, killing himself in the bunker on May 1, 1945, the day after his Führer's suicide. For his part, Hess was the only senior Nazi to survive. After the war he was imprisoned at Spandau in Berlin until 1987, when, at the age of 93, frail and blind, he managed to commit suicide by strangling himself with a length of electric flex.

by the Pripet Marshes to the north and the Carpathians to the south. In the middle of this gap it ran into the Soviets' most powerful forces, the 56 divisions of the Kiev Special Military District with 5580 tanks. Instead of a blitzkrieg, the advance of Army Group South became a slog of attrition.

By July 22 German command was locked in disagreement. Hoth and Guderian wanted

to press on to Moscow; Hitler, arguing that the Soviet armed forces were the real objective, not the capital, demanded that forces be diverted towards Leningrad and Kiev. The decision was by no means straightforward, and it took until August 21 for Hitler to exert his authority. Army Group Centre's panzers began a swing south and on September 12 linked up with forces in the Ukraine, thus

SOVIET CASUALTIES Advancing Germans pass Russian corpses during the offensive towards Kiev in September 1941. Below: A German guard looks out over a sea of Soviet prisoners, like this captured Russian Jew.

encircling Kiev. After six days of heavy fighting 600 000 Soviet troops surrendered, the largest number of prisoners ever taken, short of the general capitulation of a country.

It now seemed almost impossible for the Germans to lose. In the south their troops had finally occupied Kiev and were preparing to assault the eastern Ukraine, an industrial area vital to the Soviet war effort. In the centre they were less than 200 miles (320 km) from Moscow. Yet the Germans' situation was less commanding than it appeared. For instance, they had lost serious amounts of equipment. Of the Wehrmacht's 200 000 trucks, only a few had been made in Germany. The rest were either requisitioned from Czechoslovakia, the Netherlands, Belgium and France or bought from Italy, Sweden and Spain. With more than 200 different models to cater for, it proved hard to find spares to repair those that broke down.

Outside Germany, meanwhile, no action of Hitler's won such widespread approval as his invasion of the USSR. Pope Pius XII described Operation *Barbarossa* as 'high-minded gallantry in defence of the foundations of Christian culture'. Nor did Germany advance alone: it had, or would soon have, Finns, Romanians, Hungarians, Italians and Croats, while Franco's Spain sent the volunteer Blue Division. The SS, too, was raising volunteer divisions in occupied Europe: the Viking from Scandinavia, the Wallonie from Belgium and the Netherlands, the Charlemagne from France.

Moreover, in eastern Poland, the Baltic states and the Ukraine, German troops were hailed as liberators. The nightmare of Stalinist Communism was over, and nothing again would ever be as bad. After the

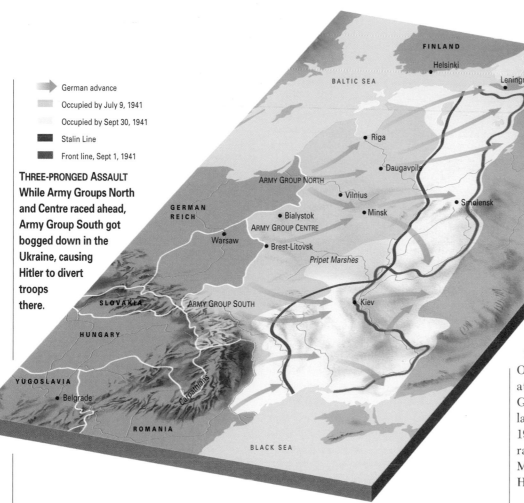

German advance

Occupied by July 9, 1941

Occupied by Sept 30, 1941

Stalin Line

Front line, Sept 1, 1941

FINLAND

Helsinki

BALTIC SEA

Leningrad

Riga

USSR

Daugavpils

ARMY GROUP NORTH

Moscow

Vilnius

Smolensk

GERMAN REICH

Minsk

Bialystok

ARMY GROUP CENTRE

Warsaw

Brest-Litovsk

Pripet Marshes

SLOVAKIA

ARMY GROUP SOUTH

Kiev

HUNGARY

Carpathians

YUGOSLAVIA

Belgrade

ROMANIA

BLACK SEA

THREE-PRONGED ASSAULT
While Army Groups North and Centre raced ahead, Army Group South got bogged down in the Ukraine, causing Hitler to divert troops there.

peoples of eastern Europe starved. By the autumn this apprehension was uniting them; the majority had no love for Stalin's system, but the alternative was even worse.

A typhoon in the east

Hitler ordered the launch of Operation *Typhoon*, a renewed assault on Moscow, for October 1, 1941. The generals were aghast at an attack so late in the season, but German meteorologists were sure that the late wet spring and blazing hot summer of 1941 betokened a late warm autumn. If the rains held off from mid to late October, Moscow was theirs. It was a gamble, but Hitler had been gambling all his life.

The attack began brilliantly. On October 2 Guderian's panzers reached Orel, south-west of Moscow. It fell so suddenly that the trams were still running; passengers waved to the

STUCK IN THE MUD The German advance into Russia became more and more difficult as wear and tear and then the weather took their toll of transport.

FATAL DIVERSION?

Could Hitler have defeated the USSR? The key to the Soviet Union was Moscow, hub of its political and communications networks, and on July 16, 1941, German troops were only 175 miles (280 km) away. Then in early August Hitler became obsessed with encircling the Soviet armies around Kiev. He had mistaken the enemy's army for its 'centre of gravity'. The Soviet Union could recover from losses around Kiev far easier than it would have recovered from the loss of Moscow.

---

eliminated to make way for Aryan colonisation. In the late summer of 1941, Wehrmacht forces began harvesting the Ukrainian and Belorussian grain crops for themselves. In villages all the way from the Baltic to the Black Sea, the conclusion was inescapable: that the new occupiers did not mind if the

German front-line forces passed through, the *Einsatzgruppen* arrived, and thousands of locals volunteered for service with Himmler's 'special action' squads. Anti-Semitism already had deep roots in eastern Europe, and by August 1941 the most extensive pogrom the region had ever seen was under way. Many of those who carried out a massacre of Jews at Vilnius, for instance, were Lithuanian collaborators.

If at this point Hitler had granted independence to the various subject peoples of the Soviet Union, the Communist apparatus would have collapsed. Nazi policy, however, was to treat them as *untermenschen* (sub-human creatures) who would themselves be

SPECIAL ACTION – EINSATZGRUPPEN

On Sunday, September 3, 1939, in Lower Silesia, thousands of young Polish men, their patriotism inflamed from the pulpit and their aggression stoked by post-Mass vodka, descended on their ethnic German neighbours and slaughtered an estimated 13 000 of them. Bringing 'to justice' those responsible for the 'Bloody Sunday' massacre was one of the first jobs of the Special Action Squads, or *Einsatzgruppen*. Across Poland the squads conducted brutal investigations, operating on the principle that it was better that 100 innocent Poles should die than that one guilty Pole should escape.

The *Einsatzgruppen* were expanded hugely for *Barbarossa,* tasked with the 'elimination of actual or potential opponents of German rule behind the front lines, particularly officers and members of the Communist Party'. Tens of thousands of Estonians,

MERCILESS MASSACRES German executioners deliver the fatal shots in the back of the head.

Lithuanians, Latvians and Ukrainians volunteered, many of whom had scores to settle with Communist Party apparatchiks. Inevitably, they also settled scores with other groups, including large numbers of Jews. By the start of 1942, the *Einsatzgruppen* had killed more than 500 000 Soviet citizens, the great majority of them Jews. Many of the massacres were witnessed by Wehrmacht personnel and letters of protest poured into Berlin. It was largely because of the messy, very public nature of these activities that the Nazi leadership decided on a different approach: the Final Solution.

panzers thinking they were Russians. Two weeks later Hoth's panzers took Kalinin, 100 miles (160 km) north-west of Moscow.

On October 6 Guderian noticed a change in the weather: that evening he felt the first showers of autumn. Panic gripped Moscow on October 15, following a report that two German tanks had reached a suburb. By October 18, however, rain was sheeting down. The rains had arrived exactly on time, heralding the *Rasputiza*, the 'time of mud'. As the roads disappeared into quagmires, the German advance slowed to a crawl.

On November 7, the 24th anniversary of the Revolution, Stalin addressed masses of Soviet infantry in Red Square. Speaking with renewed confidence, he proclaimed: 'The German invaders want a war of extermination against the peoples of the Soviet Union. Very well then! If they want a war of extermination, they shall have it!'

The USSR now looked in a better position than at any time since June 22. A large-scale evacuation of Soviet factories was under way along the railway system; more than 3000 had been moved to regions east of the Urals. Meanwhile, around Moscow the Soviets used the breathing space offered by the *Rasputiza* to increase their defences. The best news was from Tokyo, where the Soviet spy, Victor Sorge, had evidence that Japan was going to strike at the USA and the British and Dutch empires. With the Japanese tied up, Stalin could afford to relax his eastern defences. Trains trundled westwards, bringing Marshal Georgi Zhukov's 50 divisions to Moscow.

In mid November the temperature fell below zero. The ground froze and the *Rasputiza* was at an end. The panzers again moved

SABOTEURS AT WORK Soviet partisans lay the explosives to blow up a railway bridge in Belorussia. Resistance grew as the Germans alienated local populations.

forward, and by November 27 had battled their way to the Volga canal, a mere 18 miles (29 km) from the Kremlin. On December 1, Army Group Centre made an all-out attempt to take Moscow. On December 5 the advance ground to a halt. At dawn the next day, Zhukov's Siberian divisions crashed through the extended flanks of Army Group Centre. The German front fragmented, then reformed and held on in a series of mutually supporting positions through the winter of 1941-2.

During the winter the Wehrmacht requisitioned food, clothing and transport from the local population, thousands of whom died as a result; partisan bands began springing up across the occupied regions. In a moment of clarity, on December 6, Hitler turned to General Alfred Jodl, chief of his operations staff, and admitted that 'victory could no longer be achieved'. It was going to be a long war.

COLD FRONT A German unit photographed at Stara-Fomiwek, just 15 miles (25 km) outside Moscow, on December 16, 1941.

THE WAR WIDENS

ON DECEMBER 7, 1941, JAPAN ATTACKED THE US FLEET AT PEARL HARBOR AND TURNED A EUROPEAN WAR INTO A WORLD WAR. BY 1943, ONLY SEVEN NATIONS OUTSIDE SOUTH AMERICA REMAINED NEUTRAL. GERMAN U-BOATS OPERATED FROM JAVA, BRAZILIAN SOLDIERS FOUGHT IN ITALY, AND TIBETAN YAK HERDERS, CONSCRIPTED INTO THE SOVIET ARMY AND THEN, AS PRISONERS, INTO THE GERMAN, PREPARED TO DEFEND HITLER'S ATLANTIC WALL AGAINST FRENCH CANADIANS.

JAPAN HITS OUT

PEARL HARBOR, SINGAPORE, BATAAN – JAPAN'S ONSLAUGHT SEEMED UNSTOPPABLE, YET BY MID 1942 THE TIDE WAS TURNING

During the first week of December 1941 tension in Tokyo reached breaking point. Accusations of Western aggression dominated the headlines as newspapers traced the largest-ever movement of US and British personnel, aircraft and warships to South-east Asia and the Pacific. The US Commander in Chief Pacific, Admiral Husband E. Kimmel, now commanded more than 70 warships at Pearl Harbor, the US base on Oahu in the Hawaiian Islands. Another large US fleet had been assembled at Cavite and Subic Bay in the Philippines, while squadrons of the new B-17s, the world's most heavily armed long-range bombers, flew in to Philippine airfields.

Farther south, British reinforcements were pouring into Malaya and the fortress of Singapore. Singapore expected at any moment the arrival of a powerful British task force built around the battleship HMS *Prince of Wales* and the battle cruiser HMS *Repulse*. British

COMMANDERS IN CHIEF Admiral Yamamoto (left) and General Tojo (right) directed, respectively, Japan's naval and army strategy. Unfortunately for Japanese war aims, they had different agendas, which rarely supported one another and sometimes conflicted.

and Australian forces had also moved into the Dutch East Indies (Indonesia) where they garrisoned strategic locations.

Japan had been set on a collision course with the United States since 1937 when its policy of creeping expansion in China had turned into outright invasion. In December that year Japanese attacks on British and US gunboats on the Yangtse had prompted a proposal for an Anglo-American blockade of Japan. Japan's abject apology on Christmas Day 1937 forestalled that, but during the next 18 months the American press whipped up strong anti-Japanese sentiments.

In September 1940, the Japanese marched into northern Indochina and signed the Tripartite Pact – for mutual military and economic assistance – with Germany and Italy. Then, in early June 1941, they occupied the southern part of Indochina. This was a mistake as General Tojo, the war minister, was soon forced to admit. The Roosevelt administration responded by freezing all Japanese assets abroad, and Japan's international trade ground to a virtual standstill. By late 1941, despair pervaded Tokyo. Japan's envoys in the United States were trying to negotiate their way out of the mess, but for every concession they made, Washington made more demands. On November 26, the Japanese Imperial Council decided that war was now the only honourable course of action.

For its part, Japan's Navy had been planning for war since spring. The commander in chief, Admiral Yamamoto, knew America and the West well. By the spring of 1941 Japan had acquired naval parity with the USA, but for how long? Japan's five-year crash building programme, started in the mid 1930s, was being overtaken by a massive American programme started in July 1940. Yamamoto did not expect to gain victory over the USA. But he did hope to conquer

territory and to damage the USA sufficiently for a compromise peace to be negotiated some time in 1943.

The scale of the Japanese operation was extraordinary, and everything depended on surprise. Japan's forces were to embark on a series of virtually simultaneous attacks against the encircling Westerners across a quarter of the planet, from Hawaii to the Gulf of Thailand. Both the Americans and the British could read Japanese codes, but they were not exchanging information, and thus an overview of the Japanese intentions never emerged.

Tora! Tora! Tora!

At 7.49 am on Sunday, December 7, Commander Mitsuo Fuchida of the Japanese Navy's Air Service spotted Pearl Harbor through a gap in dense cloud banks. US battleships lay anchored in inviting lines off 'Battleship Row' in the centre of the nearly landlocked anchorage. He realised that, almost miraculously, the Americans were still unaware of his approach. '*Tora! Tora! Tora!* (Tiger! Tiger! Tiger!)' he radioed back to the

STRIKE FROM THE BLUE The mighty US battleship *Arizona* founders after being struck by Japanese torpedoes. Inset: Flames and smoke billow from Pearl Harbor's naval air base, as shattered aircraft litter its runway.

carrier task force – then 200 miles (320 km) north of Hawaii – to indicate that surprise had been achieved. He slid back the canopy of his cockpit and fired a blue flare, the attack signal. Seeing this Lt Commander Shigeharu Murata, leading 40 Kate torpedo-bombers, radioed them to dive. The pilots brought their Kates down to 100 ft (30 m), turned towards the outer line of battleships and at a painfully slow 150 mph (240 km/h) flew straight for them, releasing their torpedoes

literally at the last minute. Some torpedoes plunged into the mud at the bottom of the harbour, but most struck home, into the hulls of USS *Nevada*, *Arizona*, *West Virginia*, *Oklahoma* and *California*. *West Virginia* was hit simultaneously by a torpedo from a Japanese midget submarine, one of a flotilla of six that tried to penetrate Pearl Harbor.

Meanwhile, Val dive-bombers screamed down on the inner row of battleships, dropping armour-piercing naval shells onto the

ABANDON SHIP The crew of the sinking HMS *Prince of Wales* scramble for the lifeboats. In all, 840 men were drowned on December 10, 1941; 1285 survived.

Maryland, *Tennessee* and *Pennsylvania*. Zero fighters, under the command of Lieutenant Shiga, swept down on American airfields, machine-gunning parks of aircraft invitingly massed in the centre of runways. At 8.55 am another 170 Japanese aircraft swept down; by 9.30 am it was all over. From the sea Oahu looked like an erupting volcano. The smoke from hundreds of fires had thickened into a gigantic pall which rose into the stratosphere. The devastation was unprecedented. For the loss of fewer than 30 aircraft, the Japanese had inflicted staggering casualties on the Americans: more than 4700 dead and wounded; eight battleships, three cruisers and three destroyers, either sunk or badly damaged; and 400 out of a total of 480 aircraft either destroyed or rendered unserviceable.

Blow after blow

Ten hours after the attack on Pearl Harbor, 200 Japanese aircraft based on Formosa (Taiwan) flew over Clark Field on the Philippine island of Luzon, the largest US air base in the world. They saw runways neatly parked with the most modern bombers and fighters in the USAAF, B-17s and P-40s. By 1 pm Japanese attacks on Clark and other Luzon airfields had destroyed 105 of the island's

300 American warplanes for the loss of only seven of their own.

Across the South China Sea, the British, too, staggered under repeated blows. They had no excuse since, expecting an attack, they had been in a state of high alert for a week. Japanese bombers destroyed two British air bases in northern Malaya, but the worst disaster occurred at sea. Admiral Tom Phillips, receiving reports of Japanese landings on the east coast of Malaya, took Force Z – HMS *Prince of Wales*, *Repulse* and four destroyers – out of Singapore to intercept them. Japanese bombers from southern Indochina, flying at the very limit of their range, located the ships shortly before 10 am on December 10. This was the first time that large warships, fully alert and armed, moving at speed in open sea with plenty of room to manoeuvre, had been attacked by aircraft. The ships, cutting

HEARTBREAK AND SURRENDER A Malayan mother grieves over her son, killed during the Japanese attack on Singapore. An Italian illustration shows blindfolded British officers being led to the surrender negotiations.

through the water at more than 30 knots (55 km/h), put up a murderous wall of anti-aircraft fire and dodged torpedo after torpedo. Then the Japanese changed tactics. Coming simultaneously from both port and starboard, the bombers made it impossible for the ships to manoeuvre. A torpedo hit the *Prince of Wales* in her rudder and she veered into a drunken circle. Shortly afterwards Japanese bombers hit the *Repulse* from both sides, and she capsized. Churchill was horrified when he heard the news in London. 'In all the war', he later wrote, 'I never received a more direct shock.'

The Japanese continued to sweep all before them. Hong Kong surrendered on December 25. In the Philippines, where the American commander was General Douglas

OILFIELD ADVANCE   Japanese infantry crawl into the attack around Burma's Yenangyuang oilfields. In the end, the British fired the wells rather than let them fall into Japanese hands.

MacArthur, an army landed on the Lingayen Gulf coast on December 22. MacArthur's forces outnumbered the Japanese at least two to one, but after a desultory exchange the majority of the Filipinos fled. In Malaya, an army commanded by General Yamashita proved unstoppable. Riding on bicycles, the Japanese raced south, reaching the Straits of Johore separating Singapore from the mainland on January 31, 1942.

Singapore was not yet lost. Unfortunately for the British, however, its commander, General Arthur Percival, though one of the brightest officers in the British Army, was no leader of men. As disaster followed disaster

AMERICA FIRST

America First was the largest of the isolationist organisations that sprang up in the USA after the fall of France, its membership standing at 800 000 on the eve of Pearl Harbor. Its line was well expressed by the aviator Charles A. Lindbergh, addressing a rally in Des Moines, Iowa, in September 1941. He warned about the enemy within – the Jews who were 'agitators for war'. If the Jews succeeded in dragging America into war, he asserted, they would be held responsible because of 'their large ownership and influence in our motion pictures, our press, and our government'. America First was not powerful enough to prevent Roosevelt from progressively aiding Britain and then the USSR. Until Pearl Harbor, however, it did impose a brake on more direct forms of intervention.

Percival disappeared into the bowels of Fort Canning, an underground bunker complex from where he tried to control the battle as though it were a staff college exercise.

Percival had some 83 000 men, as opposed to Yamashita's 30 000, and more than 200 guns. Yamashita's logistics were at breaking point. In addition, he had quarrelled violently with Major General Nishimura, commander of the Imperial Guards Division. Yamashita had told Nishimura to go to hell along with his division, thus reducing his attacking force by a third.

Yamashita's troops crossed the straits onto the north-west shore of Singapore on the night of February 8/9. The initial waves suffered heavy casualties, until newly arrived Australian reinforcements began to break and run. By dawn the Japanese were across in strength. Over the next five days discipline in Singapore almost collapsed as mobs fought to get onto the last ships to leave. On Saturday, February 14, Percival surrendered to Yamashita in the greatest humiliation ever suffered by British arms.

Breaking the chain

Disaster had also overwhelmed the British in Burma. Lt General Shojiro Iida's 15th Army had invaded from Thailand on January 12. The British tried to rush reinforcements into Rangoon, but the Australian government thwarted this when it countermanded an order from Churchill dispatching the 7th Australian Division to Burma. A new commander was sent out, Harold Alexander, who managed to extricate British and Indian forces from Rangoon on March 7. Alexander

ALLIES OF A KIND: CHURCHILL AND FDR

One of many myths to emerge from the Second World War was of a close personal bond between the British prime minister and the US president. In fact, the relationship was very one-sided – Churchill pursued, while Roosevelt kept his distance. Both men came from the aristocracy of their respective countries, but were different in tastes and outlook. Crippled by polio while still a young man, Roosevelt was forced to keep regular hours and follow an ascetic regime. By contrast, Churchill was a bon viveur, fond of good food, good brandy, good cigars and late hours. The two men liked each other and there was mutual respect – but little more.

Churchill began wooing Roosevelt when he became First Lord of the Admiralty in September 1939. Many notes and telegrams, apparently dashed off carelessly, were the products of several drafts, designed to appeal to the American's emotions as well as his reason. On hearing the news of Pearl Harbor, Churchill felt overwhelming relief and acted quickly to build on the relationship. From mid December 1941 to mid January 1942, he virtually moved into the White House where the two leaders conferred in the oddest of places, on one occasion in a bathroom while Churchill was drying himself after a shower. When, inevitably, the towel slipped from his waist, the prime minister said with mock solemnity: 'You see, Mr President, I have nothing to hide.'

By the Tehran conference of November 1943, the first signs were emerging that the USA no longer regarded Britain as particularly important. The warmth and charm that Roosevelt had once displayed to Churchill were now offered to Stalin, and the British prime minister felt hurt and rejected. During the last 18 months of their relationship (Roosevelt died on April 12, 1945), Churchill felt increasingly cut out of important decisions.

ATLANTIC LEADERS   Roosevelt and Churchill during the Atlantic Conference in August 1941.

JAPAN'S WAR ON CHINA

THE FIGHTING WAS BRUTAL AND STUDDED WITH ATROCITIES, BUT IN THE END IT WAS THE SHEER SIZE OF CHINA THAT DEFEATED THE JAPANESE

European and US residents of Shanghai's International Concession enjoyed a ring-side seat in August 1937 as battle raged in the city between Chiang Kai-shek's Guomindang (Nationalist) army and invading Japanese. From their luxury hotels they photographed and filmed the ebb and flow of the fighting, particularly the bombing raids along the waterfront, first on Chinese, then Japanese warships. The Guomindang fought well. It was not until December, after suffering 80 000 casualties, that the Japanese managed to break the Chinese front. Frustrated and humiliated, they surged up the Yangtse to Nanjing (Nanking), the Guomindang capital. Japanese discipline had already begun to collapse. That December in Nanjing they descended into an orgy of murder, rape and looting on a scale unparalleled in the 20th century. Drunken soldiers heaped corpses into huge piles in the streets, poured petrol on them and attempted to burn them, but in the December drizzle ignition proved difficult. Most of the piles were only partly burnt, and some of those burnt were still alive. The Japanese eventually admitted to 20 000 civilian deaths, but the Chinese claimed 200 000. What was so extraordinary about the 'Rape of Nanjing' was that it was carried out in front of newsmen from America, Britain and Germany. Japan was not able to stop the Westerners wandering around the battlefields, taking pictures. It was a phenomenon that would become common later in the century.

What the journalists witnessed was the culmination of 40 years of expansionist activity by elements of the Japanese Army. Not all the army had favoured expansion into China (there was one faction that wanted to expand into Siberia) but the dominant military faction, the *Tosei Ha* or Control Faction, was fanatically committed to it. The navy disagreed profoundly, and pursued its own policy of penetrating South-east Asia in order to secure supplies of strategic raw materials like bauxite, tin, rubber and oil – all of which Japan had to import.

It was easy enough to start a war in China, but Japan's army soon discovered that it was less easy to finish it. By 1938 the Japanese had driven Guomindang forces west towards Chongqing, where Chiang Kai-shek set up a new government. In the meantime guerrilla activity, orchestrated by Mao Zedong's Communist Party, was breaking out in supposedly secure Japanese-held territory. The Japanese tried to win the 'hearts and minds' of the Chinese by establishing a puppet government in 1940 under a Guomindang defector, Wang Ching-wei. But any illusion of stability this created was destroyed by a mass uprising in northern China in autumn 1940, inspired by Mao Zedong. The Japanese Army responded with the Three All Policy – kill all, burn all, take all – which was effectively a policy of genocide, and bound to fail when applied in China with its vast population. The Three All Policy only made the situation worse. By 1941 Japan was already on a total war footing, with the vast bulk of its army tied down in China. And for the majority of Japanese soldiers, fighting in China was what the Second World War was about.

SCENE OF HORROR Chiang Kai-shek (left) led a spirited resistance to the Japanese, who in their fury unleashed the 'Rape of Nanjing'. Above: Smouldering Chinese bodies litter the Nanjing streets.

ISLAND FASTNESS After 25 days of bombardment, Corregidor is a smoking ruin, its defenders hidden in a network of tunnels.

was now faced with conducting a 1000 mile (1600 km) retreat through central and northern Burma into India – a retreat that could end only in disaster in the jungle-clad mountains of the Burmese-Indian frontier.

Alexander, an officer of the Irish Guards, had many friends in London, including Churchill. They determined that he would not have his career ruined by commanding a hopeless retreat. As a result, he was promoted to theatre command, and a newly appointed lieutenant general, William Slim, was detailed to take his place. Slim was the son of a Birmingham ironmonger, who in 1938, aged 47, had still been a major. It did not matter if he lost his career, Alexander's friends reasoned – he was a nobody.

Slim flew into Magwe in central Burma on March 19, 1942. Unlike Percival, the first thing he did was to commandeer a jeep and drive to the front line to see for himself what was happening. Tired and frightened men recalled their first sight of the stocky, pugnacious figure, his lower jaw jutting out from under a bush hat. A few words from their new general and they knew that not only were they going to survive, but that they would one day return and conquer the Japanese. Against all the odds, Slim counterattacked the Japanese, knocked them off balance and then brought the bulk of British and Indian forces through the longest retreat ever conducted in British military history.

Meanwhile, the Japanese had also moved into the Dutch East Indies, where a new Allied command had been created: the American, British, Dutch and Australian (ABDA) command. ABDA built up a force of 15 US, British, Dutch and Australian cruisers and destroyers, and on February 27 it clashed with 17 Japanese cruisers and destroyers in the Java Sea. Only a handful of Allied ships survived. Once ashore on Java, the Japanese quickly overran Allied ground forces. They entered Batavia on March 9, marching down roads packed deep with cheering Javanese, for whom the invaders were liberators.

MACARTHUR'S MEN The general himself (right) escaped from Corregidor, leaving his men to the horrors of the Bataan 'death march'.

Thus Singapore, Rangoon and Batavia all fell, but on the Bataan peninsula which forms the northern arm of Manila Bay and on the fortress island of Corregidor at the entrance to the bay the US flag still flew. After the disaster at Lingayen Gulf, General MacArthur had withdrawn all his forces – more than 100 000 men – into prepared positions there.

Bataan and Corregidor

MacArthur regarded the Japanese as his opponents, but he also had enemies in Washington. He was a right-wing Republican who thought of Roosevelt's Democrats as little better than Communists. As chief of staff in 1935 he had clashed bitterly with the president, who eased him out of office and dispatched him to the Philippines. Another enemy was the chief of staff, General George Marshall.

The officer in charge of drawing up war plans for the Pacific was Colonel Dwight D. Eisenhower, who only two years earlier had been MacArthur's chief of staff in Manila. Eisenhower briefed Marshall on MacArthur's increasingly erratic behaviour. MacArthur,

WEAPONS OF WAR

THE SECOND WORLD WAR WAS A 'HIGH TECH' WAR WHOSE HEROES INCLUDED THE SCIENTISTS WHO DEVELOPED EVER-BETTER WEAPONS

Sir Henry Tizard, a former test-pilot and now Churchill's leading scientific advisor, arrived in the United States in September 1940 with a black bag containing blueprints of virtually all Britain's weapon

systems then under development. Churchill had instructed Tizard 'to tell them what they want to know . . . give them all the assistance you can to enable the armed forces of the United States to reach the highest

level of technical efficiency'. Thus it was that the USA jumped a generation in the development of radar and the jet engine.

What Tizard offered the Americans was a technological dowry. It epitomised the most important aspect of modern industrial warfare: not natural resources, money or manpower, but the brainpower of scientists and technicians. All wars fought since the beginning of the industrial era had witnessed improvements in weapons, a process that culminated in unprecedented developments during the First World War. Armies which in

POOR PERFORMERS Neither Soviet armoured cars (above) nor the Vickers Comet (right) performed well in combat, a fact which operations analysis had predicted.

1914 fought with bolt-action rifles and horsed cavalry were by 1918 equipped with light machine guns, submachine guns, flame throwers and man-portable mortars; they rode into battle in infantry-carrying tanks, supported by self-propelled guns and heavily armed low-flying ground-attack aircraft.

The Second World War saw a similar development, but this time the technological advance was much swifter and organised more methodically. In previous conflicts, new weapons, sometimes invented by a single man in a small workshop such as Nathan Lewis with his drum-fed light machine gun of 1911 – were introduced in a haphazard, often chaotic way. In the late 1930s, RAF Fighter Command developed a more systematic approach which quickly spread to other services and other countries. Increasingly, teams of scientists and technicians were attached to various commands where they had the job of rapidly analysing battlefield experience, correcting faults in existing machines and designing new ones. This technique, known as 'operational analysis', compressed into a few short months developments which under other circumstances might have taken decades.

By 1942 all the main belligerents had worked out a few basic systems for organising weapons development. The first step was to build a research team around the weapon. Some of these teams became very large and grew into scientific-industrial mini-cities, like General Groves's nuclear physicists at Oak Ridge and Los Alamos in the United States.

ASSAULT RIFLE The father of modern infantry assault rifles, the Sturmgewehr 44 was compact and light. Although ineffective above 1200 ft (370 m), it was ideal in cities or close country.

1942 British infantry equipped with PIAT
Mass production of Bazooka begins in USA
Germans develop Panzerschreck

POUNDING THE ENEMY   The American Bazooka (left) packed a mighty punch, launching 8oz (225 g) of pentolite high explosive that could penetrate 5in (13cm) of armour at 300yd (270m). Below: An impressive part of Germany's Atlantic Wall defences, 28 cm guns like this could fire a 284 kg shell more than 22 miles (35 km).

Another system saw teams of scientists attached to particular fleets or armies. A third method, favoured by the British and the Soviets, was for governments to recruit scientists directly into state-run laboratories; the British created a new Civil Service category of Scientific Officer. A fourth system depended upon private industry. Firms like I.G. Farben, Siemens and Krupp in Germany and Du Pont, Ford and Boeing in the USA expanded their own laboratories, directly employing thousands of scientists.

The major drawback with all these systems lay in compartmentalisation. Experts specialised in particular subjects, permitting little intellectual cross-fertilisation, if any. The Americans hit on a way round this: the establishment of defence research laboratories within existing universities like Harvard and the Massachusetts Institute of Technology (MIT). Scientists, stimulated by undergraduate teaching and postgraduate supervision on the cutting edge of research, would be more likely to come up with fresh ideas.

The infantry hits back

In six years these systems of weapons development changed the nature of war. For example, in 1940 British infantry had tried to stop German tanks with solid shot from the Boyes antitank rifle; the rounds bounced off oncoming armour and the recoil of the rifle usually resulted in severe bruising and sometimes a dislocated shoulder. By 1942 British infantry were equipped with the Projector Infantry Anti-Tank or PIAT, which could propel a 2½ lb bomb about 300 ft (90 m). The PIAT was effective against most types of armour at about 90 ft (27 m), but cocking was

difficult and recoil horrific. The Americans followed a different line of development. In 1942 they began mass production of the 2.36 in Rocket Launcher, known universally as the Bazooka after a comic wind instrument played by Bob Burns, a well-known US entertainer. In late 1942 the Germans captured some Bazookas which the Americans had supplied to the Russians and set about developing their own version, the *Raketen Panzerbuchse* 54 (*Panzerschreck*).

The PIAT, Bazooka and *Panzerschreck* meant that by 1943 infantry were stalking tanks, rather than fleeing them. In addition, they could lay thousands of antitank mines

which could immobilise even the heaviest tank, making it vulnerable to antitank gun fire. The British antitank gun had increased enormously in power and size, from the 2 lb gun of 1940 to the 17 lb gun of 1943. The Germans had started the war with a 37 mm gun, but had quickly realised that their 88 mm anti-aircraft gun was also a superlative antitank weapon.

The leap in techniques for destroying tanks was matched by developments in the size and capabilities of armour. The Germans discovered during their first summer in Russia that their 27 ton *Panzerkampfwagen* (PzKw) Mk IV was massively outclassed by the 30 ton Soviet T34, the finest medium tank of the war. Daimler Benz was told to find an answer and eventually produced the

1943 German PzKw V Panther tank comes into operation
Vickers begin to develop Centurion tank in Britain

1944 American B-29 Superfortress bomber comes into service
First V-1s and V-2s land in England
Antisubmarine Squid developed by British

1945 First Centurion tanks roll off production line in April
Britain develops 'Grand Slam' bomb

SEA EXPLOSIVE The contact mine, a spherical ball fitted with 'horns' and filled with 600 lb (270 kg) of explosives, was the single biggest hazard to shipping.

PzKw V, the Panther. At 43 tons this was heavier than the T34 but with the same 75 mm gun. Unfortunately for the Germans, problems with the transmission system delayed its deployment until summer 1943.

By this time German industry had produced exactly the right tank for defensive warfare of attrition, the very antithesis of the blitzkriegs of 1939-41. Development of the PzKw VI Tiger began a month before Operation *Barbarossa*; it would probably never have reached production stage, however, had it not been for the Wehrmacht's encounters with the massive 50 ton Soviet KVs, at that time the largest tank in the world. Germany needed something that could match the KV, and the Tiger was the answer. The first of the 57 ton Tigers reached the Russian front in August 1942. They were also deployed in Tunisia in December 1942

where their 88 mm high-velocity gun came as a nasty surprise to Anglo-American forces. There were only a few ways to destroy a Tiger – heavy bombing, naval gunfire or a lucky shot with the heaviest high-velocity tank or antitank gun.

Anglo-American armour progressed along very different lines. The American offensive position required a tank that should be fast, manoeuvrable and mechanically reliable. The Sherman (which fulfilled these requirements) was the equal of all German tanks up to and including the PzKw IV, but considerably inferior to both the Panther and the Tiger. The Sherman's high profile made it an easy target for antitank gunners, and it had a propensity to explode when hit. The British, who also used the Sherman, called it the 'Ronson' after the American cigarette lighter because, in the words of a wartime advertisement, 'it lights the first time'.

Having led the world in tank design in the 1920s and early 30s, the British had fallen well behind the Germans, Soviets and Americans. Part of the blame lay with Treasury-induced cuts, but there was another problem; when rearmament did take place the contracts for tanks did not go to firms like Vickers with a tradition of building armoured vehicles, but to inexperienced manufacturers who constructed a number of markedly inferior models – the Churchill, Crusader, Valentine and Cromwell. In 1943 Vickers began designing a tank – the Centurion – which incorporated all the best features of the German and Soviet models. The first six Centurions rolled off the production line in April 1945 and were rushed to Europe, but reached Montgomery's army literally as the Germans

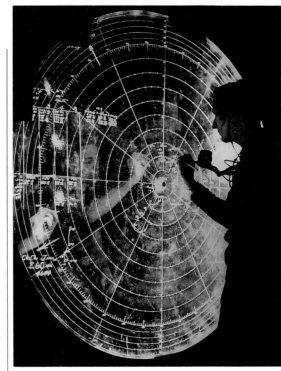

SEEING BY RADAR An SCR 270 radar aboard USS *Saratoga* could detect approaching Japanese *kamikazes* at a range of more than 140 miles (225 km).

were signing the surrender documents. Over the next four decades, the Centurion served with many armies and dominated the battlefield. Had it entered service only a year earlier, the battle for Normandy could have developed very differently.

Weapons at sea

Navies had also witnessed radical changes. All admiralties in 1939 anticipated big-gun duels between battleships and consequently poured resources into ships like the *Prince of Wales*, *Roma*, *Bismarck* and *Yamato*. They all learned that big-gun ships were vulnerable to aerial torpedoes, delivered by either land-based or carrier-based aircraft. The success of the British aircraft carrier *Illustrious* in its attack on the Italian battle fleet in Taranto in November 1940 was spectacularly confirmed at Pearl Harbor in December 1941. There were some gun duels, for example the sinking of the *Bismarck* in the Atlantic and the battles of Guadalcanal and the Surigao Straits in the Pacific, but the majority of battleships

TINY BUT TERRIBLE Germany, Japan and Italy all developed midget submarines, but none was as successful as the British X-craft which badly damaged the German battleship *Tirpitz* in September 1943.

were sunk by either aircraft or submarines. By 1945 the largest, most heavily armed ships were aircraft carriers.

The submarine also established itself as a potent weapon, capable of cutting the lines of communications of overseas armies, or threatening with starvation heavily populated island nations like Japan and Britain. The

TAILOR-MADE FIGHTERS

Alexander A. Novikov, Commissar of Defence for Aviation, introduced operations analysis into the USSR in 1942-3. The results were fed to factories east of the Urals, and fighters like the Yakovlev Yak 9 and Yak 3 were developed, enabling the Soviets to achieve air parity with the Luftwaffe.

mainstay of the German effort in the Atlantic was the Type VII U-boat, with a surface speed of 14 knots (26 km/h) and a range of 6800 miles (11 000 km). Having survived the U-boat campaign of the First World War, the Royal Navy had developed ASDIC (named after the Allied Submarine Detection Investigation Committee), which the Americans called Sonar; this used sound pulses to detect underwater objects. Most U-boat attacks, however, were made at night with the U-boat on the surface. To deal with this threat the British equipped ships with a refined form of radar, the Type 217 4 in (10 cm) set, which could detect a target as small as a periscope at 5000 yd (4600 m). Radar was also installed in coastal command aircraft. Known as ASV (Air to Surface Vessel) radar, it was used in combination with a Leigh Light, a 22 million candle-power searchlight which could illuminate a U-boat on the surface at a range of more than a mile (1.6 km). The ASV radar and Leigh Light combination scored its first success in July 1942. Soon U-boat commanders were so worried that they would risk surfacing to post lookouts only during the day.

For their part, the Germans developed countermeasures like a weighted buoy with a tinfoil mast which gave the same radar signature as a U-boat conning tower. In addition, by 1943 most U-boats were equipped with a *Schnorkel*, an air tube with a valve that was attached to the conning tower. This remained above the surface when the U-boat was under water, allowing it to obtain the external air

INDUSTRIAL ORGANISERS

Britain owed much to its minister for aircraft production, Lord Beaverbrook. Churchill appointed the ruthless Canadian press magnate to this key post when the Battle of Britain hung in the balance, and eventual victory had as much to do with Beaverbrook's streamlining of fighter production as with Air Marshal Dowding's strategy.

The Second World War was a total war, in which the belligerents mobilised industry to support their war efforts. The Soviet achievement after the German onslaught in 1941 was astonishing. Stimulated by a mix of terror of their own leadership and hatred of the Germans, Soviet railway workers shifted 1360 major industrial plants eastwards in the second half of 1941, most of which were back in production by the spring of 1942. For the Americans, the key figure was General Brehan B. Somervell. He was given the task of translating the outlines of the 1941 Victory Program – an army of some 9 million men and 215 divisions – into a statement of requirements for industry. In a series of blazing rows with top strategists, Somervell insisted on being included in strategic planning sessions, because it was all very well for Marshall, Eisenhower and MacArthur to draw arrows on maps, but only he knew if the forces were available that could translate these grand schemes into reality.

Theoretically, the central position in the German war economy was held by Fritz Todt, minister of armaments and munitions. But he died in an air crash on February 8, 1942, and was succeeded by Hitler's architect, the 37-year-old Albert Speer. The new minister used his architectural training to produce a flow diagram model of the German economy to expose bottlenecks and inefficiencies. During the next three years Speer performed miracles in expanding Germany's war production in spite of heavy bombing. By 1944 production had pulled well ahead of Britain, was equal to the USSR but was still only about one-third of the USA's. Speer squeezed out about as much as was possible, but Germany simply could not compete with the resources of the North American continent.

TWO FACES OF PRODUCTION In Leningrad (left) children working in an unheated factory put the fuses into bombs. In Seattle's Boeing works (below) seemingly endless streams of B-17 heavy bombers roll off a semi-automated production line.

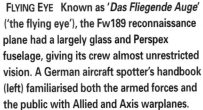

needed for its engines. By 1945 the Germans had also developed the Type XVII Walter Boat, driven by a Walter turbine which used 'Ingolin' hydrogen peroxide fuel and thus did not need external air; the U-boat was able to stay submerged indefinitely. By this time, however, the British had developed an effective means of attacking a submerged boat. Previously the attacking ship had rolled depth charges off the stern as she passed overhead, thereby breaking ASDIC contact. In 1944 the Squid was developed, which fired three depth charges ahead of the U-boat; this meant that contact could be maintained until the vessel was destroyed.

Fighters, bombers and bombs

It was in the air that the effects could best be seen of competition between industrial states with highly developed techniques of systems analysis. Despite some impressive achievements, this was an area in which the Italians, Japanese and Soviets were left behind. At the beginning of the war Britain and Germany still had biplanes in service like the Gloster Gladiator and the Henschel Hs123A. By 1944 both were using jet fighters like the Gloster Meteor and the formidable Me262.

'FLYING FORTRESS' The B-17 deserved its nickname. It had eleven .5 calibre machine guns including two in the belly turret shown here.

FLYING EYE Known as '*Das Fliegende Auge*' ('the flying eye'), the Fw189 reconnaissance plane had a largely glass and Perspex fuselage, giving its crew almost unrestricted vision. A German aircraft spotter's handbook (left) familiarised both the armed forces and the public with Allied and Axis warplanes.

High-performance fighters like the Spitfire and the Fw190 underwent constant modification; they had about 1000 improvements apiece, which added approximately 100 mph (160 km/h) to their top speeds.

A major transformation came in bombers, as the light and medium machines of 1940 and 1941 gave way to heavy four-engined aircraft like the Avro Lancaster, which could carry 10 tons of high explosives. The US B-17 ('Flying Fortress'), originally a maritime patrol aircraft, was heavily armed, and although it had only a relatively modest bomb load, it could survive in daylight operations over Germany. When, near the start of the war, it appeared that Britain might be defeated, the Boeing company began designing an intercontinental bomber, which entered service in June 1944 as the B-29 ('Superfortress'). With an unprecedented range of 5000 miles (8000 km), its operations against Japan were on a truly intercontinental scale. B-29s based in India would fly over the Himalayas, refuel at advanced bases in China, and then fly on to bomb Japan. It was B-29s that dropped the atomic bombs on Hiroshima and Nagasaki in August 1945.

Bombs grew ever larger. By 1942 the RAF was using the so-called blockbuster, the 4000 lb (1800 kg) 'Cookie', and worse was to come. By early 1945 British technicians had perfected the largest conventional bomb in the world, the 10 ton 'Grand Slam', which when dropped from a height of 10 000 ft (3000 m) would penetrate more than 30 ft (10 m) into the earth and detonate, starting an earthquake that

RADIO WARS

The Anglo-German radio war was fought by sophisticated, well-organised, state-supported machines – one run by Joseph Goebbels; the other from July 1941 until the end of the war by the Irish-Australian, Brendan Bracken.

For the Germans, their most effective radio propagandist in the early part of the war was William Joyce, an Irish-American who had been a member of Sir Oswald Mosley's British Union of Fascists. Joyce's affected upper-class drawl and sneering delivery earned him the nickname Lord Haw Haw. His impact depended on the accuracy of the news he broadcast, and while Germany was winning he was able to give listeners more details than those some-times transmitted by the BBC Home Service. The Germans scored another coup when they persuaded the writer P.G. Wodehouse, interned after they overran Belgium and France in 1940, to make six broadcasts in 1941. He thought it would be a harmless piece of fun,

LORD HAW HAW William Joyce's broadcasts for Radio Hamburg earned him execution by hanging in 1946.

but many at home, including Churchill, were disappointed and angry. The author had behaved with the same blithering idiocy he had conferred on his character Bertie Wooster, and there was no Jeeves to help him out.

By far the most effective radio propaganda organisation was the BBC itself. By 1942 it employed more than 10 000 personnel directly and was broadcasting regular programmes to 25 European countries in their own languages. The German service carried mainly news and was careful to be accurate in details which could easily be checked. The Gestapo estimated that the BBC's German audience was 1 million in 1943; as Germany's situation deteriorated during 1944 it grew to 10-15 million. The BBC's most famous radio cam-paign was the one to daub occupied Europe with the letter V for victory. Refinements were soon added. The Morse signal for V – dot dot dot dash – was used, then the corresponding opening notes of Beethoven's Fifth Symphony. Chalked Vs appeared everywhere, a relatively safe but nevertheless effective form of protest which reminded the Germans that there were many who wished to see them gone.

could shake even heavily fortified structures to the ground. The most devastating British aerial weapon, however, was the incendiary, tens of thousands of which destroyed cities like Lübeck, Rostock, Hamburg and Dresden.

Germany responded with the *Vergeltungswaffe* (Reprisal Weapon) programme. From among a proliferation of plans, two weapons were to be significant: the Luftwaffe's pilotless jet aircraft, the V-1; and the Army's large rocket, the V-2, developed by Wernher von Braun's team at the immense weapons-research project at Peenemunde on the Baltic Coast. The Luftwaffe argued that its device was cheap. Von Braun argued that the V-2 would produce greater damage, because of the high-pressure shock wave produced by its speed of arrival, roughly four times the speed of sound. In the end Hitler decreed that both weapons should be developed; the first V-1s landed on England in June 1944, followed three months later by the first V-2s. Both the United States and the USSR developed these weapons further after the war, and they are with us today as the Tomahawk cruise missile and the Scud.

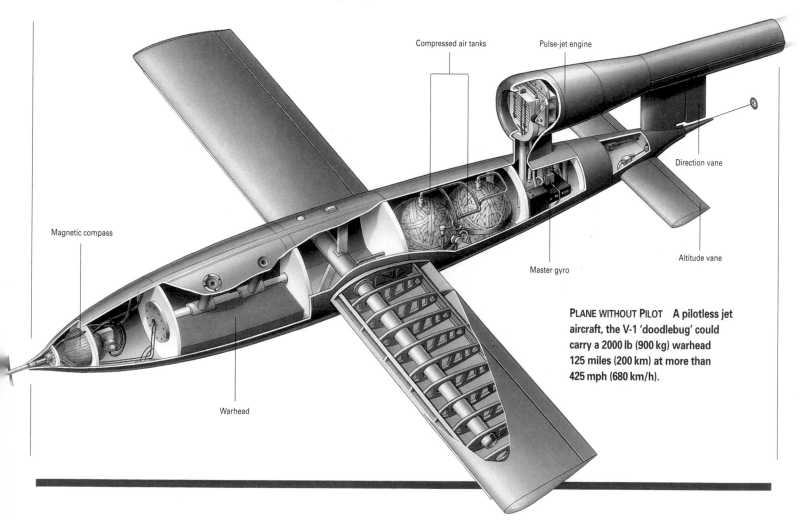

Compressed air tanks

Pulse-jet engine

Direction vane

Magnetic compass

Master gyro

Altitude vane

Warhead

PLANE WITHOUT PILOT A pilotless jet aircraft, the V-1 'doodlebug' could carry a 2000 lb (900 kg) warhead 125 miles (200 km) at more than 425 mph (680 km/h).

THE WAR AT SEA

HOW COULD THE GERMAN NAVY BEST CUT BRITAIN'S VULNERABLE TRADE ROUTES – WITH SURFACE RAIDERS OR WITH U-BOATS?

From the point of view of the Oberkommando der Marine in Berlin, Germany's prospects at sea in September 1939 looked bleak. Even if Italy eventually entered the war and kept the French Navy busy in the Mediterranean, the strength of the Royal Navy remained crushing. Britain outnumbered Germany four to one in battleships, five to one in aircraft carriers, six to one in destroyers and four to one in submarines.

If Britain was vulnerable at sea, it was in its merchant marine. This amounted to more than 3000 large freighters and tankers – 26 per cent of the world's total shipping. Each year Britain imported over 50 million tons of raw materials and food. Any disruption to its trade would have serious consequences for its ability to wage war. The question facing Germany was: how best to disrupt this flow? It became the subject of a dispute between the Commander in Chief of the German fleet, Grand Admiral Erich Raeder, and his most powerful subordinate, Commodore Karl Dönitz, in charge of Germany's 57 U-boats. Dönitz had commanded a submarine in the First World War and was convinced that Germany's U-boat campaign in 1917 had come within a hair's breadth of knocking Britain out of the war. Raeder had commanded a cruiser squadron. He did not oppose the use of submarines; he merely pointed out that they had failed to knock Britain out of the war.

Ten days before Britain's declaration of war, Raeder sent to sea two pocket battleships, *Admiral Graf Spee* and *Deutschland*. Each displaced only 12 000 tons, but their main armament of six 28 cm and eight 15 cm guns, and their ability to cruise 21 000 miles (34 000 km) without refuelling, made them potentially the most formidable commerce destroyers ever designed. On September 30 *Graf Spee* sank a British freighter off northeastern South America; five days later *Deutschland* sank another freighter halfway between Bermuda and the Azores. Within the week powerful Anglo-French task forces were scouring the Atlantic. After one more kill Raeder ordered *Deutschland* back to Germany; he had no desire to lose a major warship with a name like Deutschland. To make sure, her name was changed to *Lützow*.

Even in the South Atlantic, *Graf Spee* was under pressure. In December, its commander, Captain Hans Langsdorff, decided to return to Germany. He had captured or sunk only nine Allied vessels, but his engines were beginning to malfunction. He decided on one last run to the estuary of the River Plate, where he hoped to intercept British ships loaded with cargoes from Uruguay and Argentina. Instead, on December 13, he ran into a British squadron – the heavy cruiser *Exeter*, and two light cruisers, HMS *Ajax* and *Achilles*. He steered directly for the cruisers, concentrating his fire on *Exeter*. His 28 cm guns pounded the British ship well beyond the range of *Exeter*'s 8 inch guns, but *Ajax* and *Achilles* closed and landed direct hits on *Graf Spee*.

Graf Spee managed to drive off the cruisers, but in the confusion and smoke her gunnery officer reported to Langsdorff a positive sighting of the British battleship *Renown*. Already damaged, Langsdorff put about for Montevideo, where the Uruguayan authorities allowed him just 72 hours to effect repairs. Under Hitler's instructions to avoid the humiliation of surrendering his ship, Langsdorff took *Graf Spee* out into the Plate on December 17 and scuttled her. A week later, wrapped in the German battle ensign, he shot himself.

Surface raiding

The first foray of Germany's major warships into the Atlantic had ended in defeat, but by now Raeder had devised a new form of attack, auxiliary cruisers. These were large

GERMAN SUPREMOS Hitler's admirals Erich Raeder (left) and Karl Dönitz (right) disagreed violently about how best to defeat the British at sea. Raeder favoured surface warships, while Dönitz wished to expand the U-boat fleet.

| | October 1939
U-boats raid
Scapa Flow | December 1939
Battle of the
River Plate | | March 1941
Battle of Cape
Matapan | May 1941 *Bismarck* sunk
British capture naval
Enigma machine | | December 1941
Vaagso raid | March 1942
Saint-Nazaire
raid |

MALTA GC

In June 1940, when Italy declared war and France was transformed from an ally into a sullen, hostile neutral, the Admiralty proposed abandoning the Mediterranean – until an incredulous Churchill vetoed the proposal. The Royal Navy stayed, and by mid 1941 had established superiority over the surface components of the large, modern Italian navy. On the night of November 11, 1940, Swordfish torpedo-bombers from the carrier *Illustrious* had sunk three Italian battleships in Taranto harbour. On March 27, 1941, a British fleet had defeated an Italian one off Cape Matapan, Greece's south-western tip.

It was a different story in the air and under the sea, however. Key to the Allies' hold on the Mediterranean was Malta, a British colony lying strategically in the middle of the sea. The Axis went for it with all they had. From December 1941 to October 1942, their bombers kept up constant attacks on the island. Between January 1 and July 24, 1942, there was only one 24 hour period when no bombs fell; in March and April the Axis dropped twice the tonnage of bombs on Malta that the Luftwaffe devoted to London during the Blitz.

The population moved underground, health declined and in the summer there was an outbreak of typhus; about 1500 civilians died. A combination of German U-boats and Italian frogmen, meanwhile, sank the carriers *Ark Royal* and *Eagle* and three battleships, and virtually destroyed two of six convoys sent to Malta. In April 1942, King George VI awarded Malta the George Cross, Britain's highest award for civilian bravery. In June 1942 the daily ration was cut to 1500 calories, and the governor set a date at which he would have to surrender to prevent mass starvation. The arrival of the battered remnants of a convoy in August saved the island at the last moment.

From the Allied point of view, Malta had been worth the defending. During 1942 aircraft and submarines based there sank 230 Axis ships bound for North Africa. This did not prevent Rommel from fighting, but it did make it impossible for him to advance farther east than El Alamein, and so had a crucial impact on the war.

modern merchant ships, armed with up to eight 15 cm guns and torpedo tubes. Their volunteer crews were fluent in several languages, and by using canvas awnings could change the appearance of the superstructure within minutes, thereby disguising their identity. Between the spring of 1940 and the summer of 1943 Germany sent ten of these raiders to attack Allied shipping. In the end, however, most of them were tracked down.

The Kriegsmarine, meanwhile, had suffered heavily in the Norwegian campaign of April-June 1940, but after the fall of France Raeder again risked his big ships. The pocket battleship *Admiral Scheer* rampaged through the Atlantic in November and December, sinking 17 ships. From December 1940 to March 1941 she was joined by the cruisers *Admiral Hipper*, *Scharnhorst* and battle cruiser *Gneisenau*. *Scharnhorst* and *Gneisenau*, in particular, sank 115 000 tons of shipping.

Delighted with these successes, in May 1941, Raeder sent Germany's newest and largest battleship, the 42 000 ton *Bismarck*, accompanied by

the heavy cruiser *Prinz Eugen*, into the North Atlantic. The Royal Navy, alerted by naval intelligence officers in Sweden, prepared a warm reception; Britain's largest battlecruiser, the 42 000 ton *Hood* and its newest battleship, *Prince of Wales*, steamed to intercept the German ships in the Denmark Strait between Greenland and Iceland. At 5.53 am on May 24, *Hood*'s radar picked up the German ships. *Hood* opened fire on what her commander, Vice Admiral Holland, believed was the *Bismarck* but was in fact the *Prinz Eugen*. *Prince of Wales* fired, too, but her salvos went wide. At exactly 6 am a combined salvo from *Bismarck* and *Prinz Eugen* straddled *Hood*. A fire broke out amidships, there was an enormous explosion and by 6.03 *Hood* had disappeared, taking with her all but three of her 1400 crew.

Bismarck had not escaped unscathed. Three hits from one or other of the British warships ruptured her fuel lines, so that she was now leaving a trail of oil. British light cruisers, following just out of range, radioed her position to the carrier HMS *Victorious*, but nine torpedo-bombers sent out during the evening made little impact. That night both *Prinz Eugen* and *Bismarck* managed to shake off their British pursuers and turned southwest, heading for Brest in Brittany. The British were desperate – their worst nightmare, a

April 1942
George Cross
awarded to Malta

July 1942
Convoy PQ17: British
lose 23 ships

August 1942
Dieppe raid

May 1944
Dönitz withdraws
U-boats from Atlantic

November 1944
Tirpitz sunk

large German battleship at loose in the Atlantic sea lanes, had come true. But the following morning the *Bismarck* accidentally betrayed her position by a long radio message to Kriegsmarine HQ. Later in the day 15 Swordfish torpedo-bombers from HMS *Ark Royal* lumbered through the battleship's

BRITAIN'S LIFELINE   Attacks by Brittany-based German bombers (left) in 1940 forced convoys to abandon the south-western approaches to the British Isles. Sailing in line astern (below) are some of the 3000 freighters which sustained Britain's war effort.

heavy flak defences and managed to hit and disable her steering mechanism, leaving her capable of sailing only in a wide arc.

Bismarck was doomed. During the night of May 26-27 she fought off attacks by British destroyers, but dawn brought the battleships *King George V* and *Rodney* within range. The British pounded *Bismarck*, until she was nothing more than a battered hulk. At 10.30 am the cruisers *Norfolk* and *Dorsetshire* closed in and delivered the coup de grâce with torpedoes.

The sinking of the *Bismarck* dealt a serious blow to Raeder's strategy. Hitler, appalled at the loss, forbade any further use of major warships in raiding operations. He now agreed with Dönitz that a vastly expanded U-boat fleet was the best option.

The frustrated admiral

The first months of the war had been a time of enormous frustration for Dönitz. During the First World War, the British had developed the convoy system – merchant vessels sailing together with armed escort ships – to counter the U-boat menace; the Admiralty lost little time in reintroducing it with the outbreak of the Second World War.

In six months the handful of U-boats operating in the North Sea and the eastern Atlantic managed to sink just on 700 000 tons of merchant shipping, much too little to have any effect on Allied commerce. But indications of the potentially devastating effect of a mass U-boat campaign abounded. On October 14, 1939, for example, Lt Commander Gunther Prien took *U-47* through minefields and antisubmarine nets into the

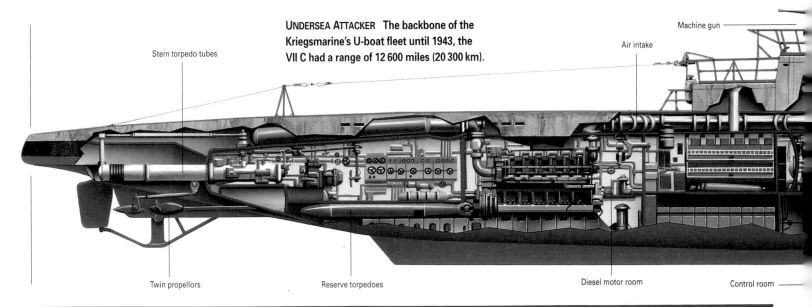

UNDERSEA ATTACKER   The backbone of the Kriegsmarine's U-boat fleet until 1943, the VII C had a range of 12 600 miles (20 300 km).

Stern torpedo tubes

Machine gun

Air intake

Twin propellors

Reserve torpedoes

Diesel motor room

Control room

British base of Scapa Flow, torpedoing the battleship *Royal Oak*, which sank.

The capitulation of France on June 22, 1940, opened up an additional 2000 miles (3200 km) of Atlantic coastline from which U-boats could operate. Dönitz also reorganised the way his boats attacked; instead of a single craft trying its luck, from now on when a convoy was sighted, any attack was to be delayed until nearby boats had time to join up and attack in unison – 'the tactics of the wolf pack'. In July and August 1940 a combination of U-boats and Luftwaffe Condors sank 700 000 tons of shipping.

By the beginning of winter 1940-1, it was clear that the Royal Navy was losing what Churchill now called the Battle of the Atlantic. By March 1941 Britain was losing a staggering 500 000 tons per month. It was at this point that the Royal Navy had an astounding piece of luck. On May 9, while protecting a convoy south of Greenland, the destroyer *Bulldog* managed to force an attacking U-boat, the *U-110*, to the surface. The explosive charge the U-boat's commander set to scuttle his craft failed to detonate, and a British boarding party seized the hitherto undecrypted Kriegsmarine Enigma cipher machine and a full set of code books.

Forewarned by Bletchley Park, the Admiralty was now able to route convoys around wolf packs, a strategy which had immediate results; by July 1941 British shipping losses had fallen by nearly four-fifths. The steady decline in the performance of the U-boats was masked, however, during the

first eight months of 1942 by the array of targets that America's entry into the war presented to the wolf packs. Commander in Chief of the US Navy, Admiral Ernest King decreed that America would not introduce the convoy system; instead US warships would 'hunt the hunters' on 'America's ocean frontier'. It was nearly five months before the US Navy sank a U-boat. In the meantime, wolf packs worked up and down the east coast, sinking hundreds of thousands of tons of unorganised and unescorted shipping. It was only in August that the Americans belatedly introduced convoys.

Channel dash

On February 11, 1942, while Dönitz's U-boats rampaged through the western Atlantic, *Scharnhorst*, *Gneisenau* and *Prinz Eugen* slipped out of their exposed anchorage at Brest and steamed at full speed up the English Channel. The British hit them with everything they had – torpedo-bombers, motor torpedo boats, gun fire – but still they surged on, clearing the straits of Dover and reaching

AIR TO SEA ATTACK Improvements on the Allied side in both aircraft range and airborne radar made it more and more difficult for U-boats to operate on the surface.

Kiel a day later. *Gneisenau* was badly damaged by a mine, but *Prinz Eugen* and *Scharnhorst* soon sailed for northern Norway, where they joined *Lützow* (formerly *Deutschland*), *Admiral Scheer*, *Hipper* and Germany's newest and last great battleship, the 42 000 ton *Tirpitz*.

Since the previous autumn Britain had been sending convoys carrying arms from Scotland to Murmansk in the USSR, a route so inhospitable in the mid winter that the Germans had refrained from operations. With the spring, the Germans came to life. A deadly combination of powerful surface ships, Luftwaffe bombers and submarine wolf packs began to exact a fearful toll on the convoys. On July 4 the British suffered

CLOSE QUARTERS With no space for a mess even on large boats, the crews ate on their bunks in the torpedo storage area.

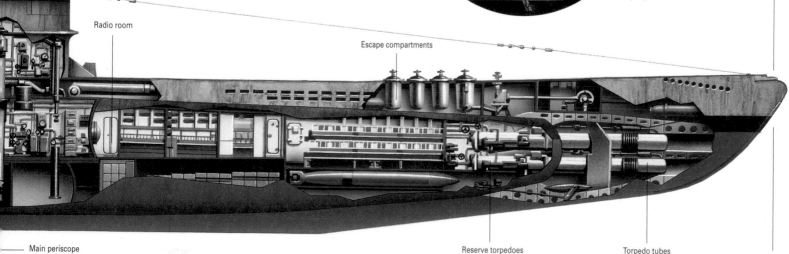

Bridge

Radio room

Escape compartments

Main periscope

Reserve torpedoes

Torpedo tubes

COMBINED OPERATIONS

BRITISH AMPHIBIOUS RAIDS WERE THE SPECIALITY OF COMBINED OPERATIONS, BUT SUCCESS AT VAAGSO AND SAINT-NAZAIRE LED TO DISASTER AT DIEPPE

On June 3, 1940, Churchill sent a minute to the chiefs of staff: 'The completely defensive habit of mind which has ruined the French must not be allowed to ruin all our initiatives . . . we should immediately set to work to organise raiding forces on those coasts [of German-occupied Europe] where the population are friends.' What was needed was a new headquarters dedicated to amphibious raiding, an organisation which might one day also plan an invasion of the Continent. On July 17, 1940, Churchill appointed his old friend, Admiral Sir Roger Keyes, to the new post of Director Combined Operations.

Things did not go very well. Amphibious raiding required months of training and the construction of special landing ships. Raid after raid was cancelled. Finally, on October 26, 1941, Churchill removed Keyes and replaced him with the naval hero Lord Louis Mountbatten, a cousin of the king, young and dynamic. Combined Operations HQ suddenly became the place to be. It grew and grew, staffed by handsome young aristocrats and pretty Wrens. Officers of the other services began calling it Wimbledon – all balls and rackets.

Despite this disparagement the first major raids were outstandingly successful. On December 27, 1941, commandos attacked and seized the Norwegian town of Vaagso, killing, wounding or capturing 209 enemy soldiers, and sinking 16 000 tons of coastal shipping. On March 27, 1942, commandos and Royal Navy volunteers attacked Saint-Nazaire, ramming an old destroyer against the gates of one of the few dry docks in north-western France capable of taking *Tirpitz*. At 10.30 am the next day, as 300 German engineers swarmed over the destroyer, 4.5 tons of depth charges exploded, damaging the dock gates so badly that they could not be repaired until the mid 1950s.

TARGET NORWAY The attack on Vaagso gave a great boost to British morale and was immortalised in several feature films in 1942.

In the euphoria produced by Saint-Nazaire, Combined Operations began planning an operation against Dieppe. It was symptomatic of the atmosphere in the headquarters that no one seemed to have worked out an aim for the attack; nor did anyone point out that raids have to be small and invasions large and well supported. Anything between a raid and an invasion was likely to end in disaster. Before dawn on August 19 five squadrons of landing craft, escorted by destroyers, approached the French coast. At about 4 am the landing force blundered into a German convoy, and a confused, close-quarter naval battle ensued, in which the British sank two German escorts. Though the element of surprise, so essential in this type of operation, had been lost, the landing went ahead. At 5 am landing craft carrying the Royal Regiment of Canada ground onto the shingle beach leading up to Dieppe's main esplanade. But the Germans were waiting for them, and over the next few hours virtually annihilated the Canadians. Of the 6100 men involved, 1027 were killed and 2340 captured. The reputation of Combined Operations never recovered.

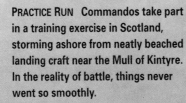

PRACTICE RUN Commandos take part in a training exercise in Scotland, storming ashore from neatly beached landing craft near the Mull of Kintyre. In the reality of battle, things never went so smoothly.

MENACE IN HIDING *Tirpitz* spent nearly three years moving from fiord to fiord, presenting a threat to British shipping and tying down the resources of the Royal Navy.

the single worst convoy disaster of the war, when U-boats and aircraft sank 23 of the 33 ships of Convoy PQ17.

The British did not resume Arctic convoys until the autumn, and these now sailed under heavy escort. On December 31, 1942, *Admiral Hipper* and *Lützow*, accompanied by six destroyers, attempted to intercept Convoy JW51B. Instead of scattering, five destroyers of the escort closed on *Hipper*, hitting her three times. In the meantime, the merchantmen, concealed by a snow storm, made it safely to Murmansk.

In a fury Hitler denounced the cowardice of the Kriegsmarine and threatened to scrap what remained of the surface fleet. In January 1943, Raeder resigned; in his stead came Dönitz. The change in policy was dramatic. U-boat wolf packs deployed to the western Atlantic, their endurance increased by 'Milch Cow' U-boats, supply craft which carried an additional 600 tons of fuel and extra torpedoes. By February Dönitz had an unprecedented 116 U-boats in the North Atlantic. In March 1943 Allied shipping losses soared to 482 000 tons.

On May 4, east of the Grand Banks off Newfoundland, 60 U-boats closed on the 43 ships of Commander Peter Gretton's Convoy ONS5. It should have been a walkover, but as the submarines closed on the surface for the kill, a heavy fog rolled in obscuring the targets. Gretton's escorts, however, equipped with the Type 271 M radar, could 'see' the submarines. In the ensuing melee a handful of small Flower class corvettes rammed, shelled and depth-charged their way through the U-boats, sinking seven and damaging many more. A dumbfounded Dönitz could scarcely credit the reports; it was the single worst day for German U-boats in either of the world wars. Believing it was some ghastly fluke, Dönitz ordered his wolf packs to attack another four convoys, but the results were almost as bad. During May Dönitz lost 41 U-boats, more than the total number of merchant ships they sank. On May 22 he withdrew his boats from the central Atlantic.

There was no single cause for this reversal of fortune. Escorts were more numerous, their radar equipment better and their crews better trained. Merchantmen, too, had become more disciplined in maintaining station in convoy. There had been an increase in the number of aircraft allocated to maritime reconnaissance, and US shipyards were now launching escort carriers capable of launching antisubmarine aircraft; soon almost every convoy would have its own escort carrier.

A turning point?

Dönitz went to his grave believing that victory in the Battle of the Atlantic had been within his grasp in May 1943. In fact, the U-boats did come close to winning the battle, but it was not in 1943. The real turning point had

been earlier, in the summer of 1941 when *Bulldog*'s capture of the Kriegsmarine's Enigma machine allowed the Admiralty to save Britain's merchant marine from almost certain destruction. Because Ultra – intelligence obtained by deciphering Enigma signals – remained a closely guarded secret for more than 30 years after the war, this brilliant action has often been overlooked.

The withdrawal of U-boats from the central Atlantic in May 1943 signposted the transformation of the Kriegsmarine into a force designed to defend the coastline of *Festung Europa* (Fortress Europe). By 1944 German destroyers, minesweepers and coastal protection vessels guarded Europe's coast from North Cape to Bordeaux, and carried on operations in the Mediterranean, the Black Sea and the Baltic. The German Navy still had the capacity to harass Allied landings, but no longer the ability to influence the outcome of the war.

THE ICE RUN Between August 1941 and April 1945, about 4.5 million tons of supplies were shipped to the Arctic ports of Murmansk and Archangel by crews who knew that to be torpedoed meant almost certain death.

EL ALAMEIN AND BEYOND

AFTER VICTORY AT EL ALAMEIN AND THE AMERICAN TORCH LANDINGS, THE WAR MOVED FROM NORTH AFRICA TO SICILY AND UP ITALY

HANDS UP   A German tank crew surrender to British infantrymen during the Battle of El Alamein. The Axis lost 2300 killed in the battle, and nearly 28 000 taken prisoner.

In the first three weeks of 1942, as Japanese forces overran Britain's empire in the Far East, there seemed to be one consolation for the British: at least Rommel had been 'knocked for six' in North Africa. On January 12 the Commander in Chief Middle East, General Claude Auchinleck, dismissed the Afrika Korps as a 'busted flush'.

Then, shortly before dawn on January 21, Rommel struck. He had not bothered to inform German high command (OKW) and so Bletchley Park was ignorant of his intentions. Pushing at high speeds through sandstorms, two panzer divisions trapped the British 1st Armoured Division south of Benghazi and destroyed it. On January 29 Rommel recaptured Benghazi, seized supplies there, and pushed on for another 150 miles (240 km) to Gazala, only stopping when he ran out of fuel.

UP PERISCOPE   An observer of the Afrika Korps keeps watch, using an ingenious pair of periscope binoculars.

Never again would the British be complacent when facing Erwin Rommel. There was a lull in the fighting; then he attacked again on May 26. By mid June he had destroyed a series of fortified Eighth Army 'boxes', and his panzers were racing to Tobruk. Tobruk fell on June 21, giving him a haul of 30 000 prisoners and much-needed petrol. Once more ignoring orders, Rommel raced for Halfaya Pass, bypassed the retreating British and swept on into Egypt. Eighth Army seemed to be in danger of disintegration.

Ash over Cairo

Panic now gripped Cairo, where a pall of smoke rose from the British headquarters as staff burnt confidential documents. To planners in London and Moscow, it seemed possible that Rommel's forces could advance from Egypt to the Caucasus to meet up with German forces which were then advancing through the eastern Ukraine.

In fact, things were not quite as dire as they seemed. Auchinleck moved his reserve to El Alamein, a small station west of Alexandria, where the coastal plain becomes, in effect, an isthmus – a neck of land between the Mediterranean to the north and the quaking, impassable bog of the Qattara Depression to the south. Rommel, at the limit of his logistics, attempted to break through, but after three days gave up.

On August 3 a troubled Churchill flew to Egypt. Disappointed by a confused briefing given by an exhausted Auchinleck, the premier decided that the present team would have to go. His first choice to take over command of Eighth Army was 'Straffer' Gott, one of the most experienced desert commanders, but as Gott flew across the Western Desert to assume his post his aircraft was shot down and the general killed. So it was Lt General Bernard Montgomery who flew into Cairo on August 17. General Harold Alexander took over from Auchinleck as Commander in Chief Middle East.

Personally, Churchill disliked the puritanical Montgomery who neither drank nor smoked and disapproved of people who did. He also disliked Montgomery's public and wholly un-English avowals of self-confidence. These went to absurd lengths. All Whitehall had been talking about a briefing he began by saying: 'As God once said . . . and I think rightly . . .' But this was the right approach for raising an army's morale. Within days of Montgomery's arrival people noticed his tonic effect. One staff officer recalled: 'We were different people . . . we suddenly had a spring in our step.'

Watching the desert war from England, Montgomery had been convinced that he knew what was wrong. British commanders had adopted what they thought were Rommel's techniques but had not made them work. Montgomery decided that he was going to impose a defensive, attritional battle on Rommel, the sort of battle at which the British had become past masters during the First World War.

He had his troops in their new positions just in time. On the evening of August 30,

Zealand and 4th Indian. For the Germans, the attack could not have come at a worse time. Since September 23 Rommel had been on sick leave in Germany due to a chronic stomach complaint.

Although ill, Rommel flew back at once. Reaching his headquarters on October 25, he sent his panzers into a furious counter-attack which stopped Montgomery's advance. On October 29 Montgomery did something he did not like admit-ting, but which was the hallmark of a truly tal-ented general: in the middle of the battle he

THE FOX HIMSELF
Rommel consults
with his aides.

MONTY VERSUS ROMMEL

Erwin Rommel and Bernard Montgomery were both egotists with supreme confi-dence in their leadership abilities. As generals, however, they favoured different techniques, the result of different experiences in the First World War. 'Monty' had served as a staff officer in the static conditions of the Western Front where he learned the importance of meticulous staff work. Rommel had served in an Alpine battalion in Romania and northern Italy, where he penetrated deep into the enemy lines, taking large numbers of prisoners. He learned to value aggres-sive action, seizing the moment and doing the unexpected. El Alamein showed both men at their best. Montgomery's thorough preparations had placed him in an apparently unbeatable position, but Rommel's counterattack badly unsettled the British. Like all good generals, both were capable of using each other's techniques. Rommel proved him-self adept in defensive warfare in Tunisia and Normandy; Montgomery launched daring offensives like the one that breached the Mareth Line in March 1943 and the one that failed at Arnhem in September 1944. But while Rommel revelled in his flexibility, Montgomery insisted that he had never changed a plan in his life. The claim was absurd and did much to damage his reputation after his death.

1942, Rommel made a mock attack towards the coast to draw British reserves north, and then swung south along the northern rim of the Qattara Depression. Two things went wrong. First, the Afrika Korps found itself mired in dense minefields. Second, instead of coming out to fight, the tanks of the British 10th Armoured Division remained hull down – concealed below the horizon apart from their turrets – on Alam Halfa Ridge, fighting defensively. After three days of unsuccessful attacks, Rommel gave up.

Having won a defensive battle Mont-gomery came under pressure from Churchill to launch an offensive. He was firm: 'I won't do it in September,' he told Alexander. 'But if I do it in October it'll be a victory.' Churchill was not pleased – his doubts about a man who neither smoked nor drank seemed well founded. Montgomery made meticulous preparations, and with every passing week he became stronger, while Rommel's position deteriorated.

On October 23 at 9.40 pm the eastern sky at El Alamein burst into sheets of orange light as 900 guns opened up the largest bar-rage yet seen in North Africa. Following behind the barrage, five crack divisions from the Commonwealth and Empire advanced into the Axis positions – 9th Australian, 51st Highland, 1st South African, 2nd New

THE STIFF UPPER LIP Monty receives a salute from General von Thoma of the Afrika Korps, captured during the fighting at El Alamein.

FREE FRENCH FIGHTBACK
Crowds in North Africa welcome arriving Free French forces (right). A poster (above) promotes General Giraud, de Gaulle's bitter rival as leader of the anti-Vichy French.

completely changed his plan. Ninth Australian Division turned on its axis and, now advancing directly north, smashed a wedge between 164th and 90th German Light Divisions. Fearing that one of his divisions would be trapped against the coast, Rommel threw his panzer reserve and virtually all his remaining aircraft against the Australians.

Shortly after midnight on November 2, the thunder of a great barrage announced the beginning of Operation *Supercharge*. Montgomery's massed armour – nearly 800 tanks – tore through the Axis front well to

the south of the Australian advance. In Rommel's place, most commanders would have given all up for lost, but with the remnants of two panzer divisions, just 90 tanks, the Desert Fox counterattacked and for two more days blunted the British offensive. He bought time, extricating the Afrika Korps from an almost impossible position. By November 24 he was back at El Agheila.

Meanwhile, a new front had opened up to the west in Morocco and Algeria, when, on November 8, 100 000 Allied troops came ashore in Operation *Torch*. Vichy French resistance was spasmodic, and ended with a ceasefire on November 11, 1942. Hitler responded to this 'treachery' by occupying the hitherto unoccupied Vichy sector of

France and rushing troops to Tunisia. On the Allied side, the new Commander in Chief North Africa was an American, Lt General Dwight D. Eisenhower. A rising star among his subordinates was Lt General George Patton.

By early March 1943 Axis forces were compressed into a single area of Tunisia. On March 9 Rommel was invalided out of Africa, never to return. Three weeks later Eighth Army attacked the Mareth Line, a fortified zone along the Tunisian-Libyan border, forcing the Afrika Korps to withdraw hurriedly to the north. Here the Germans and Italians were penned into a relatively small bridgehead around Tunis. The Germans defended the hilly, broken country tenaciously; some of the small battles for these hills were among the bloodiest of the entire war. On May 13, 1943, however, the last of 275 000 Axis soldiers surrendered; the war in North Africa was over.

Where next?

In January 1943 Churchill, Roosevelt and their staffs had met at Casablanca on the Moroccan coast. The meeting was hailed in the Press as the 'unconditional surrender' conference, because this is what Churchill and Roosevelt demanded of the Axis powers.

At the highest level all seemed amicable, but the staffs of the president and prime minister were locked in a wrangle over the

DESERT RAIDERS

To British officers who had mapped the Western and Libyan deserts in the 1930s, it seemed obvious that these were 'seas of sand' through which raiding forces could move to attack targets on the coast. Major Ralph Bagnold formed the Long Range Desert Group (LRDG) in June 1940, and in 1941 developed a close relationship with Colonel David Stirling's Special Air Service (SAS). By summer 1942 they had secured scores of US Jeeps in which they mounted machine guns. With all guns firing, a single jeep could produce 5000 rounds a minute. The LRDG and SAS crossed the Qattara Depression again and again, their Jeeps sometimes 18 abreast as they swept onto Axis airfields. By the time Rommel began his retreat to Tunisia, he had lost 400 aircraft in these raids. He admitted that no other British unit of its size caused him more damage than the LRDG.

LONG HAUL UP THE BOOT From the Allied landings on Sicily in July 1943 and in Calabria in September, it took nearly two years to defeat the Germans in Italy.

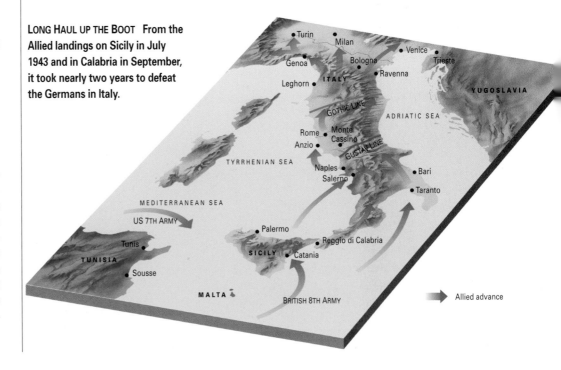

July 1942
First Battle of
El Alamein

August 1942
Montgomery takes
over Eighth Army

direction of the war. The Americans wanted to open a second front in north-west Europe as soon as possible. The British, and this meant Churchill, wanted a Mediterranean strategy in which Anglo-American armies would advance through Italy, and later the Balkans, into central Europe. For the moment both could agree on Operation *Husky*, the invasion of Sicily, but what would happen after that was by no means clear.

Things were no better among the commanders. Montgomery was now in regular contact with US generals, giving patronising briefings on how to fight. At the first lecture Patton attended, the chain-smoking American lit a cigarette. Montgomery, stopping in mid sentence, barked, 'I do not allow smoking in my lectures – kindly extinguish that cigarette!' Nonplussed, Patton ground it under his heel. He spent the rest of the lecture noisily chewing gum, moving it exaggeratedly from one side of his mouth to the other.

The planning for Sicily was shambolic, riven by Anglo-American rivalry. The result was that on July 10, the vast armada – 2500 ships and 180 000 men – which approached Sicily was really two forces, whose commanders, Patton and Montgomery, had not the slightest intention of cooperating. A lack of coordination dogged the entire campaign,

DOWN WITH *IL DUCE* Italian anti-Fascists wave portraits of King Victor Emmanuel as they celebrate Mussolini's downfall.

allowing the Germans to evacuate the island safely by August 17, having inflicted heavy casualties on the Allies.

In his so far fruitless attempts to persuade the Americans to join in an invasion of the

TARGET SICILY In a rare moment of cooperation, Montgomery and Patton ponder a map of Sicily. Below: A US patrol in Messina hunts down enemy snipers.

October 1942 Start of Second Battle of El Alamein	November 1942 *Torch* landings	January 1943 Casablanca Conference	May 1943 Last Axis troops in North Africa surrender	July 1943 Mussolini overthrown; Allied landings in Sicily	September 1943 Allied landings in Italy

Italian mainland, Churchill had taken to calling the peninsula 'the soft underbelly of Europe'. American planners were unconvinced. The 800 miles (1300 km) from Calabria in the south to the Po valley in the north were a mass of mountains and deep river valleys, which a comparatively small army could defend against all comers.

Then, on July 25, newspapers carried the headline 'Musso Out'. As the Sicilian campaign drew to a close King Victor Emmanuel, fearing that the Italian peninsula was the

Allies' next objective, tried to avoid conflict by engineering a coup. He dismissed Mussolini and imprisoned him at Gran Sasso in the Abruzzi Mountains north-east of Rome. Ironically, the king had made war in Italy a certainty. With Mussolini ousted, the Americans decided that a rapid thrust into the peninsula might after all be possible.

On September 3, Montgomery and the Eighth Army crossed the Strait of Messina, landed in Calabria and then headed across the peninsula for the Adriatic coast. For

Montgomery this was an anticlimax, and he was bitter. His archrival Patton was still in Sicily, his future under a cloud after the widely reported slapping of a battle-shocked soldier. Despite that, Montgomery had not secured the command of the major Allied landing, scheduled to take place at Salerno a week later. So anxious was Churchill to secure American involvement that this had been given to an inexperienced American, General Mark Clark, and a newly formed Anglo-American Fifth Army.

On the evening of September 8, the soldiers of Fifth Army were in transports heading for the Gulf of Salerno when General Eisenhower broadcast the news of Italy's surrender. Cheers went up from the convoys, and men relaxed. American landing

MONTE CASSINO German paratroopers (left) bring in supplies to Monte Cassino. By the time the Germans had been dislodged, the scene was one of awesome desolation.

craft grounded before dawn near the magnificent ruins of Paestum, just to the south of Salerno. Suddenly a harsh metallic voice boomed out of the darkness from a dozen loudspeakers and echoed out to sea: 'Give up now, or you are dead!' Parachute flares exploded into blinding white lights which hovered in the dark sky, transforming night into day. From all along the coast machine guns, mortars and artillery opened up, mowing down Europe's hapless liberators.

The Italians may have surrendered, but the Germans had not. Responding with astonishing energy, the German commander in Italy, Field Marshal Kesselring, had rushed six divisions to Salerno. Over the next week the Germans counterattacked violently, almost cutting the beachhead in two.

Monte Cassino

Having lost some 7000 men and inflicted more than 15 000 casualties on the Fifth Army, Kesselring withdrew north of Naples on September 18 to the Gustav Line. This was a zone of carefully surveyed defensive positions lying between the swift, steeply banked Volturno river and the mountaintop town and thick-walled Benedictine monastery of Monte Cassino. Here, the Allied advance was brought to a juddering stop. The fighting came to resemble that on the Western Front during the First World War. For seven months, from October 1943 until May 1944, the front moved no more than a few miles.

In December, Montgomery and Eisenhower both returned to England to begin preparing for Operation *Overlord*, the invasion of France. With them went many veteran divisions, so that Allied forces in Italy became ever more polyglot with Brazilians reinforcing Moroccans, Canadians, Indians, South Africans and the representatives of a dozen other nationalities. In Montgomery's place came General Oliver Leese. A former officer of the Coldstream Guards, Leese, was about as different as it was possible to be from the earnest, ruthlessly ambitious Mark Clark. The two soon quarrelled and Leese moved his headquarters as far away from Clark's as he possibly could.

On January 22, 1944, despairing of breaking the Gustav Line, General Alexander, now

ROME AT LAST Troops of the Anglo-American Fifth Army march past the Colosseum after the liberation of the capital on June 5, 1944.

Commander in Chief Mediterranean Theatre, launched an amphibious operation at Anzio, a small port to the north of the line. A move to outflank the Germans was sensible but the landing force, just 50 000 men, was too weak for the job. The Germans responded with their customary speed, and Anzio became another Salerno, but it went on for months.

In a series of bitter battles between May 11 and 25, the Allied armies finally broke the Gustav Line. The key was massive aerial attacks on Kesselring's lines of communication which cut supplies to German front-line forces; they literally ran out of ammunition and were forced to withdraw.

Military logic dictated that Clark should now swing his Fifth Army to the east to join up with Leese and cut off the German retreat. But military logic had never played much part in the Allied conduct of operations in Italy. Instead, as Patton had done to Montgomery, and as Montgomery had done to Clark, the American general now ignored his ally and headed straight for Rome. Clark had his day of triumph – June 4, 1944, the liberation of Rome – but the Germans escaped yet again to form a new defensive system north of Rome, the Gothic Line. Another long winter was to pass before Allied armies reached the plains of the Po valley. Churchill could not have been more wrong; Italy was far from being Europe's 'soft underbelly' – it was a tough old gut.

GIRAUD, DARLAN AND DE GAULLE

Who would run French North Africa? In December 1942 Eisenhower's choice for the job, Admiral Jean-François Darlan – the Vichy commander in chief, who happened to be in Algeria at the time of the *Torch* landings – was assassinated. There were two

WORKING TOGETHER? At the Casablanca Conference, from left to right, Giraud, Roosevelt, de Gaulle and Churchill.

possible successors – and they hated each other. General Henri-Honoré Giraud was the closest thing France had to a war hero; he had been captured in May 1940 but had escaped from a German prison camp. General Charles de Gaulle headed the Free French committee in London. In the end, Churchill and Roosevelt at the Casablanca Conference forced the two men to work together. They became joint chairmen of the French Committee for National Liberation established in Algiers in June 1943.

THE EASTERN FRONT

TWO EPIC BATTLES – STALINGRAD AND KURSK – SYMBOLISED THE TURNING TIDE AS THE SOVIETS BEAT BACK THE GERMAN INVADERS

For the men of the SS Totenkopf (Death's Head) Division, Valentine's Day of 1942 acquired a legendary status. Cut off by a Soviet offensive, they were forced to dig in around the town of Demyansk, about half way between Leningrad (St Petersburg) and Moscow. It was bitterly cold but they survived by requisitioning food, vodka and clothing from the local peasants. They could not, however, requisition ammunition. They fought off attack after attack, but by February 14 they no longer had the shells and bullets to survive another assault. It was then that Luftwaffe

Ju52s flew overhead, parachuting supplies. The troops in Demyansk held on, sustained entirely by an airlift, until ground forces broke through on March 20, 1942. The cost had been huge. Totenkopf had 17 265 men at the start of *Barbarossa*; by March, three quarters of these were casualties.

All along the Eastern Front there were similar stories – the Russian offensive of December 1941 and then the winter itself cost the Germans about 600 000 casualties, of whom 100 000 were dead. Back in Berlin, however, the Führer's confidence, badly

shaken by the Soviet offensive at the end of 1941, was well on the way to recovery by spring 1942. Russia's great allies, generals December, January and February, had done their worst, and the Wehrmacht had survived. Its survival, Hitler believed, was due almost entirely to his own intervention. At the crisis point on December 20, 1941, when the nerve of many Prussian generals cracked, Hitler had assumed command of the armed forces and forbidden withdrawal.

Operation *Blue*

During the spring thaw both Germans and Soviets made preparations for a summer offensive. The Soviets launched theirs on May 12. General Erich von Manstein managed to encircle its spearheads, however, and by May 19 some 200 000 Soviet prisoners were marching westwards. Hitler's own offensive, Operation *Blue*, was designed to strike south-west into the Donets basin and the Caucasus to obtain vital raw materials. Hitler ordered 60 per cent of all front-line aircraft (about 1500) to the Ukraine and divided his forces there into Army Group A and Army Group B. Together they comprised 100 divisions, of which only 50 were German; 27 came from Romania, 13 from Hungary, nine from Italy and one from Slovakia.

The Germans struck at the end of June. Spearheads closed around Staryj Oskol on July 2 and Voronezh on July 5. On July 23, Army Group A

SOLDIERS FOR THE REICH More than 250 000 Hungarians, most of them poorly equipped, advanced with the Germans in summer 1942 (right). By spring 1943 most were dead or prisoners.

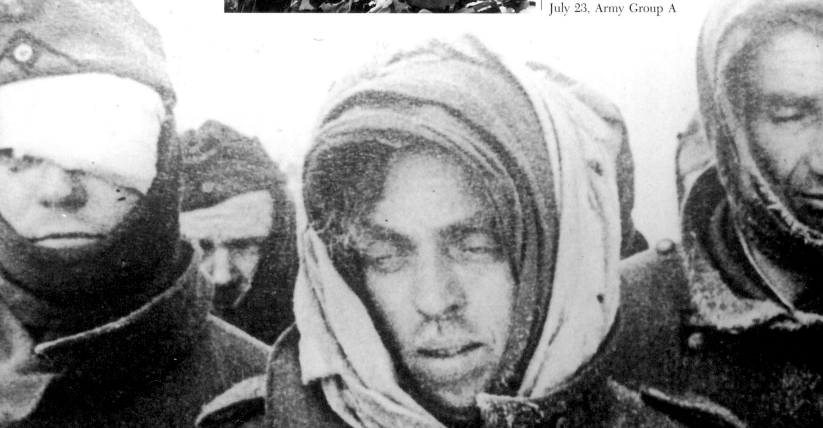

HELL IN STALINGRAD In the largest urban battle in history, Soviet and German battalions fought floor by floor for single buildings, and suffered enormous casualties in the process.

began pouring across the Donets into the Caucasus. On August 23 patrols of General von Kleist's First Panzer Army reached the shores of the Caspian Sea and tried to buy sturgeon eggs from startled local fishermen. But all was not well; on the same day von Kleist's tanks ran out of fuel about 15 miles (24 km) north of Grozny, the gateway to the oilfields of Baku. The Germans had come a long way since the beginning of July – more than 400 miles (640 km) – but this was as far as they were going to get.

Meanwhile, the spearhead of Army Group B, General Friedrich Paulus's Sixth Army, advanced due east, crossing the Donets and the Don. On August 23 it reached the mile-wide Volga north of Stalingrad (Volgograd). Paulus's infantry began probing attacks into the city on September 12, and at first the going was easy. Stalingrad's suburbs were composed of wooden houses; a burst of machine-gun fire and a quick blast with a flamethrower was usually enough to silence any resistance. But as the Germans neared the Volga they came to industrial Stalingrad, huge buildings of reinforced concrete like the ten-storey grain silo, the Machine Tractor Station and the Red October Factory. It was here that the advance bogged down.

On the Soviet side, meanwhile, Stalin had decided that the city named after him required the strongest possible defence. His choice to command the forces there was General Vasili Chuikov. Determined to succeed or die in the attempt, Chuikov set up his headquarters on the eastern side of the Volga. Massing artillery, he fired into German concentrations, and at night infiltrated enough reinforcements and supplies across the Volga to keep the battle going.

Soviet high command (Stavka), headed by Marshal Georgi Zhukov, watched the fighting closely and gradually a plan for a counter-offensive took shape. On November 19 and 20

LENINGRAD – HERO CITY

By July 8, 1941, German panzers had cut Leningrad off from the rest of the USSR, the start of a siege that lasted 933 days until January 1944. During that time the only way of supplying the city was across the ice of Lake Ladoga in winter, or by flotillas of small boats in summer. It is estimated that a million people died, out of a population of around 2.6 million. The first winter was the worst. Horses, cats, dogs, crows and sparrows had all disappeared by December, rats a month later. In unofficial markets some stalls sold meat pasties for colossal prices; it was acknowledged that these were made from flesh hacked from frozen corpses piled by the Neva river.

STARVED TO DEATH Hunger and cold took a lethal toll on Leningraders in the winter of 1941-2.

FACES OF DEFEAT Exhaustion and despair are etched on the faces of these German prisoners at Stalingrad in January 1943.

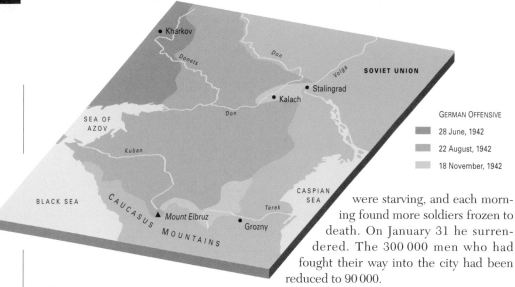

GERMAN OFFENSIVE
- 28 June, 1942
- 22 August, 1942
- 18 November, 1942

TIDE CHECKED August 1942 was the high water mark – the German offensive into the Ukraine and Caucasus would get no farther.

massive bombardments heralded Soviet attacks on both sides of the 80 mile (130 km) corridor that connected Sixth Army to the German forces on the Don. Forty-eight hours later the two Soviet thrusts met near the town of Kalach, cutting off Sixth Army.

On January 10, 1943, seven Soviet armies began attacking into the Stalingrad pocket. They pushed Sixth Army back, until by January 30 Paulus held only the Machine Tractor Station, the Red October Factory and a few other large buildings. His troops

TANK TACTICS At Kursk, the largest armoured clash in history, the latest Soviet models like the T84/85 proved more than a match for their German counterparts.

were starving, and each morning found more soldiers frozen to death. On January 31 he surrendered. The 300 000 men who had fought their way into the city had been reduced to 90 000.

Crisis in the Ukraine

While Hitler's attention was focused on Stalingrad, two Soviet army groups struck across the Don. During 1942 new Soviet divisions, corps and armies had been formed and now, like a steamroller, they crashed through Italian, Hungarian and depleted German units, advancing into the Ukraine and retaking Kursk, Belgorod and Kharkov.

Manstein, now commanding all German forces in the south, allowed the advance to continue until it faltered for lack of supplies. Then, on February 20, he struck. By mid March the situation in the Ukraine and southern Russia had been restored, except for a Soviet salient around Kursk. Manstein urged Hitler to order an immediate attack on Kursk, but the Führer refused. He would attack later in the summer when his armies had been equipped with the new Panther

MARSHAL GEORGI ZHUKOV

Georgi Zhukov (1896-1974) was the luckiest of Soviet commanders. In 1937, when Stalin was murdering other senior officers, Zhukov was out of the way in the Far East. In August 1941 Stalin appointed him to command the Leningrad Front, just as Hitler ordered Army Group North not to enter the city. But Zhukov had talent as well as luck. He helped to plan and partly directed the successful counter-attack outside Moscow in December 1941, the battle for Stalingrad and the battle of the Kursk salient. He was then appointed to command a series of army groups in the offensives of 1944-5.

Zhukov had been an NCO and understood the concerns of the ordinary soldier. He was popular with the rank and file, and would give soldiers lifts in his staff car whenever the opportunity arose. He was a product of the Soviet system at its best, a mixture of sentimentality, competence and brutality.

BEMEDALLED VETERAN By 1945 Zhukov was the USSR's most heavily decorated commander.

April 1940
Katyn
massacre

June 1941
Operation
Barbarossa

July 1941
Leningrad
besieged

June 1942
Operation
Blue

KATYN MASSACRE

In spring 1943 Wehrmacht engineers building a road through the Katyn Forest, north of Smolensk, uncovered mass graves. They thought they were the work of SS 'special action squads', but the local SS commander said that these were not his graves. In April the Germans made public their discovery. Forensic tests produced evidence that 4429 Polish officers had been murdered by the NKVD (forerunner of the KGB) in April 1940. The Kremlin denounced the report, claiming that the Germans had carried out the massacres in 1941.

In October 1992, Boris Yeltsin admitted Soviet responsibility, and informed the Poles of other sites near Kharkov and Kalinin, bringing the total murdered to about 10 000. Those killed were not just officers, but doctors, teachers and lawyers: the leadership of the Polish nation.

SCENE OF HORROR   The bodies discovered at Katyn proved an immense embarrassment to the Soviet authorities.

tanks. The two men conducted these discussions on Enigma net; within days British intelligence had provided the Soviets with details of Hitler's impending offensive.

Forewarned, Stavka decided to impose on the Germans the sort of battle Soviet armies could win, a grinding battle of attrition. In April 300 000 civilian workers equipped with picks and shovels began transforming the countryside around Kursk into a massive fortress. By the beginning of July it consisted of seven separate defensive lines. Stavka poured two army groups, totalling 1.5 million men, into the salient. By July 1, 67 per cent of all Soviet assets – tanks, self-propelled guns, artillery and aircraft – were concentrated in the Kursk salient.

On the night of July 4-5 German forces on the northern and southern shoulders of the salient moved forward to their start lines. At 3 am a sheet of light burst from the salient. Some 17 000 Soviet guns and mortars swept a hurricane of steel and explosives through the German formations. This was the heaviest bombardment thus far conducted in history, and it shredded entire battalions into mangled heaps of flesh and bone. It says much for the German leaders that they were able to move up reserves in time to attack when their own barrage started.

The German northern and southern assaults developed in very different ways. In

the north Ninth Army took three days to push just 2 miles (3.2 km) into the Soviet defences. In the south the SS Panzer Corps advanced nearly 30 miles (50 km) in a week's heavy fighting. On the morning of July 12, the 1000 tanks of Totenkopf, Das Reich and Leibstandarte divisions were advancing north up what appeared to be a gap in the Soviet defences – a long corridor between the swampy Psel river to the west and a steep railway embankment to the east. That same morning the 1000 tanks of the Soviet Fifth Guards Tank Army were advancing south down the corridor. Two thousand German and Soviet tanks were on a collision course on a front just 2 miles (3.2 km) wide.

At around 10 am, near the village of Prokhorovka, they smashed into each other.

Firing at point-blank range, Soviet and German commanders called in air support. By midday, in the largest dogfight ever, about 1000 German and 1000 Soviet aircraft were struggling for control of the patch of sky over Prokhorovka. In the end, the two sides fought each other to a standstill. German losses numbered more than 300 tanks, while the Soviets lost about 900. In a numerical sense the Germans had won, but they could no longer advance. It was at this point, July 12, 1943, that Germany's hope of defeating the Soviet Union finally passed; from now on it was the Soviets who would be attacking.

TIGERS AT KURSK   Weighing 55 tons and with a high-velocity 88 mm gun, the Tiger I was a formidable machine but suffered from chronic mechanical unreliability.

August 1942
Germans reach Volga
and Caspian Sea

September 1942
Germans attack
Stalingrad

January 1943
Germans at
Stalingrad surrender

July 1943
Battle of
Kursk

WAR AGAINST JAPAN

THE US ONSLAUGHT HAD BEGUN, BUT RIGHT ACROSS THE PACIFIC THE JAPANESE MADE THEIR ENEMY FIGHT EVERY INCH OF THE WAY

In the last week of June 1942 more than 100 warships of Japan's Combined Fleet anchored in the vast lagoon of Truk Atoll in the central Pacific. Set against its turquoise waters, they made an impressive sight. Dwarfing all others was Admiral Yamamoto's flagship, the battleship *Yamato*, at 80 000 tons the largest and most powerful warship ever built. Yamamoto spent hours each day in his cabin with brush and paper, indulging his passion for calligraphy. He could still hardly believe his defeat at Midway earlier that month. It was like some ghastly accident, and in the event Japan's military hierarchy had decided to hide the truth from their people; it was not until the autumn of 1945 that most Japanese learned about Midway.

Yamamoto was very much aware that the US onslaught, when it came, would be overwhelming. He reckoned that Japan could retain the initiative for another 18 months, and he had no intention of squandering the time. While Japan's forces in the north and central Pacific consolidated the perimeter of the area they had seized there, he intended to drive south-east into the Solomons, using these as stepping stones for an advance into the South Pacific. The Japanese Army, meanwhile, also had a plan: to land on Papua-New Guinea, seize Port Moresby on the south coast and from there to use air power to dominate the north-eastern coast of Australia.

As ever, the Japanese Navy and army followed separate policies, but it was the same for the Americans. US naval commanders knew that the victory at Midway had been a fluke. For Admiral Chester W. Nimitz and the navy there was only one way to defeat Japan – a thrust by a massively expanded Pacific Fleet and US Marine Corps through the islands of the central Pacific to Taiwan and the coast of China. Here Nimitz's forces would link up with America's Chinese allies for the final advance on Japan.

General MacArthur, however, had his own plans. On arriving in Australia after his escape from the Philippines, he had told newsmen: 'I came through and I shall return.' The last three words were the essence of his policy. He had to return. Together with the US South

THE ALLIES FIGHT BACK In the space of six months up to June 1942, Japan had spread its net across much of the Pacific. Now began the slow and bloody unravelling.

Pacific command MacArthur planned an offensive against the Japanese fleet base at Rabaul on New Britain. He also ordered an Australian brigade to advance from Port Moresby in Papua north along the Kokoda Trail – a 90 mile (145 km) native path, the only route over the rugged Owen Stanley Range.

The Japanese struck first. On July 22, 1942, Maj General Horii's South Seas Force landed on the north coast of Papua and then advanced south along the Kokoda Trail. They were checked by the Australian 39th Militia Battalion, dug in at the village of Isurava, but managed eventually to break through with the help of reinforcements. At the end of August, Japanese marines landed at Milne Bay on Papua's eastern tip where they were repulsed by Australian infantry after several days of hand-to-hand fighting.

By September 16 Horii had reached a ridge 30 miles (48 km) north of Port Moresby. This was as close as his men would get. They faced five veteran Australian brigades, and no more reinforcements were available. With rations virtually exhausted, they retreated. After about ten days without food, some Japanese killed and ate Australian prisoners. The pursuing Australians found evidence of these 'cannibal feasts' and were inspired to fight with cold fury. By early December they had pushed the Japanese back into their beachhead – Horii himself was drowned attempting to escape across a swollen river.

The pursuers were now faced with a well devised system of bunkers. This was the first time Allied troops had attacked the Japanese in strong defensive positions. The Australian

AIR ELITE Highly trained airmen like these had given Japan superiority over much of the south-west Pacific. But they were few in number and would soon be overwhelmed.

June 1942
Battle of
Midway

7th Division managed to take the villages of Sanananda and Gona with grenades and bayonets. The US 32nd Division, going into action for the first time, was repulsed at Buna and refused to go into action again. Eventually, Buna fell to a combined Australian-American attack, but the price had been heavy.

Guadalcanal by land and sea

Martin Clemens was a British colonial official who had remained in hiding on Guadalcanal after the Japanese arrived in order to report on their activities. At dawn on August 7, 1942, he climbed a hill to check shipping movements off the island's north coast. What he saw took his breath away: 'a fleet majestical', he wrote later. About 50 transports and warships were unloading US marines under Maj General Vandegrift on beaches close to where Japanese engineers had been working on an airfield.

The US landing was like a red rag to a Japanese bull. Before the day's end seven cruisers and a destroyer had left Rabaul for Guadalcanal. At 1.30 am on August 9 they surprised and sent a spread of torpedoes into the heavy cruisers USS *Chicago* and HMAS *Canberra*. *Chicago*

ALLIES RESURGENT At Milne Bay (right), the Australians inflicted the first defeat on the Japanese, literally driving a landing force back into the sea. Below: US marines on Guadalcanal.

July 1942
Japanese land
on Papua

August 1942
Americans land
on Guadalcanal

February 1943
Japanese evacuate
Guadalcanal

April 1943
Death of
Yamamoto

July 1943
US landings on
New Georgia

November 1943
US landings on
Gilbert Islands

April 1944
Battles of Imphal
and Kohima

June 1944
US landings in
Marianas

BRIDGE ON THE RIVER KWAI

In the summer of 1942 the Japanese started work on a 260 mile (420 km) railway along the River Kwai and through the mountainous jungle of the Burma-Thailand border. From then until early 1945, 270 000 Asian labourers along with 61 000 Australian, British and Dutch prisoners of war laboured on the railway. The Japanese had huge logistic problems feeding the work force – their own men suffered malnutrition. The Asian labourers and prisoners received a starvation diet and virtually no medical treatment. What starvation and brutal treatment by some of the guards started, diseases like malaria and cholera often finished. An estimated 90 000 native labourers and 12 000 Allied prisoners died.

Between December 1941 and May 1942 the Japanese took nearly 300 000 Allied military and civilian prisoners. Most of the Asians were soon allowed to go home; the 30 000 white civilians were interned in camps where their chief enemies were boredom, malnutrition and disease. Military prisoners, however, were different. The Japanese simply could not understand soldiers who surrendered. Their treatment in the period after capture was often barbaric. The most notorious case was the Bataan 'death march' when malnourished US and Filipino prisoners were driven 90 miles (145 km) from Marivales at the tip of the Bataan peninsula to a railhead at San Fernando. Some 3000 men collapsed with exhaustion during the march and were bayoneted or shot.

Most military prisoners ended up in dreadfully overcrowded complexes such as Singapore's Changi. It has been estimated that about a quarter of Allied servicemen who fell into Japanese hands did not survive their captivity. But the story did not end in 1945. There is medical evidence that Japanese captivity shortened the average life expectancy of the survivors by between ten and fifteen years.

PRISONER'S TESTIMONY Most visual evidence of the appalling conditions in Japanese labour camps came from drawings made by POWs and hidden at great personal risk.

TRUE GRIT **The US marines (above) bore the brunt of much of the land fighting in the Pacific War, taking part in some of the bloodiest battles in history.**

survived, although her bow had been blown off, but *Canberra* was soon ablaze and sinking. Three other US cruisers were also lost.

Japanese destroyers and transports now began a nightly dash from Rabaul, bringing extra troops to Guadalcanal; the Americans dubbed it the Tokyo Express. The Americans, too, poured in reinforcements and by mid September were engaged in a naval battle of attrition. All of America's and Japan's carriers were sent to the southern Solomons.

At first, the Japanese came off best. In August and September, carrier aircraft and submarines sank the carrier *Wasp* and damaged two others, *Enterprise* and *Saratoga*. Only *Hornet* remained undamaged. Nimitz, despairing of the battle, reshuffled his command, sending in Vice Admiral Kinkaid and Admiral 'Bull' Halsey. But they could not avert disaster off the Santa Cruz Islands on October 26, when Japanese carrier aircraft damaged *Enterprise* yet again and so badly damaged *Hornet* that she was abandoned and sunk. On the other hand, US aircraft badly damaged the carriers *Zuiho* and *Shokaku*. Then, in two night actions in November, the Americans sank two Japanese battleships and two cruisers. The Americans finally had control of the waters of the southern Solomons.

On January 10, 1943, American land forces attacked and drove the Japanese towards the western end of Guadalcanal from where elements of Japan's Combined Fleet managed to evacuate 12 000 survivors during the first week in February.

Yamamoto dies

On April 16, 1943, Admiral Halsey flew into Brisbane for his first meeting with MacArthur. They agreed on a two-pronged advance, one from the north coast of Papua, the other from the south-eastern Solomons. Admiral Yamamoto, meanwhile, had gone on a tour of front-line Japanese bases. But his itinerary was radioed ahead and decrypted by the Americans. When his aircraft came into land at Bougainville on April 18, 16 USAAF P-38 Lightnings from Guadalcanal dived from the clouds and sent the admiral to a fiery death.

The twin drives of Operation *Cartwheel* got under way in the summer. Halsey's forces struck New Georgia, north-west of Guadalcanal, on July 2. Despite massive superiority, it took six weeks to capture the enemy base at Munda. Early August was a time of deep depression for the US Joint Chiefs of Staff (JCS) in Washington. If each island took as long to fall as New Georgia the war would still be going on in 1973. The JCS decided on a change of strategy, from 'island hopping' (taking each base in succession) to 'leapfrogging' (bypassing large Japanese concentrations and using naval and air forces to seal them up). It fell to Halsey to put this into effect. On August 14 his forces sailed past the heavily defended island of Kolombangara. The next morning, they landed on Vella Lavelle to the

THE WAR IN BURMA

WITH 'UNCLE BILL' SLIM IN CHARGE, BRITAIN'S XIV ARMY TAUGHT THE JAPANESE THAT THEY COULD NOT ONLY HOLD THEIR GROUND BUT ALSO FIGHT BACK

The Burma campaign was one of the most politically complicated ever fought, since the Allies all had different objectives. The Americans were there because they were building a road from Ledo to Chongqing in south-western China; they would use it to send supplies to Chinese Nationalists waging war against Japan. The Chinese also had troops in north-eastern Burma and had no intention of withdrawing them once the road was finished; they regarded these provinces an integral part of China lost to the British Empire. Neither the Americans nor the Chinese were interested in helping the British to drive the Japanese from central and southern Burma.

In May 1942 Lt General William Slim had brought British and Indian forces out of Burma in the longest retreat ever conducted by the British Army. In December, the British launched a limited counter-offensive when the 14th Indian Division started advancing down the Arakan peninsula. In January 1943, however, it ran into heavily defended Japanese positions at Donbiak. By April the situation had the makings of a disaster – at which point General Noel Irwin, commander of Eastern Army, appointed 'Uncle Bill' Slim to take charge. For the second time in little over a year Slim had been handed a poisoned chalice, and for the second time he extracted his men from a near-impossible situation. Irwin tried to pin the blame on him. Instead, General Auchinleck, Commander in Chief India, sacked Irwin and appointed Slim in his place.

Slim transformed Eastern Army. He instituted new and more realistic training and gave the bewildering variety of races that composed it – Gurkhas, Rajputs, Sikhs, Baluchis, East and West Africans, Chinese, British – a common purpose. To signpost the change he altered the name to XIV Army, insisting that it should be written using Roman rather than Arabic numerals. It was a simple device, yet even today it is sacred to veterans. Another fillip to Allied morale came in October 1943 when Lord Louis Mountbatten arrived as supremo of a newly created South-east Asia Command (SEAC).

The new spirit was soon evident. In February 1944 men from General Mutaguchi's Fifteenth Army infiltrated around British forces in the Arakan, expecting them to panic. Instead, the British pulled back into defensive boxes supplied from the air. The same happened in April when they attacked into the Indian state of Manipur and surged around Imphal and Kohima; the British stayed put. The British also showed that they could attack. In March gliders carried brigades of Chindits deep into the Japanese lines of communication. The Chindits were the brainchild of Maj General Orde Wingate, a fanatical prophet who had inspired Churchill with his vision of an airborne armada hopping from jungle clearing to jungle clearing. Although the Chindits failed to achieve all Wingate desired (he himself was killed in an air crash in March), they came as a nasty surprise to the Japanese. By July 1944 the remnants of Mutaguchi's army were recrossing the Chindwin river, leaving behind a staggering 65 000 dead.

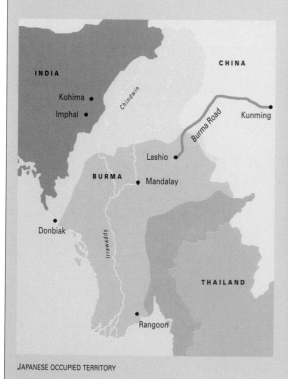

JAPANESE OCCUPIED TERRITORY

Beginning of 1944

End of 1944

June 1945

INDOMITABLE William Slim (right) was probably one of the greatest British generals of all times. Of all the forces in Burma at his command, the Gurkhas (above) adapted best to jungle conditions, and were soon the equals of the Japanese.

DEATH PLUNGE A Japanese dive-bomber is one of more than 400 victims of the 'Marianas' Turkey Shoot'. A US torpedo-bomber sits, wings folded, on the deck of a carrier.

north-west, surprising the small garrison. A brilliant success, the operation set the pattern for landings on Bougainville in November.

Meanwhile, in New Guinea in October, Australian troops from MacArthur's forces captured the Huon peninsula. The JCS had decided that the 140 000 Japanese in Rabaul were too strong to attack directly; instead, the Allies captured islands that dominated the sea approaches. With Rabaul isolated MacArthur pressed ahead for Hollandia. The landing on April 22, 1944, completely

surprised the Japanese, many of whom ran in panic for the first time in the Pacific War.

For much of 1943 the story in the central Pacific had been one of remorseless build-up. The US Fifth Fleet, commanded by Admiral Raymond Spruance, the victor of Midway, was the most powerful the world had ever seen: 7 battleships, 11 aircraft carriers with 1000 aircraft and 44 cruisers and destroyers. There were also 150 000 marines specially trained for amphibious operations.

In mid November 1943 this mighty force struck into the Gilbert Islands (Kiribati) and on November 20 stormed ashore on Makin and Tarawa. Makin fell quickly, but Tarawa was different. A 4700-strong Japanese garrison had tunnelled into the heart of the atoll,

converting it to a fortress. In four days' fighting, the marines suffered 3000 casualties, including 1000 killed. All but 28 Japanese died. Tarawa made Nimitz re-evaluate strategy. When Spruance's fleet surged into the Marshalls in January 1944 it bypassed heavily defended atolls on the rim of the group. While carrier task forces wreaked havoc as far apart as Eniwetok and Truk, the Americans attacked and captured Kwajalein, suffering relatively light casualties. By June 15, 1944, they had reached Saipan, the main island of the Marianas – within bombing range of Tokyo.

Japan's Combined Fleet had been husbanded for just such an occasion. Admiral Ozawa, its commander, hoped that his aircraft would tip the balance in Japan's favour, but disaster struck almost at once; US submarines and aircraft sank three carriers, while fighters shot down 411 Japanese planes in what became known as the Marianas' Turkey Shoot.

Meeting at Pearl Harbor

On July 26, 1944, President Roosevelt arrived at Pearl Harbor aboard the cruiser *Baltimore* to confer with Nimitz and MacArthur. Nimitz was still intent on bypassing the Philippines, MacArthur equally determined that their liberation should take precedence over all else.

When *Baltimore* docked, Nimitz and the naval staff waited in a reception line for the president. MacArthur was notably absent. Deciding that he was not going to come the president and naval high command prepared

WADING ASHORE Keeping together and following the shallowest areas around the reef, US marines pass a crashed Japanese plane as they land on Guam in the Marianas.

FACE OF THE ENEMY On Saipan US marines encountered Japanese civilians for the first time – terrified women and children.

to go ashore when, according to one witness, 'there raced onto the dock . . . the longest open car I have ever seen. In front was a chauffeur in khaki, and in the back one lone figure – MacArthur.' A waiting crowd went wild and MacArthur stopped to acknowledge their cheers on his way to greet the president.

It was an election year, and Roosevelt was too good a politician not to get the message. MacArthur's popularity was such that he could seriously damage Roosevelt. It was not surprising that MacArthur got his way.

THE RIVALS: MacARTHUR AND NIMITZ

In 1952 US television audiences were offered two documentaries about the Pacific war. NBC's *Victory at Sea* was a masterpiece of sound and vision, with a score by Richard Rodgers. It carried little commentary, though occasionally, to underline a point, words were used, such as: 'Bataan . . . Corregidor . . . way stations to America's Calvary. . . . ' At the same time CBS ran *Crusade in the Pacific* in which the treatment was very different. The commentator intoned: 'Bataan and Corregidor . . . it was here, isolated and outnumbered, that General MacArthur derailed Japan's juggernaut. . . .' *Crusade in the Pacific* was partly funded by the Republicans for the MacArthur Committee, dedicated to securing for MacArthur the 1952 nomination as Republican candidate for the presidency. MacArthur himself had scripted much of the film. In contrast, *Victory at Sea* had been scripted by a retired naval officer – Chester Nimitz.

Clashes between MacArthur and Nimitz were almost inevitable; it would have been the same between any general and any admiral both claiming primacy in the Pacific war. By 1945, as they closed on Japan, their 'turf disputes' became more and more intense; by August they were publicly countermanding each other's orders. With Japan's surrender Nimitz gathered his fleets and sailed for Tokyo Bay. On August 28, 1945, while still some distance away, he received a report that USAAF transports from the Philippines were on their way to Atsugi, an air base outside Tokyo. Nimitz ordered his fleet to increase speed, but he was too late. When he sailed into Tokyo Bay, MacArthur was waiting to greet him. The general had flown into Atsugi three days earlier, accompanied by a planeload of journalists and cine camera crews. For the navy it was a bitter moment.

FRIENDS OR FOES? Posing for a publicity shot in 1944, MacArthur (left) and Nimitz give an appearance of unity which was far from reality.

THE BOMBER OFFENSIVE

THE BOMBER ONSLAUGHT SAW SOME OF THE HEAVIEST CASUALTIES OF THE WAR AS ALLIED BOMBERS POUNDED THE HEART OUT OF GERMANY

In 1944 George Orwell wrote the first draft of his novel, *1984*. In his nightmare future world Britain is Airstrip Number One, the launching pad for Oceania's continuous air assaults on Eurasia. Orwell reflected what was a common perception at the time. Since 1939 the landscape of eastern England had been transformed as RAF Bomber Command and the Eighth Air Force of the United States Army Air Force (USAAF) constructed more than 200 major air bases. In area, airfields covered about 2000 sq miles (5200 km²), roughly 4 per cent of the area of England.

Except when the weather was absolutely foul, the skies over East Anglia, Lincolnshire and the East Riding of Yorkshire were full of bombers either leaving for or returning from raids. Many of the latter limped back damaged, smoke streaming from burning engines. Crashes were common – about four per day – and not all belly-landed on airfields. Travelling through Norfolk could be hazardous; between the summers of 1942 and 1945 a number of vehicles were hit by B-17 Flying Fortresses ploughing through fields and hedges and across roads.

HASTY REPAIRS Ground crews in April 1943 strip down the engines of one of 39 B-17s damaged in a raid on Bremen a week earlier.

The streams of bombers flew around the clock. In the morning US B-17s and B-24s would be taking off, as British and Canadian Halifaxes, Lancasters and Stirlings were coming in to land. They were all part of the same effort, the Combined Bomber Offensive, agreed by the Combined Chiefs of Staff at Casablanca in January 1943. The 'Casablanca Directive' stated their aim as 'the progressive destruction and dislocation of the German military, industrial and economic system, and the undermining of the morale of the German people to a point where their capacity for armed resistance is fatally weakened'.

Night versus day

But although they were following the same directive, the British and Americans disagreed on how to achieve its objectives. Immediately after the declaration of war, Bomber Command had attempted daylight precision raids against military targets in Germany, and paid dearly. German fighter defences had shot large numbers of Wellingtons, Blenheims, Whitleys and Hampdens out of the sky. Daytime attacks were abandoned, and flights over Germany confined to the hours of darkness. But because of the danger of hitting civilians the only cargo the bombers carried was propaganda leaflets.

Such niceties disappeared with the German assault on the Low Countries and France in May 1940. Bomber Command responded with night attacks on rail junctions and oil refineries. From August 25 British bombers began night attacks on military and industrial targets in Berlin. Over the next ten months the list of targets expanded as bomber strength grew and the first four-engined heavy bombers, the Stirlings and Halifaxes, joined

August 1940
RAF night raids
on Berlin

February 1942
Harris appointed C in C
Bomber Command

March 1942
RAF raid on
Lübeck

April 1942
RAF raid on
Rostock

squadrons. But there seemed to be a problem. The bombers went out, yet according to photographic reconnaissance flights, some of the 'targets for tonight' had sustained no damage. At the instigation of 'the Prof' – Lord Cherwell, Churchill's chief scientific advisor – the Cabinet Office ordered a detailed study. This concluded that over a 53 day period only two-thirds of aircraft had reached their target areas.

It was 'the Prof', a ruthlessly logical Oxford don, who came up with a solution. Bomber Command should concentrate its resources on the area bombardment of one or two large cities each night. He proposed that the bombers attack in waves. The first would drop high explosives to break gas and water mains and force fire and rescue services under cover. The next waves would shower tens of thousands of small

incendiary bombs into a relatively concentrated area in a city centre. With donnish sophistry, Cherwell claimed that the object was 'the dehousing of the German work force'. The unspoken corollary was that Bomber Command's primary target would be women and children living in large cities.

On February 22, 1942, Air Marshal Arthur Harris was appointed Commander in Chief of Bomber Command. He at once set about testing the Prof's hypothesis. On March 28, 234 bombers attacked the largely wooden medieval city of Lübeck. It burnt beautifully; the later raiders could see the conflagration

SKY GIANT Dwarfed by a Halifax (below), the men of the 'Shining Tenth' Squadron of Bomber Command pose on an airfield in the East Riding. The navigating officer of each bomber maintained a log book (left). An RAF instructor (above) uses models to demonstrate the most vulnerable points of enemy fighters.

THE GREAT ESCAPERS

Most of the RAF and USAAF men who survived being shot down over enemy territory spent time in Stalag Luft III, a prisoner-of-war camp at Sagan south-east of Berlin. One was a US officer, Colonel Delmar T. Spivey, who arrived in the summer of 1943. He was astounded when the most senior British officer took him into his confidence. The British had three tunnels under way, Tom, Dick and Harry. In succeeding days Spivey learned about the prisoners' forgery operation, covert communications with London and Washington, impressive education and theatrical programmes and athletic activities.

The British were constantly breaking out, and though few made 'a home run', they sometimes occupied thousands of German troops in searches. At first the Germans regarded these as 'jolly japes', but as the RAF's area bombardments killed thousands of German civilians attitudes began to harden. This was the situation on March 24/25, 1944, when 80 prisoners managed to get through Harry. Four were captured at the mouth of the tunnel, but 76 cleared the camp area. Hitler issued his infamous Sagan Order, which led to the death by shooting of 50 escapees. Only three made it home. On April 6 when the camp commandant told the remaining prisoners of the fate of their colleagues, he apologised for his inability to protect them once they were beyond the wire.

100 miles (160 km) ahead. Harris then turned his attention to Rostock, another medieval city. Between April 23 and 27, 521 bombers destroyed 70 per cent of its built-up area. On May 30 came a much harder target. By borrowing aircraft from Coastal Command and training squadrons, Harris put 1050 bombers over Cologne. The aircraft formed a single stream, 70 miles (110 km) long, which simply overwhelmed the German defences. For a terrifying 75 minutes an apparently endless stream of planes rained bombs on Cologne, destroying the city centre where only the cathedral remained standing.

But Cologne was a one-off. Bomber Command could not yet sustain raids on this scale. New four-engined Lancasters were arriving but it would be 1943 before the majority of Harris's aircraft were modern. Navigation, too, was a problem. Even with electronic aids like OBOE – using radar pulses emitted from stations in Britain to indicate when a plane should drop its bomb load – a high proportion of aircraft failed to reach the target. This improved, however, after August 1942, when Harris appointed an Australian,

Wing Commander Donald Bennett, to command the Pathfinders, a force of highly skilled pilots and navigators, who would show the others the way to the target and then mark it.

Firestorm over Hamburg

By the spring of 1943 Harris believed that he at last had the aircraft and techniques to start destroying Germany's ability to wage war. From March 5, Bomber Command kept up a constant attack on the cities of the Ruhr. In 16 major raids the British dropped 24 000 tons of bombs and began to have an observable effect on German morale. For Harris, however, the campaign was only partly satisfactory. In 30 days Bomber Command had lost 310 aircraft, the highest casualty rate thus far.

He needed another spectacular raid to maintain the momentum of his campaign. He later recalled: 'I had always wanted to have a real dead set at Hamburg. It was the second biggest city in Germany and I wanted to make a tremendous show.' On July 24, 791 aircraft flew in a stream some 200 miles (320 km) long towards the German coast. At a distance of about 80 miles (130 km) the crews threw out bundles of 'Window', a new wonder weapon which was, in fact, very prosaic – bundles of aluminium

OVER THE TARGET A pilot (left) checks his instruments as he waits for the signal, 'Bombs away'. Below: 88 mm anti-aircraft guns mounted on towers in the Berlin zoo.

chaff which confused short-range German radar. Pilots saw antiaircraft shells hose skywards towards the falling chaff. The British flew on almost unmolested – they lost only 12 aircraft – and dropped 2300 tons of bombs which burnt out the centre of the city and killed about 1500 people.

The bombers came back on July 27. The temperature during the day had been around 32°C (90°F). As the incendiary bombs fell the heated air rose much more rapidly than usual. The hot air above sucked in surrounding cooler air to produce a firestorm. A raging

BRITISH BOMBER The Avro Lancaster was the backbone of Britain's bomber offensive, but suffered heavy casualties. More than half of the 8000 built were lost in action or accidents.

wind fed an enormous pillar of flame, picking up large fire engines and propelling them into the flames as though they were children's toys. Very few of Hamburg's population were caught in the streets. The city had been bombed many times and tens of thousands were sheltering in deep, well-constructed cellars. This time it did not help them. The firestorm raised temperatures so that asphalt melted, and oxygen was sucked from the atmosphere to feed the pillar of flame. When the fires began to subside on July 29 rescue workers discovered cellar after cellar packed with what looked like blackened monkeys; most had died from asphyxiation, after which the intense heat had shrivelled their bodies.

The work of removing the corpses had barely begun when the bombers came back on the night of July 29 to pulverise the smouldering ruins. And they were back again on August 2 to smash what was left. By this time, 40 000 people had been killed in the firestorm, and another 4500 in the later raids. In Berlin the minister of armaments, Albert Speer, calculated that another six raids like the one on Hamburg would finish the war. But astonishingly production in Hamburg did recover; within five months the main war factories were up to four-fifths of their previous output.

WHAT PRICE GOMORRAH? The shrunken corpses of two children lie amidst the rubble of Hamburg. The view from Cologne Cathedral in 1945 bears witness to the deadly effectiveness of incendiaries, small bombs which burned the hearts out of Europe's cities.

Harris, too, was sure that he had won an outright victory in Hamburg, one he wished to follow up. So, for five months from November 1943, Bomber Command pounded Berlin. This time the results were disappointing: no firestorm, no cessation of normal life. Part of the problem was the target. Berlin was a sprawling city of stone and concrete with broad avenues and parks. A fire might burn out a district but it would not spread. There was another factor: German scientists had developed a radar which could see the British bombers through clouds of Window.

In December 1943 Harris lost 316 heavy bombers. A crew now had only a one-in-four chance of surviving the statutory 30 missions,

and in a few squadrons morale began to crack. When Harris finally agreed to call the battle off in March 1944, it had cost Bomber Command 1128 aircraft.

Flying Fortresses

Nearly two years earlier, on August 17, 1942, 12 US B-17s commanded by General Ira C. Eaker had flown across the Channel to bomb marshalling yards at Rouen. For the next five months, Eaker's bombers developed their skills in daylight raids on targets in northern France and the Low Countries, all in range of British fighter support. But Eaker was convinced that his air force could also carry out daylight precision raids on targets beyond

DEATH OF A B-17 Filming from another bomber, an Eighth Air Force cameraman catches the moment when the port wing of a B-17 is hit by flak and explodes into flame. The chances of the crew bailing out and surviving are very small – no more than one in five.

OPERATION CHASTISE

DAMBUSTER TRIALS A Mosquito drops a prototype of Wallis's 'bouncing bomb'.

On the evening of May 16, 1943, 19 Lancasters, each laden with a 5 ton 'bouncing bomb', took off from Scampton in Lincolnshire. Their targets were dams on the Möhne, Eder and Sorpe rivers, tributaries of the Ruhr. The Ruhr supplied water for numerous industrial enterprises, and the dams helped to control its level. They were obvious targets and heavily defended, but Vickers' engineer Barnes Wallis, an eccentric genius, had developed a spherical bomb to overcome the defences. It would skip over the protective torpedo nets, sink to the bottom when it reached the wall, then detonate. The commander, 24-year-old Squadron Leader Guy Gibson, led the first six Lancasters onto the Möhne. Four missed, one was shot down, but the last scored a direct hit; the dam crumbled. Meanwhile, four of the five aircraft attacking the Eder had been shot down, but the last, piloted by American J.C. McCarthy, scored a hit and the top of the dam crumbled. In the end, the results were not as impressive as Wallis had hoped: 1294 dead or missing and 11 factories destroyed.

the range of escorting fighters. The B-17 was a sturdy, heavily armoured machine – not for nothing was it known as the 'Flying Fortress'. By flying in close formation, the Fortresses, Eaker believed, could fight their way through the heaviest German fighter opposition.

On January 27, 1943, 53 B-17s bombed the North Sea port of Wilhelmshaven and 50 made it back to England. During the next six months Eaker's bombers, now designated US Eighth Air Force, penetrated to targets such as Hamm, Kassel and Hanover. Losses mounted steadily, from 18 in January to 118 in July, but more aircraft and crews were arriving all the time and Eaker believed he could win this battle of attrition.

On August 17, 1943, two formations of B-17s took off to attack the Messerschmitt factory in Regensburg and ball-bearing factories at Schweinfurt. Thunderbolt fighters escorted the Regensburg group as far as southern Belgium, then peeled off and headed for home. So began one of the greatest air battles of the war, as hundreds of German fighters closed in for the kill. A US observer, Lt Colonel Beirne Lay Jr, watched 'B-17s dropping out in every state of distress, from engines on fire to control surfaces shot away, . . . and, on the green carpet far behind us, numerous pyres of smoke from fallen fighters, marking our trail'. As they approached the

HERALDRY OF TOTAL WAR The crew of B-17 'Delta Rebel' record the number of missions completed with small painted bombs and the number of enemy fighters shot down with small swastikas.

SCOURGE OF THE GERMAN SKIES The P-51 Mustang could penetrate deep into Germany with the aid of underwing 'drop tanks', and outfight any Luftwaffe fighter with the sole exception of the Me262.

target, the Regensburg group was down to 14 aircraft – from 98. Its commander, Colonel Curtis LeMay, planted his bombs on top of workshops containing the fuselages of the new Me262 fighters and flew on, unaware that he had just destroyed Germany's last hope of regaining aerial supremacy. The twin-jet Me262 would now come too late to influence the course of the war. Meanwhile, the 230 B-17s on their way to Schweinfurt had been attacked by upward of 300 fighters. The Germans dived out of the sun to rake the topmost group and continued through the US formation at high speed to hit the bottom group, sending 31 B-17s down in flames.

Eaker was not deterred. Believing he was winning the battle, he pursued his long-range daylight bombing programme and the result was disaster. From October 8 to 14, 1943, he lost 148 bombers and nearly 1500 air crew. The mood in Eighth Air Force was captured six years later in Henry King's film *12 O'Clock High*, in which Gregory Peck played a character based on Eaker, who pushes his crews and ultimately himself too far. Eventually, unescorted daylight operations over Germany were suspended, and at the end of the year Eaker was transferred to the Mediterranean. The Eighth and Fifteenth Air Forces were combined into the US Strategic Air Forces under General Carl A. Spaatz.

Spaatz's appointment coincided with the arrival of the first P-51 Mustangs – hybrid fighters with an American-designed fuselage and a British engine, which could outperform Germany's Fw190. In his Christmas message, the commander of the USAAF, General 'Hap' Arnold, stressed that the overriding aim was now the destruction of the Luftwaffe. Spaatz sent out formations with the primary objective not of reaching a target but of forcing the Luftwaffe to come up and fight.

Beginning on February 20, 1944, US bombers and fighters struck at key factories of the German aircraft industry. For the next seven days they fought their way into the Reich, losing 226 B-17s and B-24s but only 28 fighters. These losses were much heavier than those of 1943, but now German fighters were being shot down in large numbers. In March alone the Luftwaffe lost 56 per cent of its fighters and 22 per cent of its surviving pilots. The Americans could keep this up indefinitely. Having applied the principles of industrial mass production to air warfare, and having a superior long-range fighter, they tore the heart out of the Luftwaffe.

Last gasps

At the end of March the chiefs of staff ordered the US Strategic Air Forces and Bomber Command to suspend attacks on Germany and concentrate on 'softening up' German defences along the northern coast of France. Neither Spaatz nor Harris was happy with this development. Both believed that they were on the brink of winning outright victory for the Allies, but in both cases it was an illusion. Indeed, the pause in night bombing allowed Bomber Command to recover from a battle it was losing.

The suspension should have given the Luftwaffe time to recover, too, but Hitler insisted on pouring resources into offensive weapons, like the V-1 and V-2. He also demanded that the new Me262 jet fighter, just then coming off the production lines,

should be converted into a fighter-bomber. When Allied bombing of Germany resumed in the autumn, there were too few Me262s to have a decisive impact.

The climax of the bombing offensive came with Operation *Thunderclap*, a combined Anglo-American assault on Dresden. It had originally been scheduled for February 3, the eve of the conference at Yalta of the 'Big Three', Churchill, Roosevelt and Stalin. It was meant to boost Anglo-American prestige and send a clear message to the Soviets about the power of the Western bomber fleets. However, cloud cover over south-eastern Germany delayed the attack until February 13, by which time it no longer served its original political purpose.

Dresden was well suited for a demonstration raid. Like Rostock and Lübeck it was medieval with many half-timbered buildings; because it contained a large part of Europe's architectural heritage, it had not yet been bombed and was therefore full of combustibles. It was also full of people, the population having been swollen to over a million by an influx of refugees. On the

THE BOMBER BARONS – HARRIS AND SPAATZ

The 'bomber barons' of Britain and the USA epitomised different approaches to aerial warfare. Historians have likened Harris (1892-1984) to the First World War commander in chief, Sir Douglas Haig, sending his bomber crews 'over the top' night after night regardless of casualties in pursuit of an unattainable objective. By contrast, Spaatz (1891-1974) has been portrayed as the commander who realised that the air war could not be won until the Luftwaffe had been shot out of the skies. However, Spaatz's casualties were just as heavy as Bomber Command's; in fact, the approaches were complementary rather than opposed.

In 1946 Spaatz was appointed commander of the USAAF and became chief of staff of the newly independent United States Air Force in 1947. When he died he was buried at the USAF Academy at Colorado Springs, an institution he had helped to found. For Harris it was very different. In 1946, still only 54, he resigned from the RAF and left for South Africa. Unfairly blamed for the destruction of Dresden, he became a figure of hate for many. The controversy has shown no signs of diminishing. When the Queen Mother unveiled a statue of Harris in London in 1992 the ceremony was disrupted by a noisy protest.

COMPLEMENTARY PATHS Although area bombardment by night and precision bombing by day seemed very different, the strategies of Harris (left) and Spaatz (right) often ended with the same result.

DEVASTATION IN DRESDEN On February 15, 1945, police and *Volkssturm* ('People's Guard') pile some of the more than 60 000 bodies onto an enormous funeral pyre in Dresden's Altmarket.

night of February 13, 796 Lancasters hit the city in two waves three hours apart. The following day 311 B-17s dropped another 1000 tons of bombs. Conditions were ideal for a firestorm, which raged for seven days. When it subsided rescue workers retrieved 68 650 corpses, about half of whom were children. The Nazi propaganda chief Joseph Goebbels did not try to minimise the impact; he doubled the number of dead to 135 000.

In summer 1945 the survivors of Bomber Command learned with surprise, which soon turned to anger, that they would not be awarded a campaign medal. And when other theatre commanders, Alexander, Montgomery and the like, were being raised to the peerage, Harris was refused the honour. Churchill was a statesman but he was also a politician. In the aftermath of Dresden, a raid he had specifically requested, he sent Harris a memorandum critical of Bomber Command's 'pursuit of terror for terror's sake'. An incensed Harris, refusing to accept this criticism, sent back a blistering reply. He was defending 50 000 men who had died during the war in terrifying circumstances, falling from the sky at night in burning aircraft. Eighth Air Force had also lost 50 000 men.

The combined offensive killed approximately a million German civilians. But it was not the deaths of the civilians that brought about the collapse of the German war effort in spring 1945; it was the disruption of the German transport system. In this both US and British bombers had played a role.

THE HOME FRONT

NO SIX YEARS HAVE EVER BROUGHT SO MUCH CHANGE TO SO MANY SOCIETIES. ON THE ALLIED SIDE, THE STANDARD OF LIVING AND THE EXPECTATIONS OF MILLIONS ROSE DURING THE WAR YEARS, DESPITE BOMBING AND RATIONING. BY CONTRAST, OCCUPIED EUROPE AND PARTS OF ASIA WERE PLUNGED INTO A NEW BARBARISM. IN THE USSR, POLAND AND GERMANY, MILLIONS OF GIRLS GREW TO MATURITY WITH NO COMPANIONSHIP FROM ADULT MALES, AS BROTHERS, FATHERS OR LOVERS.

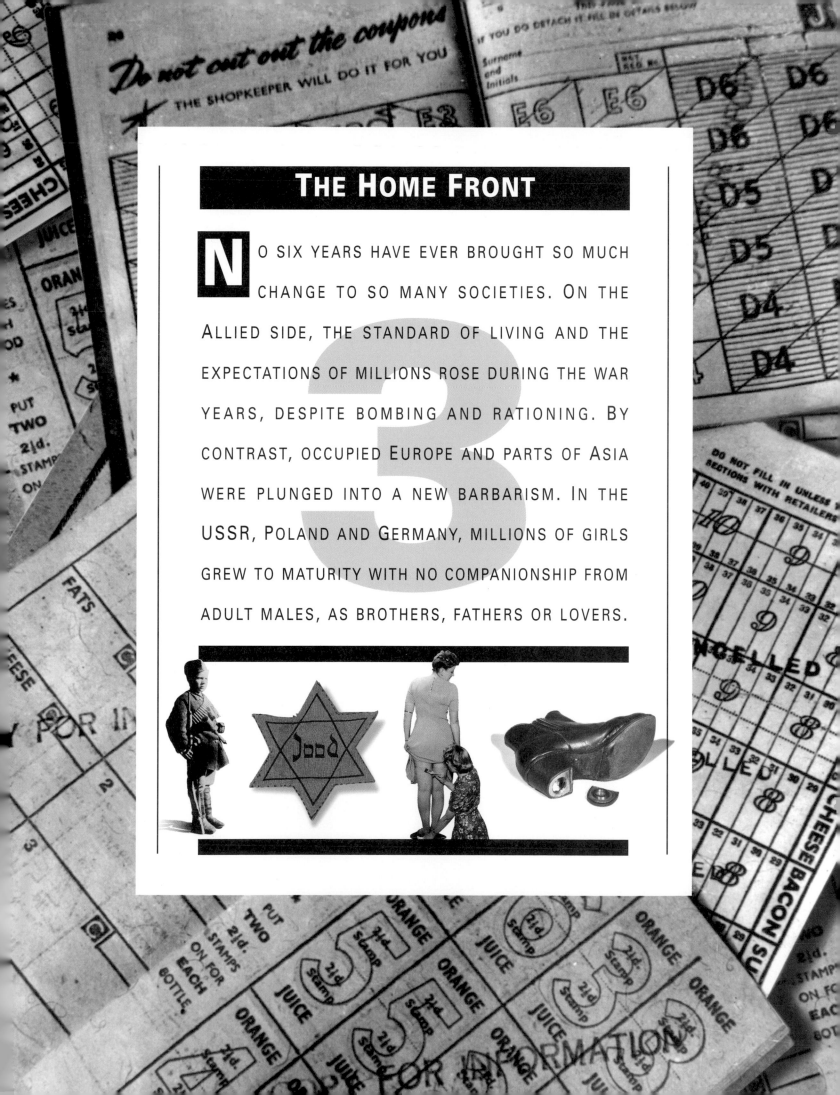

THE WAR AT HOME

IN TOTAL WAR, THE HOME FRONT BECAME ANOTHER WAR FRONT, WITH CIVILIANS SUFFERING DANGER AND HARDSHIP SIMILAR TO SERVICEMEN

The sanctity of hearth and home was the theme of one of the most popular songs of 1915; 'Keep The Home Fires Burning' urged women to tend the flame of domestic harmony while the men were away fighting. Thirty years later, in the middle of the second great war of the century, the lyrics sounded ironic. By now Britain was the home front, where the population was as much in the war as soldiers on the Italian front or in Burma. Even Allied nations whose civilian populations were far from any active front, like the United States, Canada, Australia, New Zealand and South Africa, were deeply affected by the conflict, though none so much as Britain.

Britain looked like a country at war. Its towns and cities were packed with people in military uniforms, and everywhere walls and hoardings were covered with posters exhorting people to grow more and eat less, to travel only if necessary and to 'Be Like Dad, Keep Mum'. Although similar signs could be seen in New York, Toronto, Wellington, Sydney and Cape Town, British cities were unique in bearing the scars of war: hundreds of acres of rubble and thousands of acres of bomb-damaged buildings.

In hundreds of city parks the upturned barrels of 3.7 in (94 mm) anti-aircraft guns sprouted between the trees. By 1944 England had about 50 000 anti-aircraft guns, mostly concentrated in dense belts in the southeast. Britain's air defences were operated by tens of thousands of women. Male officers and NCOs were attached to each gun actually to fire it, but this legal nicety, introduced to save 'the givers of life from being the takers of life', was increasingly ignored.

The guns were still fired in anger. The suspension of the Blitz in May 1941 marked the end of sustained heavy bombing, but the Luftwaffe continued to carry out raids. From April to June 1942, for example, German bombers heavily attacked Exeter, Bath, Norwich, York and Canterbury in retaliation for Bomber Command attacks on Rostock and Lübeck. These so-called Baedeker Raids – after the *Baedeker* tourist guides, because the raids were all against historic towns and cities – killed about 1000 people and injured many thousands more. The Luftwaffe hit London again in March and April 1944 in the 'Little Blitz', which killed 1500 and seriously injured 3000. In addition, the Germans kept up day and night 'hit and run' attacks on towns and cities from Penzance to Newcastle upon Tyne. East Anglia was very badly hit; German

GAS ALERT A cigarette card (left) explains the operation of a gas mask. Civilians in a Brighton street (below) respond to a mock gas attack in February 1941.

FLOATING DEFENCES WAAFs raise a barrage balloon, one of several thousand that formed an aerial forest over southern and eastern England.

fighter-bombers would fly beneath the British radar net, then climb at the last moment to swoop down and strafe the streets of Great Yarmouth, Maldon and a dozen other provincial centres. The last Luftwaffe operation over England was on April 10, 1945, less than a month before Germany's capitulation.

By this time England was reeling from flying bomb and ballistic missile attacks. The first V-1s came down on June 13, 1944, and within a week had killed nearly 800 and badly injured another 2700. From September 8, 1944, the flying bombs were supplemented by the V-2, a rocket carrying a 1 ton warhead which struck without warning. Every day until the end of March 1945 around 50 V-1s and 10 V-2s came down indiscriminately over south-east England, each killing and injuring a few dozen people.

Between May 1941 and April 1945 more than 17 000 British civilians died and another 40 000 were seriously injured as a result of German attacks. Life had a dangerous edge. One could never be quite sure that an Fw190

THE PEOPLE'S WAR A family in London's East End, bombed out by the first big raid of the Blitz on September 7/8, 1940, move to temporary accommodation.

EVACUEES – HOW TOWN MET COUNTRY

On the night of September 1/2, 1939, some 36 hours before Britain declared war on Germany, the country's rail system was under pressure. Thousands of trains packed with 827 000 schoolchildren, 524 000 mothers and children under school age, 7000 blind and disabled people and 103 000 teachers and helpers were moving out of the cities to evacuation billets in the country. It was the largest social upheaval Britain had ever experienced. Middle-class children from Hampstead and Highgate found themselves in labourers' cottages; slum children from Stepney, Toxteth or the Gorbals ended up in middle-class or even aristocratic households. According to one story, a Gorbals mother billeted in a country house in Ayrshire yelled at her child: 'You dirty thing, messing up the lady's carpet. Go and do it in the corner.' City and country came into contact, and produced some marvellous humour. William Brown, Richmal Crompton's 'bad boy', sees profit to be made. The evacuees, reasons William, get the best of everything. Soon he and his 'outlaws' are touring villages, passing themselves off as city children, who have never seen cows, chickens . . . or grass.

POIGNANT PARTING A soldier on leave in London in summer 1940 says goodbye to his young son, about to be evacuated to the relative safety of Wales.

would not strafe the 8.10 am from Norwich to King's Cross, or that a V-2 travelling at four times the speed of sound would not crash onto one's office in the City of London.

Queues and rationing

By 1944 queues were features of all Allied cities – even the Americans and Australians queued. There were queues for public transport, queues for cinemas, queues in shops. But whereas women queued in New York for nylon stockings, and in Sydney for coffee, in London they queued for almost everything. Unlike its allies, the small, crowded island of Britain could not have survived without a rigorously enforced system of rationing. It increased the area of land under cultivation from 16 million to nearly 23 million acres (6.5 million to nearly 9.3 million ha), and supplemented the agricultural work force with a Women's Land Army of 80 000 and some 40 000 Italian prisoners of war. As a result of rationing and increased domestic production, nobody went hungry. Meals were boring, but they were generally nutritious, and by 1945 the population was in better physical shape than it had been in 1925 or would be in 1965.

HOME FRONT MEMENTOS With the outbreak of war, many products were repackaged. Matches were sold under the labels Victory, Spitfire, even Hitler's, cigarettes under the brand name Tank. Meanwhile, cans adorned with the Stars and Stripes were crossing the Atlantic, packed with powdered milk and the soon-to-be-reviled powdered eggs.

LAND GIRLS The 80 000 girls of the Women's Land Army worked long hours and helped to keep Britain from starving.

SOCIAL REVOLUTION For most US blacks a move into the industrial work force meant a spectacular rise in living standards.

The need to wage total war pushed Allied governments towards increasingly planned economies. In the United States, Roosevelt had already sought to increase the powers of the executive branch during the 1930s when pulling the American economy out of the Depression. He now used a series of War Powers Acts to override state and local authorities if they got in the way of the war effort. However, although 12 million men were eventually drafted into the armed forces, the USA never adopted a comprehensive manpower programme; it relied instead on high pay to lure workers into the new factories springing up throughout the north-east and California. More than 6 million people entered the industrial work force for the first time, mainly white women like 'Rosie the Riveter', whose picture was seen on posters in all work places. The expansion also brought 1.5 million blacks into the northern states and more than 200 000 Mexicans into southern California. The result was a series of race riots, more serious and deadly than the better reported disturbances of the mid 1960s.

Of all the Allied nations, none mobilised as comprehensively as Australia. Fearing a Japanese invasion, the Labor government panicked in early 1942. It pushed nearly a million men into the armed forces, and directed the labour of the rest of the population into the war effort. As Australia had slightly fewer than 7 million people, these measures produced immense dislocation and precipitated a progressive collapse of the economy during 1943. The result was a partial demobilisation, with troops directed into factories.

The experience of the First World War stood Britain's civil servants in good stead and they handled mobilisation for total war more effectively. By 1944 Ernest Bevin's Ministry of Labour was 'totalitarian' in a much more real sense than its counterparts in Germany or the Soviet Union, in that it was generally competent and kept corruption under control. Women, unless they had heavy family commitments, were conscripted into war-related work. No one was exempt. One highly publicised conscript was the 18-year-old Princess Elizabeth, who served as an Auxiliary Territorial Service (ATS) mechanic and driver from the spring of 1945. Most young men were conscripted into the armed forces, but a proportion of each intake, known as 'Bevin Boys', was directed to work in coal mines; the minister of labour made the point that maintaining coal production was just as important as the business of fighting.

Moving around

During the Second World War people were constantly on the move. North America, Australia and New Zealand sent the majority of their young men aged between 18 and 36 to battlefronts thousands of miles away. About

2.5 million American men were in Britain, and another 1 million passed through Australia. The servicemen of both nations came to resent the Americans: their higher pay, smarter, sexier uniforms and a veneer of what was believed to be worldly sophistication attracted women in large numbers. They were, in the catchphrase of the time, 'overpaid, oversexed and over here'. In Britain, where the ratio of Americans to the local population was still relatively low, there was some friction but relationships were on

COAL CRISIS By the summer of 1943 the loss of 56 000 British coal miners to the armed forces had resulted in a decline in production. The government asked miners' sons (below), some as young as 14, to volunteer in the pits.

THE BIG BAND SOUND OF GLENN MILLER

IN THE MOOD Miller and his band entertain the troops.

In June 1944 an elite unit of the USAAF landed in Britain, commanded by 40-year-old Captain (later Major) Glenn Miller. The Glenn Miller USAAF Band had produced a string of hits, from 'Little Brown Jug' to 'Chattanooga Choo Choo'. In England the band maintained a punishing schedule, averaging three performances a day. At an open-air concert in August 1944, while playing 'In the Mood', a loud buzzing heralded the approach of a V-1. Instead of taking cover, Miller increased the tempo, drowning the noise of the flying bomb with massed trombones and trumpets.

Mystery has surrounded Miller's death. Officially, his aircraft iced up in bad weather while crossing the Channel on December 15, 1944, and plunged into the sea. Of the many other theories put forward to explain his disappearance, one came from RAF bomber pilots flying back from an aborted daylight raid. As they jettisoned bombs over the Channel, an aircraft suddenly appeared below them; it was blown to smithereens. The plane was a Norseman, the same as Miller's.

the whole friendly. By contrast, Australia was swamped. When Walt Disney's *Bambi* was premiered in Sydney in 1943, the most poignant moment in the film, when the baby deer is crying for its lost mother, was shattered by an Australian serviceman shouting out: 'Don't worry, Bambi, she's probably out with some bloody Yank!' Fights were frequent, and on one occasion in Brisbane in August 1942, ended in a pitched battle with several dead and seriously injured.

Within the Allied nations there were enormous internal migrations. Millions moved to new jobs, while in Britain at least 5 million were 'bombed out', many thousands more than once. Traditional family life virtually ceased to exist for the duration of the war, with women struggling to bring up children alone in the absence of their fathers. Churchmen in the USA became worried about a new phenomenon – the teenager, a term first used in about 1943. Sixteen and seventeen-year-old boys and girls had more freedom and money than ever before, and an older generation

saw in their distinctive style of dress and dance crazes the signs of moral degeneracy.

In Britain young people had neither the money nor the time to create a distinctive youth culture. That would come about ten years after the war. For the moment British youth was among the most highly regimented in the world. In January 1941 the Air Ministry had launched the Air Training Corps (ATC) for boys between 16 and 18. Volunteers were given RAF uniforms, and within six months the ATC had grown to 200 000. Sea Cadets and Army Cadets were also expanded, along with parallel organisations for girls. But despite the regimentation, British youth

MAKING NEW FRIENDS Black American men and white English girls fraternise in a club for 'colored' US servicemen (below). US airmen and British girls jive and jitterbug to the sound of a big band (bottom).

A KISS IS STILL A KISS

THE CINEMA WAS POPULAR AS NEVER BEFORE OR SINCE DURING THE SECOND WORLD WAR, AND THE FILM INDUSTRY OBLIGED WITH CLASSICS SUCH AS *CASABLANCA*

Ingrid Bergman is insistent: 'Play it, Sam, play it.' A reluctant Dooley Wilson succumbs and starts singing 'As Time Goes By'. 'Sam, I thought I told you never to play that again', snarls Humphrey Bogart, coming in. Over time, the two lines have merged in the popular consciousness.

Warner Brothers filmed the play *Everybody Comes To Rick's* in 1942; the name was changed to *Casablanca* at the last minute to take advantage of news coverage of a meeting in Casablanca between Churchill and Roosevelt. It was a straightforward melodrama, in which Rick's Café is a microcosm of the war-torn world – Rick (Humphrey Bogart), the proprietor who could restore order if he so chose but is crippled by disillusion and cynicism, is emblematic of the United States. The symbolism was so obvious it might have been laughable, but for a brilliant cast. Instead, it caught the mood of the time. Bogart and Bergman (Ilse Lund) are in love but the need to fight the Nazis means that they must put their own feelings to one side and say goodbye. It was something millions of couples were doing throughout the world.

During the war the USA produced more than 4000 feature films, and Great Britain another 400 or so. Many of the best were like *Casablanca*; they did not deal directly with battles and warfare, but themes like loss, separation, conflicting loyalties and duty. Because so many people had direct experience of war, re-creating battle on screen was generally unsuccessful, and actors such as Errol Flynn and John Wayne who starred in such films were often subjected to derision; both were booed out of US Marine Corps camps. Action frequently revolved around relationships in a platoon, invariably a cross-section of society, and showed how these disparate individuals were turned into an efficient fighting machine. The enemy were stereotyped villains, often played by Erich von Stroheim, Conrad Veidt or Raymond Massey. An exception was the Nazi in Alfred Hitchcock's *Lifeboat*, who was portrayed as competent, intelligent and ruthless, a man who knew exactly what he wanted. Critics attacked the film as pro-Nazi, and few were prepared to listen to Hitchcock's argument that it was fatal to underestimate one's enemy.

The war years were also a golden age for Hollywood comedy, either related to the domestic impact of the war, like *The Miracle of Morgan's Creek* and *Hail the Conquering Hero*, or completely escapist like *Arsenic and Old Lace*. The alternative was the bittersweet world of Rick, Ilse and Casablanca. Cinema attendance reached levels never achieved before or since. Receipts in the USA showed that more than 100 million attended the cinema each week, while in Britain numbers rarely fell below a staggering 30 million. Life in Britain had become a round of long hours, monotonous and tasteless food, and exhausted sleep, interspersed with moments of sheer terror during air raids and rocket attacks. All that millions had to look forward to was three hours of escapism in the relative warmth and comfort of a cinema.

MAKE 'EM LAUGH, MAKE 'EM CRY   A poster advertises a zany comedy of 1944, featuring two homicidal maiden aunts and their lunatic nephew.
Left: Humphrey Bogart, Claude Rains, Paul Henreid and Ingrid Bergman star in the classic wartime drama *Casablanca*.

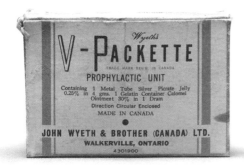

IF YOU CAN'T BE GOOD As venereal disease rates rocketed, governments swept aside old taboos and issued kits to servicemen containing condoms and antiseptic cream.

enjoyed the same music and dances as their US counterparts. In cities and towns all over the country, cavernous dance halls (some could accommodate more than 3000) were packed to capacity on Friday and Saturday nights with people swinging to the music of the big bands. There were never enough men to go around, so dances that involved rapid changes of partner and mass participation dances like the hokey-cokey were popular.

Conventional moral constraints fell away suddenly and on a large scale. In the heightened emotional atmosphere of a bombed city, with life itself seeming to hang in the balance, people who scarcely knew each other made love. In 1941 the incidence of syphilis

WESTWARD HO! Some of the more than 80 000 British women who married US servicemen board the *Queen Mary* for New York in the summer of 1945.

increased by 113 per cent and it was even higher the following year. At the same time the number of 'irregularly conceived pregnancies' skyrocketed; by 1945 British women had produced more than quarter of a million illegitimate babies. For the bored and lonely wife of a soldier serving overseas a pregnancy as the result of a brief encounter could spell disaster. In 1945 there were 25 000 divorces (two and a half times the prewar number), 70 per cent of them involving allegations of adultery. For every woman who had an illegitimate child, there were several who had recourse to abortions – in Harley Street for the Chelsea set and in backstreets for the rest.

The government was slow to take action. Churchill did not much mind about illegitimacy but the worrying increase in venereal disease threatened the war effort. In 1942 Britain launched an unprecedentedly graphic campaign to raise people's awareness of venereal disease; this included prominently displayed posters warning of its dangers. At the same time Defence Regulation 33B compelled people with venereal disease to undergo treatment. The first months of the war had seen the virtual disappearance of condoms and diaphragms, as rubber production was diverted to vital war manufacturing work. In 1942 rubber was once more made available for contraceptives, despite the fact that the Allies had just lost the world's major rubber-producing areas in South-east Asia.

The great majority of women had neither abortions nor illegitimate children, but many

FOR BETTER OR WORSE Miss Martha Coogan and Fusilier Tom Dowling refuse to allow bombing to destroy their big day. They are married on Saturday, September 14, 1940, in the gutted shell of a central London church.

hundreds of thousands plunged into marriage, sometimes within a few days of meeting. Preembarkation leave would often find young men desperately anxious to have something to come back to. Some women were married and widowed two or even three times. For some marriage would take them to new homes many thousands of miles away. In 1945 some 80 000 British women sailed for the USA as 'GI brides', and another 20 000 left for the British dominions to join their husbands. The situation in the dominions was very similar, with some 30 000 women from Australia and New Zealand marrying GIs.

Black markets

As the war dragged on the quality of life on the home fronts of the Allied nations diverged considerably. In Britain the population grew more 'proletarian' in appearance as austerity abolished class divisions, at least superficially. Utility clothing, although generally well made, was drab. In North America, Australia and New Zealand, consumer spending increased greatly, and most people were now beginning to look prosperous. In all Allied societies shortages of consumer goods produced black markets; Britain had the largest and most

sophisticated. Offenders were sometimes punished with a £500 fine and two years' imprisonment, but generally the 'spiv' was tolerated, so long as he could produce nylon stockings, cigarettes, whisky and petrol.

Full employment and the new respectability of the Communist Party, thanks to the alliance with Soviet Russia, produced an

PAINTED LADY With the disappearance of silk and nylon, many women preferred to paint their legs rather than wear stockings made from cotton or wool.

WASTE NOT Appearing in cartoons, 'Hitler's little friend' the Squanderbug inspired Britons to save everything from string to sealing wax.

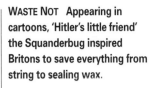

explosion in trade union membership in Allied countries. By the middle years of the war, with victory increasingly assured, trade unions began pursuing traditional industrial objectives with traditional industrial methods. The results could be unfortunate. A strike by the North Australian Workers' Union closed down the port of Darwin in early February 1942, so that freighters began to pile up in the harbour. When Japanese bombers attacked on February 19 they could scarcely believe their luck, and sent 16 ships to the bottom.

The fact that trade unions could shut down important industries in the midst of total war underlined for many people what they were fighting for. In Allied countries individuals continued to enjoy basic freedoms and there was still a limit to the power of the state. This point was made very forcibly early on the morning of Sunday, June 25, 1944, when a V-1 fell onto a farm about 4 miles (6.5 km) from Chequers, and woke everyone in the prime minister's country residence with 'a surprisingly loud noise'. After breakfast the prime minister's principal private secretary, John Martin, and the prime minister's wife Clementine, decided to visit the crater. As they were about to open a gate to enter the field, the woman who owned the farm suddenly appeared, accused them of trespass, and ordered them from her land. Martin began to explain that it was the prime minister's wife who wished to cross her field, but she cut him short. She was perfectly well aware that it was Mrs Churchill, the entire family were scoundrels, and she wanted them off her land immediately.

With that, as Martin later recalled with mock ruefulness, the party from Chequers retreated rather than face 'a fierce woman'. Less than a month later, Hitler was supervising the arbitrary arrest, torture and judicial murder of thousands of the Prussian aristocracy – in the aftermath of the bomb plot of July 20, the failed attempt by high-ranking German anti-Nazis to blow up and kill the Führer.

But while the Allied nations were fighting for freedom, it meant different things in different places. In Britain a report by Sir William Beveridge on the establishment of a welfare state after the war sold out within a few days of publication. For the postwar world, Beveridge promised the British freedom from want. The citizens of the United States were much less concerned to have their futures guaranteed by the state. In December 1941 the USA had been a confused and divided society; by the spring of 1943 it was beginning to realise its enormous power – and was revelling in it.

In July 1943 critics realised the significance of the opening song of the new musical, *Oklahoma*. 'Oh what a beautiful morning' was a celebration of America's awakening to its true destiny, for many now had a glorious feeling that everything was going America's way. In Britain people looked forward to security in decline; in the United States they looked forward to the beginning of the American Century.

LILI MARLENE: A SONG FOR ALL

In 1915 Hans Leip, a 22-year-old soldier in Germany's Fusilier Guards Regiment and an aspiring writer, penned a sentimental poem. It was about two women with whom he was in love, Lili and Marlene. Leip combined them into a composite everywoman, Lili Marlene, part angel, part mistress. Leip's barracks were close to where he had grown up in Hamburg's dockland, and he used the glimmer of a street light to illuminate his everywoman, waiting for her soldier in a bleak urban landscape. She is his 'lady of the lamplight', representing hope and desire.

In 1939 a young German popular composer, Norbert Schultze, put Leip's poem to music, a haunting melody which gave a sentimental theme a marching rhythm. First recorded by Lale Andersen in Cologne in March 1939, 'Lili Marlene' was an immediate hit. Its subsequent impact on the Allies was just as great, and it became the unofficial anthem of the Eighth Army. In May 1943, when the British 7th Armoured Division, on its way to an Allied victory parade in Tunis, passed the German 90th Division on its way to a POW camp, both columns were singing 'Lili Marlene'.

LIFE IN NAZI EUROPE

REGIMENTATION AND CHAOS, FANATICISM AND PRAGMATISM, ALL COEXISTED IN THE STRANGE AND BRUTAL WORLD OF NAZISM

Newsreels from Germany astonished world cinema audiences in the 1930s. They seemed always to show the same scene. Projected mesmerically onto the screen were rank after rank of brown-shirted *Sturmabteilungen* (SA), or the Hitler Youth, or the League of German Girls, all marching with military precision. Or there were vast crowds in Munich, or Nuremburg, or Berlin, thundering out, as with one voice, '*Ein Volk! Ein Reich! Ein Führer!*' The newsreels portrayed what the Germans called *Gleichschaltung*, a regimentation or conformity of an extraordinary kind, a unity produced by a totalitarian system with the Führer at its pinnacle.

Magazine articles reinforced this image. Germany was the most highly organised state in the world, boasted the Wehrmacht paper, *Signal*, in 1942. In a cartoon colour spread, it showed the Reich's administrative jigsaw. Starting at the bottom, there were 539 774 blocks which combined to form 121 406 *Zelles* (cells), which linked up to create 30 601 *Ortsgruppe* (local groups) which formed, in turn, 890 *Kreis* (districts), which federated to create 43 *Gau* (provinces), each under a *Gauleiter*, a high-ranking Nazi official wtih direct access to the Führer. The system created hundreds of thousands of administrative posts, each one to be filled by a National Socialist. Party membership soared from 4 million in September 1939 to 6.5 million by January 1943.

Regimentation began early. At the age of ten boys joined the *Deutsches Jungvolk* and girls went into the *Jungmadelbund*, while at 14 boys graduated to the *Hitler Jugend* (Hitler Youth) and girls to the *Bund Deutscher Madel* (League of German Girls). At 18 boys faced six months' compulsory labour service, while girls could volunteer for the female equivalent. Thereafter life diverged. For boys it was conscription and military service, for girls the 'fulfilment of their biological destiny': childbearing – either in or out of marriage, for the Nazi state was busily removing any stigma from illegitimacy, eager at all costs to boost the Aryan population.

The world of work was similarly regimented. Membership of the German Labour Front

ARYAN PURITY Members of the *Bund Deutscher Madel* (League of German Girls) put up posters proclaiming the Nazi ideal of female purity. After their 1934 Nuremberg rally, more than 1000 girls returned to their families pregnant.

HONOUR CROSS OF THE GERMAN MOTHER This medal was awarded to 3 million women on August 12 – Hitler's mother's birthday – 1939. The bronze went to mothers of four children, the silver to mothers of six and the gold to mothers of eight or more.

was compulsory for all employers, craftsmen and workers. The Front's founder and controller, Dr Robert Ley, a radical corporatist, hated capitalism, Communism, Jews and the Prussian aristocracy in about equal measure. Ley's bureaucracy controlled the hiring and firing of workers, their compensation and insurance, care for the elderly and disabled, and educational programmes. One of the Front's subsidiary organisations, *Kraft durch Freude* (Strength through Joy) provided up to 9 million German workers a year with holidays at the Front's resorts on the Baltic or in the Alps, or on one of several cruise ships. The Front was also behind the *Volkswagen* (People's Car) project, which German workers were going to be able to purchase via a generous instalment plan. The agricultural economy, too, was regulated; the 15 million members of the Reich Foodstuffs Corporation represented cooperatives, distributors, farmers and agricultural workers.

The Führer and 'creative chaos'

According to Nazi propaganda, *Gleichschaltung* had created a prosperous and a fairer Germany, a nation that was more truly democratic than the so-called liberal democracies of the West or the social democracies of the East. The Nazi emphasis on uniforms for party members had begun to erode superficial class distinctions based on differences in dress. Robert Ley, for example, insisted that each of his 40 000 employees wore a simple blue uniform, irrespective of rank. And mass activities, from a Hitler Youth camp to a *Kraft*

THE PEOPLE'S CAR Entering production in 1937, the VW cost less than 1000 marks and could be bought on a four-year instalment plan with weekly payments of about 6 marks. The war brought the scheme to an end.

Der Kdf Wagen

durch Freude holiday, broke down class barriers and promoted social cohesion.

Such was the propaganda image. And some of it was true. Germany was increasingly classless and certain aspects of life were highly regimented. But Hitler's system was far from being centrally controlled and coordinated, let alone directed. Indeed, such a system, truly totalitarian, would have gone against Hitler's intentions. Hitler believed that all life was a struggle in which only the strongest survived. Like all true revolutionaries he deeply distrusted institutions, which he believed protected the weak and promoted unsuitable people purely on the basis of seniority. Hitler deliberately created a bureaucratic and administrative jungle. He gave different organisations responsibility for the same or closely related fields of activity, with overlapping areas of authority as the rule rather than the exception. While ultimate authority resided with the Führer, the authority of Reichministers, Gauleiters and many lesser officials was only as great as they could make it themselves. Hitler believed that a stronger system, manned by the best people, would eventually emerge from the competition. It was an interesting sociopolitical experiment, but not a sensible way to organise a country for war.

Many aspects of administration became mired in very un-Teutonic chaos and confusion. Orders from Goering might be countermanded by Himmler, only to be overruled by Speer, after an appeal to Hitler. Gauleiters, too, engaged in infighting, each interpreting general and often vague instructions from the Führer in different ways. Neighbouring provinces might follow completely different policies on any number of issues, meaning that almost anything said about Nazi Germany might be true in some places at some times. Some of the 43 Gauleiters were very efficient and honest, but many were not, and corruption was

widespread. A character like Oskar Schindler, the wheeler-dealer businessman who also saved the lives of hundreds of Jews, could not have flourished in a truly totalitarian system.

One organisation with a formidable reputation, inside Germany and elsewhere, was Himmler's Gestapo. But it, too, had its limits. Its maximum strength was only 32 000, far too

few to police the Reich itself, let alone the occupied territories. The Gestapo was really an intelligence-gathering organisation, which could not have functioned without the help of hundreds of thousands of informants throughout Germany and occupied Europe. A letter of denunciation would arrive, a file be opened, and if corroborating evidence were found, an arrest would be made. The Gestapo was essentially reactive rather than proactive. Typical letters might denounce neighbours suspected of being part Jewish, or claim that someone had made a joke about the Führer. In 1937 the German judiciary had agreed with the Gestapo and other law-enforcement bodies

THE ARYAN IDEAL Urged by the Führer to be 'slim and slender, swift as greyhounds, tough as leather, and hard as Krupp steel', the Hitler Youth became all-pervasive. By 1939 it boasted a membership of 7.7 million.

January 1943 Nazi Party membership has risen to 6.5 million Milice established in France

September 1944 Pétain flees to southern Germany

to allow the 'intensive interrogation' of suspects in order to extract a confession. A suspect could receive up to 25 strokes with a bamboo cane across the buttocks – a medical officer had to be in attendance after the tenth stroke. In this way people denounced by their neighbours could quickly be made to confess.

The number of 'crimes' that carried the death penalty increased greatly after the start of the war; there was a corresponding rise in judicial executions, from just under 1000 in 1940 to nearly 6000 by 1943. The death penalty, however, was employed in a capricious and

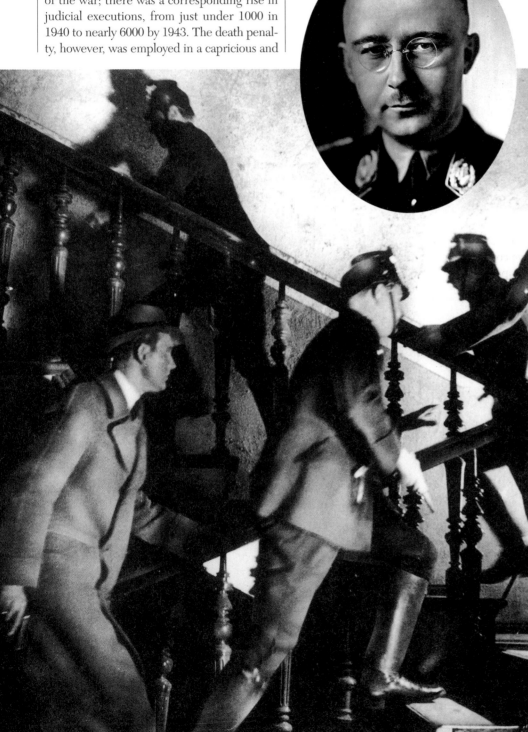

POLICE RAID Short, plump and myopic, the former chicken farmer Heinrich Himmler became the most feared man in Europe. As head of the Gestapo, he dispatched the Reich's enemies in night-time raids.

MOUNTAIN SAVIOURS

In the summer of 1940 many of France's 250 000 Jews, along with 100 000 Jewish refugees from central Europe, fled south into the unoccupied zone of Vichy France. Here, they experienced steadily increasing repression, and by summer 1942 Vichy police were rounding them up and shipping them north to transit camps, whence they were dispatched to the death camps in the East. By the time the Allies landed in 1944 the Vichy regime had dispatched about one-third of France's Jews.

Many Jews escaped with help from ordinary citizens. Throughout France for every Jew-hating bigot, there was someone who would place his or her life in jeopardy to help to smuggle Jews to the safety of Switzerland or Spain. The most extensive operation was in the Cévennes, the mountainous region to the west of the Rhône, and the most important refuge was the village of Le Chambon-sur-Lignon. The largely Protestant population had endured repeated persecutions and massacres by Catholic kings and was strongly sympathetic to the plight of the Jews.

Le Chambon's minister, Pastor André Trocmé, organised a reception service for Jewish children smuggled from Lyons, Saint-Etienne and other cities. The refugees were given false papers, which identified them as poor children from the cities sent to the country for fresh air. Le Chambon was approached only by a winding road and a twisting, picturesque railway. Gendarmerie patrols were spotted long before their arrival, giving ample time to hide Jewish children. By the end of August 1944 when the Americans reached Le Chambon, there were more than 5000 Jews hiding in the area.

arbitrary manner, depending on the attitude of the president of the local People's Court and the Gauleiter. In summer 1941 a woman in Danzig (Gdansk) was accused of sleeping with a Polish worker, and confessed under interrogation. For a German woman to sleep with a non-Aryan worker was a 'race crime', punishable by death. Yet the woman was sentenced to six months' imprisonment; her lover had to undergo phrenological tests – measuring the size and shape of his head and features such as his nose – after which he was pronounced an Aryan. In contrast, six months later in a similar case in Posen (Poznan) the woman received ten years' imprisonment and her Polish lover the death penalty.

A concern with race, eugenics – the study of how to 'improve' the quality of the human race by selective breeding – and hereditary behaviour suffused the judicial system. As a

DUTCH RESISTANCE Dutch deportees are depicted entering a labour camp in a frozen hell. However, most Dutchmen who worked in the Reich did so voluntarily, and as Aryans enjoyed the same conditions as the Germans.

result, some criminals, arraigned before a court on relatively minor matters, could find themselves sentenced to death because a jail term would not cure their 'congenital criminal inclinations'. Homosexuals suffered severely. Widely tolerated during the Weimar years, they were now rounded up and incarcerated in concentration camps.

And yet if one were not Jewish, or homosexual, or sleeping with a non-Aryan, and if one did not worry overmuch about politics, life in Nazi Germany for the first half of the war was remarkably good. Terrified that excessive hardship would bring about a collapse in

civilian morale like that of 1918, the Nazis looted food from conquered territory, and filled the shops of Germany's towns and cities with consumer goods from France, The Netherlands and Scandinavia. Rationing did not begin to approach British standards until the summer of 1944, and it was still possible to buy silk stockings in the better Berlin department stores in the spring of 1945. By that time the majority of Germany's urban dwellers were living in cellars, but in parts of the country – for example, Pomerania and Bavaria – the only indications of a war were the presence of urban refugee families and the absence of men.

Unlike Britain, Germany did not begin the conscription of women until very late in the war, and then it was relatively easy for a German girl to avoid the more unpleasant types of service. Germany had an abundance of labour, more than 8 million foreign workers and prisoners of war. For them, as with everything else in the Reich, conditions varied enormously. Many workers from Western Europe came of their own free will on lucrative contracts, and enjoyed conditions roughly comparable to German workers. So, too, did

ALLIES OF THE REICH A Ukrainian *Ost* (from the East) worker cuts out eagle badges for SS insignia. Below: Their fezzes adorned with SS eagles, soldiers of the Bosnian Muslim SS Handschar Division march through Sarajevo.

some of the Eastern workers, particularly girls from Belorussia and the Ukraine who came to work as maids in German houses and quickly adopted Western clothing, hairstyles and make-up. But for most of the workers from the East, conditions were difficult. At the bottom of the pile were Soviet prisoners of war and the non-Jewish inmates of concentration camps; they were literally worked to death in the winter of 1944-5 in places like the tunnel factories at Nordhausen in the Harz mountains of eastern Germany where they built jet and rocket engines.

Partners in the cause

Nazi rule in occupied Europe varied as much as it did within the Reich. In Western Europe the Nazis soon tried to convert Scandinavians, Dutch, Belgians and French into partners in a Europe united under German leadership. The shortages of food, clothing, petrol and coal were blamed on Europe's common enemies, the Anglo-Americans and their allies, the Bolsheviks. Proclamations stressed that

only Jews, Communists and terrorists (Resistance fighters) had anything to fear from the Germans. Recruiting offices soon opened in Paris, Brussels and Rotterdam for the Waffen

SS and for contract work in Germany. Most of the population came to an accommodation with their new masters; tens of thousands went eastwards in the new SS divisions.

For much of the war, Paris was a particularly popular posting for the Wehrmacht. It was here that the Germans could enjoy what they called '*Paris bei Nacht*' ('Paris by night'). Outside nightclubs, restaurants and brothels,

FRIENDLY RELATIONS The ink on the armistice is barely dry, but these Parisian girls in June 1940 do not seem too displeased at the attentions of a pair of German soldiers.

billboards in German enticed soldiers. They packed the Casino de Paris, Moulin Rouge, Moulin de la Galette, Scheherazade and dozens of other establishments. One French observer, surrounded by 1500 Germans at the Folies-Bergère, wrote that 'the sight of 60 naked women under fairy-like lighting seems to fill them with doleful stupor'. For much of the Occupation the streets were filled with German soldiers, arm in arm with French girls. Until 1944 very few, if any, soldiers carried weapons, because there was no danger. Law and order continued to be enforced by the '*flic*' in his familiar blue uniform.

In Western Europe, Germany preferred to rule through existing elites. The situation in the East was very different. Here was the Reich's new frontier, the *lebensraum* ('living space') of which Hitler and others had written. The existing population were in the way, and they would have to be removed. But like every other aspect of Nazi rule, there was little consistency in policy. Some of the peoples of the East – the Slovakians, for example – were allies, and treated as members of the Axis like Hungarians, Romanians, Bulgarians and Croatians. Alfred Rosenberg, minister for Occupied Eastern Territories, argued vigorously that non-Slavic Soviet peoples should be given their independence and enlisted as allies against Russia. He received the Führer's permission to form six national legions from the millions of Soviet prisoners – one each from Armenia, Azerbaijan, Georgia, the North Caucasus, Turkestan and the Volga Tartars. In April 1942 these were joined by a division formed from among Cossacks originating in the Don, Kuban, Terek and Siberia; this eventually grew into a corps. Rosenberg argued that, appearances to the contrary, the Cossacks were not descended from the Slavs but from the Goths, and were therefore Aryan.

Albert Forster, the Gauleiter of Weichsel, a province carved out of north-western Poland, followed Rosenberg's lead and argued that most Poles in his area were really descendants of the Teutonic Knights of the Middle Ages, and therefore pure Aryans. When ordered to clear his province of Poles, he simply

PÉTAIN: PATRIOT OR TRAITOR?

On April 26, 1944, more than a million people lined the streets of Paris and cheered as a motorcade swept Marshal Pétain to a Requiem Mass at Nôtre Dame to commemorate the victims of Allied bombing raids. It was one of the few times in his life that the 88-year-old Marshal felt like a popular politician. Just 15 months later a court sentenced him to death, a sentence which one of his former junior officers, Charles de Gaulle, commuted to life imprisonment.

Henri-Philippe Pétain (1856-1951) is the single most controversial figure of French history in the 20th century. At the outbreak of the First World War he was in his 59th year and still only a colonel, but his stubborn defence of Verdun in 1916 led to his promotion to the rank of Marshal. Appointed ambassador to Spain in 1939, Pétain was recalled by the Reynaud government during the crisis of May 1940. Instead of bolstering resistance, however, he opposed Reynaud's attempts to carry on fighting, negotiated an armistice with the Germans, and became leader of a puppet rump state, setting up his government in the spa town of Vichy.

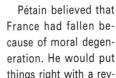
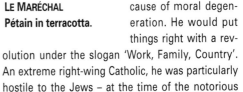

LE MARÉCHAL
Pétain in terracotta.

Pétain believed that France had fallen because of moral degeneration. He would put things right with a revolution under the slogan 'Work, Family, Country'. An extreme right-wing Catholic, he was particularly hostile to the Jews – at the time of the notorious Dreyfus affair around the turn of the century he had been deeply upset by the pardon granted to the Jewish officer, Alfred Dreyfus. Deportations of Jews began from Pétain's Vichy France even before the Germans had made an official request.

In January 1943 Pétain's regime established the Milice, a paramilitary police which operated closely with the Gestapo. By 1944 a civil war was raging between the Resistance and Milice. As Pétain's visit to Paris showed, he was still a symbol of the nation, yet only four months later crowds cheered for de Gaulle. In September 1944 Pétain fled with the Germans (he later claimed he had been kidnapped) and set up a Vichy government-in-exile in southern Germany. At the war's end he fled to Switzerland. Now in his 90th year, he decided to give himself up, reasoning that his advanced years would save him from execution. He was right; he died in prison in 1951.

NAZI GOVERNORS Three Gauleiters of Eastern provinces – from left to right, Greiser, Koch and Frank. Although they followed different policies in their fiefdoms, the end result in all was the destruction of millions of lives.

recategorised entire villages as Aryan, and set in motion a programme of Germanification. Forster was an opportunist who believed that much of the official racial theory was claptrap. He also said that anyone who looked like Himmler should think twice before making too much of supermen and racial purity, a joke which earned him the sensitive Reichsführer's undying enmity.

Life in the east

For most East European peoples life became very hard. In the autumn of 1939, Arthur Greiser, Gauleiter of Warthegau, another area of north-western Poland annexed to Germany, began supplanting the Polish population with German emigrants. By the end of 1943 Warthegau had a German population of nearly a million, while nearly twice that number of Poles had been deported to the south into Gauleiter Hans Frank's General Government, the rump of the Polish state covering the area between Warsaw and Cracow. Life here was savage. Frank had been attempting to reduce the Poles to the level of serfs. He closed

universities and high schools, and forbade primary education beyond fourth-grade level, roughly the standard achieved by German children at the age of ten. Poles were to be taught enough to allow them to follow simple instructions but nothing more. In order to accelerate the destruction of a Polish identity, Frank began the systematic extermination of Poland's intelligentsia. Many were deported to concentration camps as suspected members of Poland's underground Home Army – many were. Others were executed, sometimes as hostages in reprisal for Home Army attacks, but often on flimsy, trumped-up charges of anti-German activity, which could include anything that kept Polish culture alive. Frank boasted to a Nazi journalist: 'If I put up a poster for every seven Poles shot, the forests of Poland would not be sufficient to manufacture the paper for such posters.'

A very similar policy was followed between October 1941 and 1944 by Erich Koch, Reichskommissar for the Ukraine. In March 1943 Koch told his administrators: 'We are the master race which must remember that the lowliest German worker is racially and biologically a thousand times more valuable

HORSEMEN FOR HITLER With their hatred of Stalin and the Soviet system, many Cossacks made enthusiastic fighters for the Reich.

than the population here.' Koch closed all schools in the Ukraine, declaring that 'Ukraine children need no schools. What they'll have to learn later will be taught them by their German masters.' It is a testimony to the hatred most Ukrainians felt towards Stalin that hundreds of thousands of them volunteered to join the Wehrmacht's *Ost* battalions.

The regimes of Greiser, Frank, Koch and others give a glimpse of a nightmare world that was narrowly averted. This would have been a Germania extending from the Moselle to the Urals. Most of the Gauleiters were relatively young men – Himmler himself was only 39 when the war began – and it was unlikely that any moderation of the regime would have occurred until the Slavic peoples had gone the way of the North American Indians and Australian Aborigines. And, of course, the treatment of the Slavs was relatively benign compared to that of the Jews.

THE FINAL SOLUTION

THE HORROR OF THE HOLOCAUST EMERGED FROM BLOOD-CHILLING NOTIONS OF RACIAL SUPREMACY AND THE 'JEWISH PROBLEM'

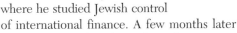

ENGINEER OF EXTERMINATION Adolf Eichmann poses proudly in his new uniform of SS Hauptscharfuhrer (Sergeant) in 1936.

In the autumn of 1918 a severely gassed Adolf Hitler spent three months recuperating in a hospital in Pomerania. He was appalled by the large number of psychological and psychiatric casualties he saw wandering the wards, men who appeared fit but lacked the mental toughness or the will to carry on. Applying his own peculiar logic, Hitler worked out what was happening. It was clear to him that the war had created conditions that favoured the weak rather than the strong. The mentally 'inferior' and the unstable cracked and were invalided out to survive, while the mentally tough, the biological 'cream' of the nation, fought on and were killed. The war, then, was resulting in the genetic weakening of the German people.

Ten years later he stated what he saw as the best way of ensuring that Germany won the next war. This was to eradicate 700 000 'inferior' children, so that a strong and stable

BIOLOGICAL THEORY Using a chart purporting to outline the scientific bases for legalised racism, a teacher shows that a German is genetically superior to a Jew, and that it is wrong to breed between higher and lower species.

generation, capable of withstanding the pressures of modern battle, could emerge. In January 1933 his first legislative enactment was to provide for the sterilisation of carriers of hereditary mental diseases. During the mid and late 30s, perhaps as many as 400 000 Germans were sterilised. Then with the outbreak of war, it no longer seemed logical to have the Reich's resources tied up in supporting insane and senile people. The gassing of the inmates of lunatic asylums began in January 1940 and by August 1941 more than 70 000 had been killed. Protests from Catholic bishops led to a reduction in the programme. Even so, in the following months, another 60 000 were killed. By 1941, Germany had developed the technology of mass extermination, and had the staff who could carry it out.

Juden Raus

But Nazi policy was not only cleansing Germany of the mentally disabled; it was also tackling the 'problem' posed by other 'undesirable' elements. In the mid 1930s children in Germany played a new board game, *Juden Raus* ('Jews Out'), in which the player who won was the first to succeed in making his or her area of the Reich 'Jew Free'. At school, meanwhile, children studied a new type of history. The great engine for change in human affairs was no longer economics but race. History, they were taught, was a constant process of racial struggle, in which the enemy of all races, sapping the vitality of host nations and producing chaos and misery, was the parasitical Jew.

Racial theories were in vogue in universities, where dozens of new institutes and hundreds of new lectureships and professorships were created to investigate this new 'science'. In October 1933, for example, Otto Ohlendorf, a graduate in law from the universities of Leipzig and

Göttingen, took up a research post at Kiel University's newly established Institute of World Economy, where he studied Jewish control of international finance. A few months later a recent medical graduate from the university of Frankfurt am Main, the 23-year-old Dr Josef Mengele, got his first job as a research fellow at the new Institute of Hereditary Biology and Race Research.

Others, too, in a world still reeling from the Depression, were finding work, thanks to the new regime and its institutions. At the age of 34, the unemployed Rudolf Höss, son of a devout Catholic shopkeeper, got his first permanent job as a block overseer at a concentration camp at Dachau. A similar case was Adolf Eichmann, who had been forced through family poverty to drop out of Linz University before finishing his engineering degree. He had been working as a travelling salesman, but now he got a 'proper' job with a new subsection of the SS, the SD (*Sicherheitsdienst* or 'Security Service'). Here, he soon headed a small office, tasked with finding a solution to the 'Jewish problem'.

The 'Jewish problem'

Like everything else in the Third Reich, the evolution of policy towards the Jews was chaotic, but it was not opportunistic. There were thousands like Ohlendorf, Mengele, Höss and Eichmann who actually believed that there was a Jewish problem. Their chief problem was that they did not know how to tackle it. Legislation during the 1930s forbade Jews to practise the professions and prohibited marriage and sexual intercourse between gentile and Jew. As the children's board game suggested, the object was to get the Jews out. From his increasingly influential office in the SD, Eichmann argued that the acceleration of Jewish emigration from the Reich was the best solution. But whereas Jewish scientists, doctors and businessmen found it relatively easy to emigrate, there were fewer and fewer countries willing to accept Germany's poorer Jews.

January 1940 Gassing of lunatic asylum inmates begins

Summer 1940 Polish ghetto policy announced

January 1942 Wannsee Conference held in Berlin to discuss the 'Jewish problem'

By 1937 about 330 000 German Jews had emigrated, leaving another 330 000 still within the Reich. Then came the *Anschluss* with Austria in April 1938, followed by the invasions of Czechoslovakia in October 1938 and Poland in September 1939. This increased the Jewish population under German control to well over 2 million. Young Nazi officials like

GETTING OUT Oblivious to the horrors lying in store, these wealthy German Jews put on brave faces as they make their way to trains bound for Holland in June 1939. Right: A Jew in occupied Warsaw is arrested and dragged away for failing to identify himself as a Jew by wearing the yellow Star of David (bottom).

Eichmann felt overwhelmed by the ever-increasing dimensions of the 'Jewish problem'.

Newly conquered Warsaw had the largest urban Jewish population in Europe. Janina Bauman, the strikingly beautiful 14-year-old daughter of a Jewish doctor, recorded her own confusion when the Germans arrived. Janina, who could speak perfect German and was immersed in German culture, felt closer to the young men who marched through the streets of Warsaw singing '*Heili Heilo*', than to her Polish neighbours. Nonetheless, within a few weeks the Germans were stopping Jews in traditional dress, forcing them to perform

humiliating and exhausting physical exercises in front of passers-by, and then cutting their beards and ringlets. Soon Janina, and all Jews over 13, were ordered to wear armbands with the Star of David.

Janina noted that whereas some Polish friends remained loyal, many became evasive, and some were hostile. The worst was her father's former chauffeur, a Mr Richter, who though he could speak no German convinced the Nazi authorities that he was *Volkdeutsche* (ethnic German). By spring 1940 Richter was an official of the local government. One morning he arrived with some henchmen

WANNSEE CONFERENCE

Set on the lake shore at Berlin Wannsee, the Interpol Building can be mistaken for a country estate. It was here that Reinhard Heydrich, head of Reich Security Service, convened a conference on January 20, 1942; the minutes were taken by Adolf Eichmann. Heydrich explained that, with more than 11 million Jews in Europe, a solution to the 'Jewish problem' was going to be more difficult than anticipated. He proposed concentrating the Jews in transit ghettos, with the able-bodied conscripted for labour gangs where 'a large percentage will be eliminated by natural attrition'. Those who remained alive 'would constitute a natural selection of the fittest who would form a new cell from which the Jewish race could again develop'. It was essential that these should be liquidated. Wannsee was not a policy meeting (the policy had been decided) but an implementation meeting. Apart from Heydrich, Eichmann and a few other SS personnel, those who attended were ordinary German civil servants. In the third year of war these men were discussing genocide in terms of 'output' and 'productivity'.

July 1942 First Jews leave
Warsaw ghetto to be
'resettled' in labour camps

April 1943
Uprising in
Warsaw ghetto

January 1945 Auschwitz
abandoned as the Russian
Army approaches

IN THE GHETTO Three pictures of Jews taken by the SS in the Warsaw ghetto as 'evidence' that the Jews were subhuman. As conditions worsened, the old and the young were the most vulnerable and often the first to succumb to starvation.

and began confiscating the Baumans' property. Shortly afterwards Richter ordered the Baumans out of their house and appropriated

it for himself. When Janina's grandfather protested, Richter's henchmen beat him so severely he died a week later.

Like thousands of other Jewish families in Warsaw, Lodz, Cracow and other Polish cities, the Baumans welcomed the announcement in summer 1940 that ghettos were to be created. Poles were beginning to avenge old grievances, real and imagined, and life was becoming increasingly unpleasant; the ghetto would be protected by walls and defended by its own Jewish militia. The Warsaw ghetto was to cover an area of about 1000 acres (400 ha). For the six members of the Bauman family, the move into a two-roomed flat with a kitchen and a WC marked a massive decline in living standards, but Janina recorded that at least she now felt safe.

The Baumans' story was repeated all over the General Government (all that theoretically remained of Poland as a separate entity), with Jewish families moving willingly into the ghettos. By autumn 1940, however, Jewish peasant families were also being moved in, until there were more than 500 000 people crammed in. And Warsaw, with 500 people to the acre (more than 1200 to the hectare), was relatively uncramped. In Lodz, the 300 acre (120 ha) ghetto contained 250 000 people, and ratios in other cities were even worse.

All this while, the ghetto policy had evolved haphazardly through a series of administrative decisions. Gauleiters of former Polish regions now incorporated into the Greater Reich were desperate to rid their provinces of Jews. So they deported tens of thousands of them to the General Government. The Governor General of the General Government, Hans Frank, simply dumped them in the ghettos, at the same time refusing to increase the amount of food allocated to the Jews. By one crude but reasonably accurate reckoning the average calorie intake from official rations fell from about 600 per day to fewer than 200, though well-to-do families like the Baumans, who had brought gold and silver jewellery with them, were able to supplement their diets by trading on a thriving black market. Polish farmers and Nazi officials became rich, exchanging vegetables for jewellery which would have cost a year's salary before the war. The poor Jews starved and were carried off in typhoid epidemics. By the summer of 1941 a combination of disease and starvation was killing 2000 a month.

Meanwhile, conquests in Western Europe and the Balkans had brought another 600 000 Jews within the orbit of the Reich.

The Commissar Order

In early June 1941 Hitler issued the so-called 'Commissar Order' giving *Einsatzgruppen* the task of exterminating the apparatus of the Soviet Communist Party. Included within the general remit were Jews and other 'undesirable' elements, though it is clear that Hitler saw Soviet Communists and Jews as virtually interchangeable. Following in the wake of the victorious Wehrmacht, *Einsatzgruppen* organised paramilitary groups from the Ukraine to Lithuania, and set about the systematic extermination of the Jews. One of the most successful, *Einsatzgruppe D*, was commanded by Otto Ohlendorf. In city after city, the Jewish population was rounded up by locally recruited militias and marched to convenient spots on the outskirts, often by a ravine or a quarry where bodies could be disposed of. Thus the 33 000 Jews of Kiev were machine-gunned into a ravine at Babi Yar, and the Jews of Minsk were shot and pushed into the Ratomskaya ravine.

The slaughters in the East in the summer and autumn of 1941 were witnessed by thousands of ordinary German soldiers and civilian contractors. Protests were soon flooding into Himmler's office, and to the Führer himself. An alarmed Adolf Eichmann had already taken action. Calling on technicians involved in the euthanasia programme, which was now winding down as German hospitals ran out of mentally disabled people, an experimental 'mercy killing' unit was opened at Chelmno to the north-east of the Lodz ghetto on December 8, 1941. A train carrying 2300 Jews from the ghetto packed into cattle trucks pulled into a siding in a forest; alongside it was parked a fleet of what looked like large prison vans. The Jews, told that they were going to complete the rest of the journey by road, were herded into the backs of the vans and the doors were closed. When all the vans had been loaded, their engines revved into life, pumping carbon monoxide into the airtight rear compartments; all 2300 were killed. In the following month, the Chelmno vans killed about 1000 per day.

Although pleased with their Chelmno pilot scheme, Eichmann and many others thought it would be better if Jews capable of working were first to make an economic contribution to the Reich, before either dying or being put out of their misery. On January 20, 1942, representatives of various Reich ministries met at Wannsee in Berlin and agreed the details of their scheme. By the spring of 1942 additional facilities – gas chambers and incinerators – had been built at existing SS labour camps at Auschwitz and Lublin, and three new camps had been built at Sobibor, Treblinka and Belzec.

Mass-production killing

Thus was born the Final Solution. This was not like other massacres in history – the Turkish massacre of the Armenians in 1915, for example, or more recent examples of 'ethnic cleansing'. Nor was it like the slow slaughter taking place in Poland's ghettos, or the work of the *Einsatzgruppen* in the Soviet Union. The Final Solution was slaughter on

GET MOVING! Following an attempted uprising in the Warsaw ghetto in April 1943, the SS round up men, women and children for immediate dispatch to concentration camps.

THE DEATH FACTORIES On arrival at the camps, the trainloads of Jews were sorted into two columns (top). The right column – mostly men – would be directed to barracks by SS guards and destined to slave in factories like the one above in Sachsenhausen camp. The left column would be marched to the 'shower' blocks and gassed. Below: An aerial photograph showing the main camp at Auschwitz.

the basis of mass production, using railways and a modern bureaucracy with filing cards and photographs. The same method was used throughout Europe. The SS announced that Jews were to be resettled in the East in new labour camps, where they would be allowed to practise their own religion. On July 22, 1942, the first Jews left the Warsaw ghetto. Janina Bauman recorded that thousands volunteered for the move, lured by tables groaning with food that the Germans set up at the station depot.

The Final Solution was such a monstrous concept that, when rumours began to circulate, they were at first given little credence. Even when the packed cattle trucks were shunted through the gates of Auschwitz and the other camps, the guards maintained the subterfuge. As the Jews crowded the platforms, guards shouted: 'First wash, then work.' The guards then sorted the deportees into two columns. Those who were young and fit would, indeed, go to shower rooms and then to barracks, where they would be fed and set to work in vast factory complexes. Those who were old, or too young, or ill, or pregnant, were sent to sealed 'shower' rooms, where they were gassed.

By this time Rudolf Höss had come up in the world. From block attendant at Dachau

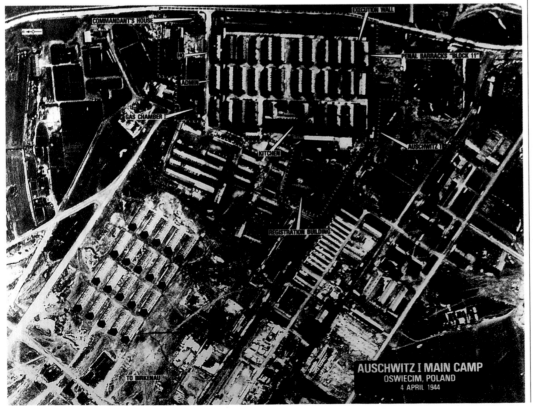

AUSCHWITZ I MAIN CAMP
OSWIECIM, POLAND
4 APRIL 1944

SCHINDLER: MAN OF THE ARK

Israel has accorded the title 'Just Among Nations' to 2000 gentiles for their actions in saving Jews during the Holocaust. Of these, Oskar Schindler (1908-1974) is the most problematic. Schindler was a Sudeten German, a lapsed Catholic, given to womanising, who joined the Nazi Party out of opportunism. After the invasion of Poland, he set up a factory in Cracow producing enamelware. He also made contact with a Jewish bookkeeper, Itzhak Stern, who proposed that in exchange for laundering Jewish funds, Schindler should employ as many Jews as possible, ensuring that they had protected status and were not liable to 'deportation to the East'. The relationship worked well. Schindler grew rich; he protected hundreds of

GENTILE HERO Jews protected by Schindler greet their saviour in Israel in 1962.

Jews and had intimate relationships with scores of women. Had this been all, he would be remembered as an exploiter of desperate people. Yet all the women who knew him – apart from his estranged wife – regarded him with affection. Moreover, he began risking his life to save his Jewish workers, once bluffing his way into Auschwitz to whisk them from the jaws of death. Stern believed that Schindler was embarrassed by his altruistic responses, and so buried them under a veneer of self-interest.

he had become commandant of Auschwitz labour camp, taking up his post on May 1, 1940. It was Höss who first realised that the fumes of a form of cyanide, known as Zyklon-B, already used in the camp as a fumigant, would be more effective against humans than any other form of gas. Auschwitz had six gas chambers, each of which could hold up to 2000 people. Höss took enormous pride in the fact that Auschwitz's extermination rate soon outstripped that of rival camps.

Dr Mengele had also arrived at Auschwitz. Deportees with any physical disorder – giants, dwarfs, hunchbacks – ended up on his dissection table, as did twins and triplets. He was an empiricist. He knew theoretically what would happen if petrol were injected into the human bloodstream, but he had to be sure. He wished to avoid wasting the Reich's precious medical resources and so he conducted his experiments without anaesthetic.

The major problem facing Höss and other commandants was the disposal of the corpses. At full production Höss's chambers were killing 16 000 per day, but Auschwitz's *Sonderkommandos* – special squads of young male inmates who cleared the chambers after each killing, and received extra food and special privileges – were having difficulty coping. The crematoria, too, were frequently overloaded, the chimneys belching forth a fiery black smoke, which smelt sickly sweet.

End of the Warsaw ghetto

By early summer 1942 rumours about the fate of the deportees were reaching Warsaw, Lodz and the other centres. Each ghetto was run by its own Jewish Council, who had the task of selecting people for relocation. Volunteers were no longer coming forward, and the Germans used force, sealing off entire blocks and dragging away anyone they could lay their hands on. In Warsaw Janina and her family survived until January 1943 and then escaped into the gentile part of the city in a blinding snowstorm, where they were passed from hiding place to hiding place until the Soviet army arrived in January 1945.

By the spring of 1943, the 60 000 Jews remaining in the Warsaw ghetto knew that very soon the Germans would try to remove the last of them. The fitter formed resistance groups, made crude hand grenades and Molotov cocktails and bought pistols from the underground Home Army. When 3000 Germans moved in on April 19 to close down the ghetto, they got the surprise of their lives. Knowing they had no chance of survival anyway, the Jews determined to take as many Germans as possible with them. In nearly three months of house-to-house, room-to-room fighting the Germans lost more than 400 dead, and about 1000 wounded. The Jews lost 14 000 dead in the fighting, and virtually all the remainder were slaughtered in gas chambers. But against all the odds about 50 resistors survived, escaping through the sewers to join up with the profoundly anti-Semitic Home Army, which was honoured to have these particular Jews in its ranks.

Even in the death camps there were those who chose to die on their feet. In October 1943, 600 Jews, many of them captured Soviet soldiers, stormed the gate and guardhouse at Sobibor, overwhelming the SS guards. About 300 were killed but the others made it to the woods. Anti-Semitic and anti-Russian Polish peasants hunted down the escapees and handed most back to the SS.

When given time to organise and arm, the Jews did not die like sheep, but few had such opportunities. The death factories continued their work virtually unabated, until the approach of Soviet armies in January 1945 led to their abandonment. But the ordeal of the survivors – some 400 000 – was far from over. The Nazi authorities had no intention of relinquishing them to the Russians. So, in the depths of a cold winter, they were

UNHOLY OVENS Incinerators at Auschwitz worked night and day burning the corpses of the gassed victims. These two were left intact when the SS hastily left in January 1945.

force-marched westwards across Germany, beaten and shot by their guards when they faltered, and strafed by Allied aircraft. About 100 000 died on the march, or succumbed to typhoid and malnutrition in their new homes, concentration camps like Belsen. Approximately 6 million had died, about one-third of the world's Jewish population.

The defence of Höss and others after the war was that they were merely cogs in a huge machine. Höss protested in his posthumously published memoirs: 'I am completely normal . . . even when I was carrying out the task of extermination I lived a normal life.' The awful truth is that Höss was right. He was completely normal, as were the hundreds of thousands of officials, policemen and railway workers throughout Europe who knew what was happening but who helped to keep the machine running. It was the relative handful who attempted to stop the machine who were the odd people out.

PARTISANS AND RESISTANCE

IN OCCUPIED EUROPE A BRAVE FEW RESISTED FROM THE START, BUT MOST PEOPLE JUST GOT ON WITH LIFE AS BEST THEY COULD

The German conquest of much of Europe between September 1939 and December 1941 was so sudden and so devastating that peoples everywhere were in a state of shock. In some places, such as Croatia, Lithuania and Latvia, there were many who welcomed the German victories – partly, at least, because they saw the Germans as liberators from more hated oppressors. Elsewhere, the majority sought an accommodation with their new masters. This was not the same as collaboration; it was a recognition that Europe was going to be under Germany's domination for at least a generation, and that nothing was likely to change this situation. As late as the autumn of 1942, it seemed inconceivable that Germany would be defeated by spring 1945.

In most places people met the Germans with sullen acceptance, which did not rule out passive resistance. This took many forms. In Paris formidable old ladies armed with umbrellas prodded their way through German parades, daring the police to arrest them. In Amsterdam, a man clad only in shoes and a hat strode through the streets, protesting against clothes' rationing. And in Copenhagen the king rode through the streets each day, acknowledging the salutes and cheers of his people. The citizens of most occupied countries soon noticed a deterioration in train services – particularly in France, where the railway workers instituted a permanent go-slow. Strikes, too, were soon common, though the Germans became less and less tolerant of these from 1943 onwards, giving the job of improving industrial relations to the Gestapo.

CHILD WARRIOR Boys like this 11-year-old Belorussian (far left), orphaned by the Germans, made formidable guerrillas.
Left: Some of Tito's men are marched off to summary execution. Bottom: A train derailed by the French Resistance in spring 1944.

January 1940
Polish Union for Armed
Struggle founded

June 1940
De Gaulle establishes
Free French

July 1940
British Special Operations
Executive founded

May 1942
Massacre at
Lidice

TITO – WILY OPPORTUNIST

Josip Broz (1892-1980), better known as Tito, was a Croatian and political secretary of the Yugoslav Communist Party when the Germans invaded in April 1941. Because of the German-Soviet Pact he did nothing to resist, until they also invaded the USSR in June. The war in Yugoslavia was particularly confusing and ferocious, and Tito displayed considerable skill, guile and lack of scruple in manoeuvring through the mess. At various times, he fought the Germans, Italians and Bulgarians as well as their local allies, the Croatian Ustashis and the Bosnian Muslim SS division, the Handschar; but he also viciously fought fellow resistance warriors like Mihailovic's Serbian Chetniks. Chased from his HQ by the Germans in May 1944, he sought shelter on the island of Vis, controlled by the British, who later flew him to Russia to meet the Soviets. By the end of the war Tito and his partisans had the enviable reputation of being the only Resistance movement to liberate their country without an Allied invasion.

In Eastern Europe anti-German gestures and passive noncooperation were a luxury few could afford. The Nazi grip here was far more tight – people either resisted outright or shut up. Yet in Poland, with its long history of insurrection against occupying powers, fighting never really stopped. On the night of September 26/27, 1939, elements of the Polish Army went underground and in January 1940 became the nucleus of General Sobeski's Union for Armed Struggle (ZWZ). There were parts of Warsaw, the Silesian industrial region and the forests and marshes of eastern Poland that the Germans were never able to bring under proper control.

Later, both Yugoslavia and the USSR would claim that their partisan forces destroyed entire German armies. In fact, research following the opening of archives in Moscow and Belgrade has revealed a much less heroic picture. Resistance in Yugoslavia started in Bosnia, when Bosnian Serbs defended themselves, not against the Germans, but against the ultranationalist Croat group, the Ustashis. At first the partisan war was a civil war fought among Serbs, Croats and Muslims, in which the Germans were scarcely involved.

In the Soviet Union, underground Communist cadres attempted to start resistance in occupied areas of Belorussia and the Ukraine, but soon found they were in more danger from local peasants than from the Germans. The terrain also made resistance difficult. Much of Belorussia and the Ukraine is open, gently undulating plains devoid of cover. Such partisan groups as did emerge were quickly hunted down by a combination of German aerial and horse-cavalry patrols. When successful resistance finally got under way in the spring of 1943, it was on the fringes of the vast Pripet Marshes and in the forests of the northern Ukraine.

Communists and Resistance

One result of the German invasion of the USSR on June 22, 1941, was to trigger serious resistance in Western Europe. Until this time Communist parties in France, Belgium, Holland and other countries had followed Moscow's line and had actually cooperated with German occupation forces. Now, that line was overturned, and the members of each party, usually young, fanatical, highly disciplined and well educated, began a programme of sabotage and subversion, which aimed at drawing as many German forces from the East as possible.

Other Resistance movements were organised by governments-in-exile based in London. The largest was General de Gaulle's Free French movement, established in June 1940. At first, its growth was very slow, as was the development of similar movements in countries such as Belgium, The Netherlands and Norway. In July 1940 Churchill established the Special Operations Executive (SOE), an organisation modelled on the prime minister's misconceptions of the largely mythical German 'Fifth Column' – a supposed network of enemy infiltrators in Britain. SOE recruited heavily from amongst European refugees, trained them to use explosives, firearms and sophisticated radio communications, and then

REVENGE KILLINGS

In May 1942, Czech patriots in Prague assassinated Deputy Reichsprotektor Heydrich, SS governor of Bohemia and Moravia. On June 9, German military police arrived in the village of Lidice, outside Prague. The next day they shot 173 men and boys; most of the women and children were sent to concentration camps, from which few returned. The village was razed to the ground. The Germans made no attempt to hide what they had done. It was a reprisal, a warning to other would-be resisters.

sent them back into Europe via parachute and submarine to 'kick-start' Resistance. Sometimes they linked up with existing groups, but more often than not they had to recruit and train their own bands. In all, SOE recruited 10 000 men and 3000 women, many of whom were captured and tortured to death by the Gestapo.

Relations between London-based and Communist Resistance movements were often difficult. As it became clear that a German defeat was inevitable, Communist and non-Communist organisations began fighting each other to decide who would form a postwar government. In France this often took the form of Gaullists and Communists

FASHION ACCESSORY The 'Cuban' heels fashionable in the early 1940s provided excellent hiding places for microfilm.

July 1944
Bomb plot
against Hitler

BOMB PLOT AGAINST HITLER

At 12.40 pm on July 20, 1944, Hitler and two dozen generals and staff officers gathered in a briefing hut at the Wolf's Lair, the Führer's headquarters in East Prussia. Laid out on an oak table in front of them was a map; they were studying the latest developments in Russia. Hitler had just leant forward when there was a crack and a blast. Everyone was hurled to the ground, some with their hair in flames.

Only a few moments earlier Colonel von Stauffenberg, a staff officer, had placed a briefcase containing plastic explosives under the table, made an excuse and left. Now as he watched from a nearby building, he saw a body carried from the wreckage wrapped in the Führer's cloak. He telephoned news of Hitler's death to fellow conspirators in Berlin, who attempted to take over the government of the Reich.

The Gestapo had long suspected a conspiracy. It was a loose confederation of Prussian officers and diplomats and Protestant churchmen, notably the radical theologian Dietrich Bonhoeffer. They had all come to agree on one thing – that Hitler represented an embodiment of human evil. But the body Stauffenberg saw beneath the cloak was not Hitler's – it was the corpse of one of four officers who had been less fortunate than the Führer. As the conspirators moved to arrest the Nazi leadership they were stunned to hear Hitler broadcast from the Wolf's Lair. The plot collapsed overnight. Stauffenberg was arrested and shot. Over the next months the Nazis exterminated his fellow plotters and many more, like Field Marshal Rommel, who had known about the plot but had not been involved in it. Bonhoeffer was one of the last to die, executed on April 9, 1945.

AFTER THE BLAST Hitler's survival led him to believe he was divinely protected. Claus von Stauffenberg (right) was a brave and decent man, but his traditional military training made him an inept conspirator.

And yet, while claims were exaggerated, the Resistance was not without influence. Movements passed on much valuable intelligence information, including early warnings of the V-1 and V-2 and details of the beaches of northern France. Moreover, on at least two occasions, Resistance forces had a direct influence on the conduct of major battles. The first was the Battle of Kursk. Between April and July 1943, Soviet partisans emerged from the Pripet Marshes to attack the German supply lines leading to the Kursk front, and significantly delayed the German build-up there. The second occasion was between June 5, 1944, the eve of D-Day, and the middle of August that year, when the French Army of the Interior (FFI), an uneasy amalgam of Gaullist and Communist groups, launched an all-out attack on German communications, and made it very difficult for the Wehrmacht to respond effectively to the Allied landings in Normandy.

The Resistance was also used to seize centres of government as the Germans withdrew. In August 1944, it was the Gaullists who took control of Paris, much to the chagrin of the Communists. The London-backed Polish Home Army was less fortunate in Warsaw. As the Russians approached the Polish capital in July 1944, the Home Army tried to seize the city, but was strongly resisted and then annihilated by the SS. Soviet armies sat a few miles away, on the eastern bank of the Vistula, letting the Germans do their work for them.

The most important legacy of the Resistance and partisan movements to their defeated peoples was a sense of pride. In 1995, during celebrations marking the 50th anniversary of the end of the war, old men in Paris, Brussels, The Hague, Warsaw and Oslo paraded with medals, showing younger generations that the Nazis had not had things all their own way. In fact, the numbers who had engaged in active resistance had been very small – until, at least, the end of the war when the Allied armies had almost reached their regions. Missing from the parades were the veterans of the various SS divisions recruited in occupied Europe and the French Milice – the Vichy militia, famous for its enthusiastic cooperation with the Germans. The truth is that as many Europeans fought for Hitler as against him, a truth that Europe is just beginning to acknowledge.

betraying each other to the Germans and the Vichy authorities. In Poland, Yugoslavia, Greece and, after September 1943, Italy, tensions erupted into open warfare.

How many heroes?

In the aftermath of the war, governments in formerly occupied countries made extravagant claims for the Resistance. Allied propaganda had done the same thing during the war with documentaries like *Men of Norway* and *The Silent Village* and feature films such as *One of Our Aircraft Is Missing*, *Desperate Journey* and *Undercover*. These created a glowing picture of heroism in which each country had a handful of collaborators – such as the Norwegian, Vidkun Quisling – but a majority who faced the Nazis with implacable hostility. It was necessary for Allied populations to believe this . . . but it was not true.

ROAD TO VICTORY

BY MAY 1944 IT WAS CLEAR THAT THE ALLIES WOULD WIN – BUT WHEN? MOST EXPERTS PREDICTED CONFLICT IN THE PACIFIC FOR ANOTHER FOUR YEARS, AND IN EUROPE A NAZI-INSPIRED GUERRILLA WAR DRAGGING ON INTO THE 1950S. THE WAR IN EUROPE AND THE PACIFIC ENDED MORE COMPLETELY AND SOONER THAN MOST HAD FORESEEN, BUT EVEN AS THE LAST BOMBS WERE DROPPING A NEW CONFLICT WAS BREWING BETWEEN THE SOVIETS AND THEIR FORMER WESTERN ALLIES.

D-DAY

METICULOUS PREPARATION PAID OFF WITH SUCCESS ON D-DAY: THE LONG-AWAITED 'SECOND FRONT' WAS AT LAST OPENED

In December 1941 Germany again faced the prospect of a war on two fronts. It was clear that the defeat of the USSR was going to take some time; it was equally clear that an Anglo-American invasion would one day strike from the west. To face this threat, Hitler ordered the construction of massive defences from The Netherlands to the Spanish frontier: the Atlantic Wall.

The Todt Organisation – responsible for mobilising labour across the Reich and set up in 1940 by the then munitions supremo, Dr Fritz Todt – started work in earnest on the project in the spring of 1942. By the time the invasion actually came in June 1944, a work force, never fewer than 100 000, had used 1 million tons of steel and 20 million tons

MIGHTY BLASTER The Atlantic Wall was the biggest construction project in Europe's history, but defences on this scale (below) were confined to the most obvious invasion beaches.

of reinforced concrete to create a zone of fortifications along 1700 miles (2740 km) of coast. In addition, by the summer of 1944 the Germans had sown 4 million antipersonnel and antitank mines along the coast. Off likely invasion beaches engineers were constructing reefs of underwater obstacles, designed to rip the bottoms out of landing craft. Knowing that the Allies would probably use paratroopers and gliderborne forces to supplement any landing, the Germans flooded low-lying areas behind the coast. In drier regions they drove sharpened wooden stakes into fields and linked them with a latticework of wire.

These defences had the great advantage that they could be manned by soldiers too old or too disabled to serve on any active front. This was as true of the commander in the West, Field Marshal Gerd von Rundstedt, 67 years old when appointed in March 1942, as it was for the men under him. One division consisted entirely of men suffering from

stomach ulcers. Placed individually in other units, each would soon have become ill but, concentrated in their own division, special arrangements could be made for acid-free rations. In late 1943 the so-called 'stomach divisions' were reinforced by divisions formed from volunteers among Soviet prisoners. One included a handful of confused Tibetans who had been press-ganged into the Soviet Army while grazing their herds near the Kazakh border. The officers and NCOs of these divisions were often reliable Wehrmacht veterans whose loss of a leg, an arm or an eye had not diminished their ability to fight well from entrenched positions.

By spring 1944 the Germans also had in France 24 field divisions, including 10 panzer ones, of which six were concentrated north and north-west of Paris. In November 1943 Hitler had appointed Field Marshal Rommel to inspect the Atlantic Wall. Rundstedt rightly sensed that Rommel's commission posed a threat to his own position, so he pushed Rommel into a subordinate post, command of Army Group B. This was responsible for the coastal area between the Dutch-German border and the Loire. Rundstedt himself maintained control of the panzer reserves. Rommel was furious. In his opinion Rundstedt was holding the reserve too far back from the coast. He confided to his aide, Hans Spiedel: 'If we are not at the throat of

the enemy immediately he lands there will be no restoring the situation, in view of his vastly superior air forces. If we are not able to repulse the Allies . . . in the first 48 hours, then the invasion will have succeeded.'

Plans and planners

When the Germans began constructing the Atlantic Wall the idea of an Anglo-American invasion was still being debated by the Allies. Churchill was haunted by memories of the fiasco at Gallipoli – an attempted seaborne invasion of Turkey and the Balkans during the First World War – and was very much against it; only enormous American pressure brought him to agree. Roosevelt had wanted a landing in 1942 or 1943, but the catastrophe at

FRONT-LINE DEFENCES Concrete and steel 'tetrahydrons' (left) were designed to rip the bottoms from landing craft. Rommel inspects rows of wooden stakes protecting France's Atlantic beaches from invasion.

Dieppe in August 1942 taught everyone the importance of meticulous planning.

In March 1943 the British logistics specialist, Lt General Sir Frederick Morgan, was appointed Chief of Staff to the Supreme Allied Commander (COSSAC) with the job of planning an invasion. This was a task of unprecedented complexity, and Morgan's offices in London's St James's Square were soon filled with the best staff the British and US armies could muster. Two months later Churchill and Roosevelt, meeting at the Trident Conference in Washington, decided that the landings should take place on May 1, 1944 – codenamed 'D-Day'. For the operation as a whole, they chose the codename *Overlord*.

The leaders had decided when to invade; Morgan's staff had to decide where. This did not take very long. The Dieppe landing had shown that a direct attack on a port was foolhardy: the landing would have to be on open beaches. The heavily defended Pas-de-Calais had narrow shingle beaches – difficult for

TAKING SHAPE COSSAC planners devised the *Mulberry* artificial harbours, made of components built in Britain (above), ready to be towed across the Channel.

tracked vehicles – dominated by high cliffs. Farther west, Brittany had excellent beaches but they were exposed to south-westerly Atlantic winds. That left only the shore from the Gironde to the Spanish border (too far away), and the coast of Normandy, from the Seine estuary to the Cotentin peninsula. The Normandy coast had wide sandy beaches, backed by dunes and low cliffs and protected from south-westerly storms by the Cotentin peninsula. The beaches were midway between Le Havre and Cherbourg. Once ashore, Allied armies could capture either or both of these ports from the landward side.

That was the easy part. Now the coast had to be mapped and plans made for getting the

March 1943
Planning for
D-Day begins

May 1943
Trident Conference,
Washington

January 1944
Eisenhower takes up
Allied command

June 1944
D-Day
landings

troops ashore. Mapping was undertaken by the French Resistance, aerial reconnaissance and miniature submarines taking swimmers by night to within a few hundred yards of the shore. Resulting maps of the invasion beaches detailed the German defences right down to barbed-wire entanglements. New steel boats, Landing Craft Assault (LCA), were designed which could be carried aboard troop transports. Armoured support would come ashore in Landing Craft Tank (LCT) barges and Landing Ship Tanks (LSTs). The invaders would also need engineering support to clear obstacles and mines, and fire support to clear bunkers. These tasks were assigned to a specialised British armoured division, the 79th.

A major problem was how to keep supplies coming in over open beaches following a successful landing. COSSAC estimated it would take at least two weeks to capture Cherbourg, and two to three months to repair it. The answer was to construct artificial harbours, codenamed *Mulberry*. In October 1943 orders were placed with shipyards from the Clyde to the Tyne for more than 200 steel and concrete caissons (watertight floats), some as much as 60 yd (55 m) long and 20 yd (18 m) high. There were also

INFLATABLE SHERMAN Dummy tanks were a key part of Operation *Fortitude*. They were arranged in large, poorly camouflaged parks in the woods of East Anglia and Kent.

to be floating pierheads and 10 miles (16 km) of steel roadway. The caissons would be towed across the Channel by 150 powerful tugboats.

In all this surprise was vital, and a massive operation (*Fortitude*) was launched to mislead the Germans into believing that the Allies would land in the Pas-de-Calais. Without this deception the Normandy landing could turn into the bloodiest massacre in history; even after the landing had taken place, it had to look like a mere diversionary tactic for the 'real' invasion. Accordingly, the fields of Suffolk, Essex and Kent blossomed with huge encampments crammed with rubber blow-up tanks and airfields packed with mock-up transports made from wooden three-ply. The phantom army even had a commander, General Patton, who was frequently seen in the south-east, apparently visiting various units in his command.

Operation *Bolero*

As COSSAC laboured to perfect the invasion plans, Britain was being transformed by Operation *Bolero*, the American build-up. By the end of May 1944, the Americans had brought in 50 000 tanks and armoured vehicles, 450 000 trucks and 450 000 tons of ammunition. In the words of General Eisenhower, chosen for the job of supreme allied commander in December 1943, Britain had become 'the greatest operating military base of all time'.

IKE – QUIETLY IN CHARGE

General of the Army Dwight D. Eisenhower had an extraordinary career. In the autumn of 1939 in his 50th year he was still a major and had never commanded troops in battle. He had spent the previous four years as chief of staff to General Douglas MacArthur in the military backwater of Manila. Just four years later Eisenhower, now a general, was

GOOD LUCK Eisenhower visits US paras on the evening of June 5, 1944, knowing that many will not see the next dawn.

appointed supremo for the planned invasion of north-west Europe – Operation *Overlord*.

The transformation in his fortunes came with his appointment in 1941 as Deputy Head Pacific War Plans in Washington. The US Army chief of staff, General Marshall, was impressed by the way he outmanoeuvred MacArthur to construct a coherent strategy for the Pacific. In June 1942 Marshall appointed Eisenhower commanding general of the European Theatre of Operations (ETOUSA), which led to the command of Operation *Torch* in North Africa. It was here that he demonstrated exceptional diplomatic skills. He kept competing French factions from each others' throats and prevented open warfare between Patton and Montgomery.

Eisenhower was nobody's first choice to command Supreme Headquarters Allied Expeditionary Force (SHAEF). Churchill wanted Alan Brooke, and Roosevelt favoured Marshall. He was a compromise candidate. He showed that he was a leader but not in the charismatic sense. He was a brilliant chairman of the board who knew how to get the best out of men who often despised his lack of combat experience. Although hurt by their insults, he never allowed the defence of a bruised ego to get in the way of the objective – the successful invasion of Europe.

After the war Eisenhower was appointed supreme commander of the Allied Powers in Europe. He became 34th president of the United States in 1953 and was re-elected in 1956.

As well as the equipment, there were 1.5 million US troops in Britain. The Canadian Army had nearly 200 000; the Poles and Free French together fielded 40 000, and the Belgians, Dutch, Norwegians and Czechs accounted for another 10 000. But the largest army, at least initially, was the British: by spring 1944 it had 1.75 million men within the British Isles. All told, the Allies had 3 million men waiting in southern England.

In January 1944 Eisenhower arrived to take over Supreme Headquarters Allied Expeditionary Force (SHAEF) in Bushy Park by the Thames. His first major problem was the refusal of the Anglo-American 'bomber barons', Air Marshal Harris and General Spaatz, to divert their air fleets from the bombardment of Germany. On March 25 Eisenhower brought them into line, threatening to resign unless they agreed to devote their forces to the bombing of the French railway system. Over the next nine weeks Lancasters and B-17s pulverised rail centres and marshalling yards, then turned their attention to the Atlantic Wall. By the start of June, bombers had destroyed 74 of the 92 German radar stations that monitored movement on and over the English Channel. The Germans were now almost sightless.

On May 15 in the model room of St Paul's School in London, Eisenhower unfolded *Overlord* before a select audience including Churchill, King George VI and scores of admirals, generals and air marshals. On D-Day, now set for June 5, eight divisions were to land in Normandy, three from the air and five from the sea. Two US airborne divisions, the 82nd and 101st, were to drop at night along the east coast of the Cotentin peninsula to secure the western flank of the beachhead. Meanwhile, the British 6th Airborne Division

WARRIORS FROM THE SKY US and British airborne forces landed by night on the flanks of the beachhead. Despite heavy casualties, they confused the Germans and thus paved the way for the seaborne invasion. Here, US paras (above) drop in to reinforce the 82nd Division. A light tank (right) disembarks from a British Hamilcar glider, and British Horsa gliders (below) land east of Caen.

was to land east of the River Orne. The other five divisions were to land on five different beaches – codenamed *Utah, Omaha, Gold, Juno* and *Sword* – between the areas secured by the airborne forces. By dusk on D-Day, the Allies planned to control a stretch of the Normandy coast 50 miles (80 km) long and some 10 miles (16 km) deep. Once ashore, there was to be a rapid and massive build-up, made possible by the arrival of the *Mulberry* harbours from D+3, the third day after D-Day. By D+90, the Allies would have 39 divisions ashore. By that time, the bulk of Allied forces would have broken out and would be well across the Seine, heading for the Low Countries and the Siegfried Line along Germany's south-western frontier. That, at least, was the plan.

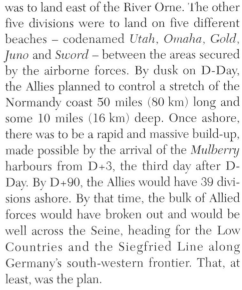

TWO VIEWS OF OMAHA Their landing craft having been sunk by German artillery, American survivors (below) are pulled ashore on *Omaha* Beach early in the afternoon of June 6. Just a week after the bloody assault, *Omaha* had been transformed into a vast logistic depot (above).

and south-west was closed to civilians: once the troops entered this area they were out of contact. The gigantic machine was at last in motion. But on June 1 the weather broke. Rain and wind gusting to gale force swept up the Channel, and did not let up. On Sunday, June 4, Eisenhower brought the machine to a halt. Then, at 4 am on June 5, meteorologists predicted a 24 hour abatement in the bad weather, beginning in the early hours of Tuesday, June 6. Eisenhower gave the most momentous order of the war: 'OK, let's go.'

Overlord unleashed

During the evening of June 5, 1400 transport aircraft and 3500 gliders carrying 20 000 men took off from southern England and flew through steadily deteriorating weather to the coast of Normandy. Shortly after midnight, the transports carrying the US 82nd and 101st swung east towards Cotentin. They suddenly hit a storm of anti-aircraft fire. The Dakota pilots took evasive action, and within minutes the formations had broken up; pilots nevertheless gave the order to jump. Some of the 101st dropped directly into streams of flak and were dead before they hit the ground. Hundreds of others were deposited far from their drop zones. Weighed down by equipment and tangled in their parachutes, they

May 1944 proved to be a beautiful month over southern England – the skies were cloudless, the temperature was well above average and the Channel like a millpond. The roads to the south coast ports were choked with military convoys, some over 100 miles (160 km) long. The coastal zone of the south

plummeted into flooded fields and drowned. Casualties were heavy but the majority did get down safely, and being scattered worked to their advantage. The Germans found it impossible to focus on a target.

While the Americans were dropping on Cotentin, the spearhead of the British 6th Airborne Division approached its landing zone. Six gliders carried an assault party of the Ox and Bucks Light Infantry to a field right next to its objective, a bridge across the Orne, soon to be known as Pegasus Bridge. The men quickly captured it, though German tanks counterattacked before dawn. The rest of 6th Airborne had been coming down farther east. Flak scattered Lt Colonel Terence Otway's 9th Parachute Battalion as it headed for a coastal battery at Merville. Otway attacked all the same with just 150 of his men. After vicious hand-to-hand fighting, they won – 110 Germans lay piled in bloody heaps in the bunkers; 65 paras lay with them.

By 3 am the invasion fleet was just off the coast, a huge armada of 7000 ships carrying 287 000 men. These included 1213 warships, from battleships to torpedo boats. The largest were three US and four British battleships, and 23 British, US, French and Polish cruisers. At 5.10 am, 1000 naval guns

JOURNALISTS ON D-DAY

THE FACE OF BATTLE With his hands shaking uncontrollably, Robert Capa snapped GIs under withering German fire as they struggled to land on *Omaha* on the morning of June 6.

What did BBC radio reporters like Richard Dimbleby and Howard Marshall, newspaper journalists like Alan Moorehead and Chester Wilmot, novelists like Ernest Hemingway and photographers like Robert Capa have in common? They – and another 2000 journalists, writers, broadcasters and photographers – all covered D-Day, the most intensively reported operation of the Second World War.

Photographer Robert Capa was with the troops who landed on *Omaha*: 'We got out of the boat and started wading and then I saw men falling and had to push past their bodies. I said to myself: "This is not so good." I hid behind some tanks that were firing on the beach. After about 20 minutes I suddenly realised that they were what the Germans were shooting at so I made for the beach. I fell down next to a guy who looked at me and said: "You know what I see up there? I see my old mother sitting on the porch waving my insurance policy at me." ' Capa had been taking pictures all along. Now mortar bombs whistled down, and he felt 'a new kind of fear shaking my body from toe to hair, and twisting my face'. He tried to reload his camera but his hands were shaking too violently. He turned, ran to an incoming landing craft and felt the blast of an explosion. 'The skipper was crying. His assistant had been blown up all over him, and he was a mess.' Capa had taken 106 photographs, which were rushed to *Life* magazine's London offices. There, an over-eager technician dried the film too quickly and ruined all but ten frames.

fired on every known German battery from Villerville in the east to Barfleur in the west.

At *Utah* and *Omaha*, H-hour – the time at which the troops were due to come ashore – was 6.30 am, an hour after low tide. Farther east, on the British beaches where the tide came in later, H-hour was 7.30 am. About 3 miles (4.8 km) off *Utah*, landing craft carrying the US 4th Division were caught in a lateral current and came ashore about a mile (1.6 km) south of their intended objective at the base of the Cotentin peninsula. They were the luckiest men of D-Day. The beach they landed on was virtually undefended.

American troops landing at *Omaha* faced a different set of problems. The transports had anchored 12 miles (19 km) offshore in a strong swell. Heavily laden troops clambered down scaling nets into rolling landing craft. As the craft pulled away, loaded to the brim, the waves came crashing down on them. Within minutes ten were swamped; most of the 300 men on board drowned. Other landing craft pushed on. As they grounded, the spatter of machine-gun bullets against their steel ramps showed that the defenders were alive and full of fight. The tide was out – in some places it was more than a mile (1.6 km)

PARLEZ-VOUS? A guide book reminds Normandy-bound British soldiers that there is more to France than German soldiers.

to the beach. The troops, weighed down with heavy equipment, landed in neck-deep water and struggled towards the shore in the face of heavy fire.

With the situation on *Omaha* desperate, the US Navy came in dangerously close. Two LCTs made at top speed for a German strongpoint, their momentum pushing them far enough up the beach to pour fire at point-blank range into the bunker. Farther

west two destroyers came within 3000 ft (900 m) of the shore; with their keels scraping the bottom, they pumped broadside after broadside into German positions. German fire began to slacken. One of the few surviving senior officers, Colonel George A. Taylor, rallied small knots of survivors within earshot: 'Two kinds of people are staying on this beach, the dead and those who are going to die. Now, let's get to the hell out of here!' A few men charged after him into the dunes. More followed, and soon the crisis was passed.

Appealing to Ernie

The slaughter at *Omaha* had been going on for more than an hour when the British started coming ashore on *Gold* and *Sword*. They expected to be slaughtered. They had cheered Ernest Bevin, the minister of labour, when he visited them on June 4, but they had also called out like doomed men: 'Win the peace for us, Ernie' . . . 'We're counting on you, Ernie. Don't let our kids starve.' It was too much for the minister. He was not a

REWRITING HISTORY As early as 1945, French accounts had General Leclerc's 2nd Free French Armoured Division storming ashore on June 6 – whereas they made a much more peaceful landing on July 29.

sentimentalist but he had to return to his car, convulsed with sobs.

Nonetheless, as the landing craft approached the French coast British morale was sky high. The Tannoys blared out 'Roll Out the Barrel', and the troops sang along. Amid the din of engines and gunfire, the Germans caught snatches of 'the gang's all here' and 'we'll have a barrel of fun'. The men had trained for months

and years for this moment. They were with their mates – the gang was all there – and they were going together.

As the ramps of the British LCTs lowered, waiting German machine-gunners were stunned to see not the expected infantry but monstrous armoured vehicles emerging, the 'Funnies' of the 79th Armoured Division. 'Crab' tanks flailed paths through the minefields up the beach. At Le Hamel, in the centre of *Gold* beach, a German 88 mm antitank gun in a concrete bunker blasted away at incoming craft. A Crab, commanded by Sergeant Lindsay of the Royal Engineers, smashed through the centre of the town, firing and flailing alternately, until it came up alongside the emplacement. Edging his tank around to the front, Lindsay (in 79th Division parlance) 'posted a letter': he swung the muzzle of his gun into the

EXCESS BAGGAGE Encumbered with bicycles which they were soon ordered to abandon and never saw again, the Canadian 8th Brigade wade ashore at Bernières on *Juno*.

GADGETRY: GENERAL HOBART'S 'FUNNIES'

The 'Funnies' were designed, built and tested by the British 79th Armoured Division, which was created in April 1943 as an experimental engineering workshop. Its head was Major General Percy Hobart, a 58-year-old with horn-rimmed glasses and a toothbrush moustache, who looked more like an eccentric professor than a general. The 'Funnies' were all designed to deal with specific problems. The 'Crab' or flail tank, for example, dealt with mines. It was a Sherman equipped with a rotating drum with lengths of chain attached; when the drum rotated the chains flailed the earth, detonating the mines. The Duplex Drive (DD) Sherman could 'swim': fitted with a propeller and a canvas skirt and air bags, it provided infantry with close fire support when coming ashore. It could easily be swamped, but it was calculated that enough would get ashore with the first wave of infantry to make a difference. These and other 'Funnies' reduced British casualties on D-Day; the Americans declined British offers to include some in their landings, and suffered on *Omaha* as a result.

FLAIL TANK Beating the ground with iron chains, the flail tank could rapidly clear paths through minefields.

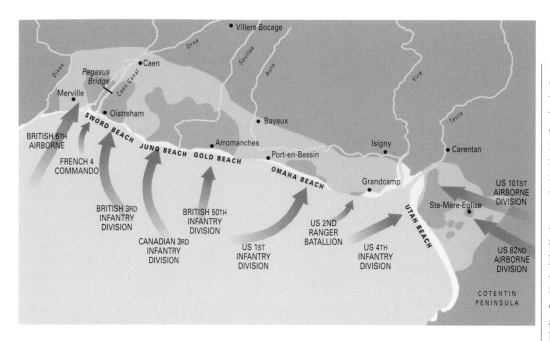

D-Day front-line objective

Front line at the end of D-Day

embrasure, fired and blew the '88' and its crew out of the back.

On *Sword* Beach, meanwhile, the first troops ashore were Commandant Jean Kieffer's Free French commandos. Here, the attack ground to a halt in front of Ouistreham's casino, converted into a fortress by the Germans. Kieffer made his way back to the beach. When he returned, he led another Funny, a tank able to lob enormous 'dustbin' charges into the casino. These cracked the German defences, and the commandos stormed in, capturing the dazed survivors.

With the exception of *Omaha* Beach, the landings had all gone surprisingly well. By the end of the day 130 000 troops had landed from the sea and another 22 500 had arrived by air, all for 10 000 casualties. The Allies held four pockets along a 50 mile (80 km) stretch of coast, and over the next two days were able to consolidate them into a single beachhead.

They've come at last

The Germans had been surprised. On June 5, as rain descended in sheets and fierce winds whipped up the breakers, Rommel had left for a meeting with Hitler at the Führer's Bavarian mountain retreat, Obersalzberg. General Friedrich Dollman, the commander of Seventh Army, which

A SUCCESSFUL START Despite capturing less ground than planned, by the end of D-Day the Allies had their vital foothold in Normandy.

manned the Normandy defences, had sent most of his staff to a war game at Rennes.

News of the landings filtered up slowly through the command chain; Dollman's headquarters remained ignorant of the British landings until 8.45 am and did not hear about the American landings until 11 am. Rommel, who had stopped at Ulm to see his family, could not be back for at least 24 hours. When Hitler was told the news at

10 am he seemed almost relieved: 'They've come at last,' he said. He and Rundstedt were convinced that the Normandy landings were a diversion; the real invasion was still to come in the Pas-de-Calais. When Rommel reached his headquarters he demanded the immediate release of the operational reserves, but only a trickle reached him in the first crucial days.

The German miscalculation allowed the Allies time to establish a beachhead. The first sections of the *Mulberry* harbours were in position by June 7, one off *Omaha* in the American sector, the other off Arromanches in the British. By June 18 nearly 25 000 tons of supplies and ammunition had rolled ashore. A catastrophic storm, however, which began on the night of June 18/19, wrecked the American *Mulberry* and badly damaged the British one. The flow of supplies dropped alarmingly for several days, and things might have been serious, except that the Germans remained transfixed by the Pas-de-Calais.

For his part, Rommel had no intention of just containing the landing; it had to be destroyed. He therefore prepared offensive thrusts to the east and west of Caen. Between June 9 and 13 German and British forces

MOVING ON British troops attack across the **N 13, the Caen-Paris highway, near the village of Cagny, south-east of Caen, in mid July.**

DEVASTATION AT TILLY In mid July British troops search for mines near the wreckage of a Bren gun carrier in what had been the main square of Tilly La Campagne.

clashed in a series of confused actions around Caen. The Germans scored a victory outside the small town of Villers-Bocage, when a Tiger and four Panther tanks under SS Obersturmführer Michel Wittmann virtually annihilated a British armoured regiment. It stopped the British expanding farther south, but the Germans lacked the strength to push on to the coast.

Meanwhile, in the American sector, Lt General J. Lawton Collins' VII Corps was inching its way forward, field by field, hedgerow by hedgerow. This kind of countryside is known in French as *bocage*, and it was a defenders' paradise with hedgerows so

---

WHAT IF?

Staff Colleges in the USA, Britain and Germany have re-enacted the Normandy campaign, and concluded that even a minor change in the parameters would have produced a German victory. What if Rommel had been at his HQ and able to respond immediately? What if he had ignored Rundstedt and Hitler and poured the armoured reserve onto the beachhead? What if the Germans had penetrated the deception of Operation *Fortitude*? The armoured forces in the Pas-de-Calais could have reached the beachheads while the *Mulberry* harbours were still being rebuilt after the storms of June 18/19.

---

thick that tanks could not break through them. It turned into an infantry battle, with troops stalking each other in sunken lanes. By June 18, however, Collins' corps had slogged its way to the western coast of Cotentin. Three divisions then turned north and captured Cherbourg on June 25. German engineers had already reduced the port to a shambles: sunken ships blocked the harbour and mines lay everywhere. It would be November before it was back in full operation.

The Americans had just taken Cherbourg when the British front erupted. On June 26, 700 artillery pieces, backed by naval guns, heralded the beginning of Operation *Epsom*, an attack by 60 000 men and 600 tanks down the western side of Caen. Two days later the British had crossed the Orne and were fighting on Hill 112, a high feature which dominated Caen to the south-west. To General Dollman of the Seventh Army it seemed that the British had broken the German line; fearing the worst, he committed suicide.

The situation was saved by Dollman's successor, Obergruppenführer Paul Hausser, a veteran of Kursk. Since June 20 Rommel, preparing for his own offensive, had concentrated elements of seven panzer divisions to the south of the beachhead. Hausser now fed these into the battle. Warned by Bletchley Park of the size of the

---

force coming at him Montgomery pulled his divisions back, pursued by a mass of German armour. To some it seemed like 1940 and Dunkirk all over again, but it was not. On June 30 hundreds of Lancasters bombed the 9th SS Panzer Division as it passed through Villers-Bocage, and wiped it and the town from the face of the earth. The other German divisions went to ground; Allied air superiority meant that major movements in daylight were now impossible.

The Germans could not destroy the beachhead, but the Allies could not break out. Both commands were plunged into crisis. On July 3 Hitler sacked Rundstedt and Eisenhower sought Churchill's support for sacking Montgomery. Only forceful intervention by the Chief of the Imperial General Staff, General Alan Brooke, saved Monty. Normandy now settled into an attritional slog, in which parts of the battlefield began to look like the Western Front in the First World War. Rommel and Montgomery, who had made their reputations as masters of manoeuvre in the North African desert, now began to behave like Ludendorff and Haig. Nothing was going to plan.

FACE OF DEFEAT Robert Capa caught the look of sullen resignation on the face of a young SS officer, captured in mid July, as he is frisked by a US military policeman.

The US front-line troops were stunned and dazed, but the attack went ahead, behind a rolling artillery barrage. The Germans were confident of stopping the Americans in the dense *bocage*, where in June Sherman tanks had 'bellied up' as they tried to smash through hedges. This time it was different. Long spikes had been welded to the front of about three-fifths of the US tanks, converting them into gigantic garden forks. Shermans now tore through the *bocage*, their advance accelerating steadily as the Germans found their

'OLD BLOOD AND GUTS'

No one felt neutral about Patton. Some hated him, like a Third Army veteran who dismissed him as 'a swaggering bigmouth'. Others would say with intense pride, many years after the war: 'I was with Patton.' The Germans feared him. The apprehension that an army under Patton was in Kent waiting to cross the Channel encouraged them to keep substantial armoured forces in the Pas-de-Calais long enough for the Normandy landings to succeed. In August 1944, when Third Army did join the battle, it quickly overran much of northern France. Almost uniquely among the generals of the Western allies, Patton understood manoeuvre war. One historian has said: 'Patton could think like an army. When the occasion demanded it he could turn it on a dime.'

Patton played out the role of dashing cavalry commander to the point of carrying pearl-handled revolvers in holsters from his belt. His men knew him as 'Old Blood and Guts', a name he encouraged, though those hostile to him changed it to 'Our Blood and Guts'. But Patton was a more complex character. Virtually every day he visited the men his orders had maimed and wounded in field hospitals. He would often kneel in prayer by the cots of severely wounded GIs. Unlike so many generals he was prepared to face the consequences of his actions.

Controversy swirled around Patton. Violently anti-Communist, in the summer of 1945 he urged rearming the SS, suspending denazification, and launching a pre-emptive strike against the Soviet forces. He died in Germany on December 21, 1945, following a car accident.

old defensive tactics no longer worked. Late on the evening of July 28 the advance guard of VIII Corps rolled into Coutances, on the western side of the Cotentin peninsula. After 52 days of grinding struggle the Americans had ripped through the extreme western end of the German line.

Patton's onslaught

On August 1 the tank columns of Patton's newly created Third Army tore through this gap, and spread over north-western France. While some divisions raced into Brittany, XV Corps struck south-east and by August 9 had reached Le Mans, 60 miles (95 km) west of Paris. German commanders in Normandy, convinced that they were about to be trapped in an enormous pocket, wanted an immediate withdrawal, but Hitler saw the situation very differently. Poring over the map of Normandy, it was obvious to the Führer that all Patton's supplies passed along a narrow corridor through the town of Avranches. Instead of withdrawing from Normandy, on the night of August 6/7 four panzer divisions attacked from Mortain to Avranches. Over the next ten days the Germans, spurred on by Hitler, poured men and equipment into what became known as the 'Mortain counterattack'.

To the south, meanwhile, Patton's tanks had been tearing eastwards. On August 8

THE RESISTANCE RISES **Expecting Allied armies to arrive at any moment, Gaullist and Communist resistors built barricades throughout Paris on August 19 and started fighting the Germans – and each other.**

Bradley ordered Patton to change direction and advance north-west via Argentan towards the British beachhead. On the same day, the Canadian First Army attacked from the beachhead via Falaise towards Argentan. Hitler seemed oblivious of the danger as more and more German divisions advanced into what was clearly becoming a pocket. The jaws of the pincers closed slowly, but by August 17 US and British forces were only 20 miles (32 km) apart. The new commander in Normandy, Field Marshal von Kluge, ordered troops to begin withdrawing. In a rage Hitler countermanded the order, dismissed von Kluge and ordered him to return to Berlin immediately. The hapless field marshal chose instead to take cyanide. His successor, Field Marshal Walther Model, took one look at the situation and he, too, ordered a withdrawal.

It was now August 19 and for many Germans it was too late. Allied forces pressed

against the perimeter of the pocket, while British and US aircraft exacted a fearful toll. The road out of the pocket reminded one German officer of Dante's *Inferno*: 'Soldiers lying in their own blood – arms and legs torn off – others driven crazy, crying, shouting, swearing, laughing hysterically – and the horses screaming terribly, trying to escape the slaughter on the stumps of their hind legs.' On August 21 the jaws of the Anglo-American pincer snapped shut.

The liberation of Paris

Forty-eight hours earlier Major General von Choltitz, the German commander in Paris, had been woken by striking gendarmes marching through the streets, singing the forbidden *Marseillaise*. Throughout August 19 gun battles were heard from all quarters of the city, as Communist and Gaullist Resistance movements attempted to seize strategic locations from the Germans. Eisenhower had intended to bypass Paris, but de Gaulle, convincing him of the danger of a Communist takeover, soon had General Leclerc's French 2nd Armoured Division racing for the capital, followed by the US 4th Division. Leclerc entered Paris on August 25, followed on the 26th by de Gaulle, who made a triumphal progress down the Champs Elysées. Diehard Germans and Vichyite *Milice* remained hidden across the city; at the Hôtel de Ville they opened fire on the crowd, and so began a furious gun battle. De Gaulle walked through the middle of it and into Nôtre Dame, where he attended a service of thanksgiving.

The last days of August 1944 were extraordinary. While gun battles flared in various

IMAGES OF LIBERATION Captured Germans in front of the Arc de Triomphe on August 24 (below). Two days later, de Gaulle walked through cheering crowds on his way to Nôtre Dame. Bottom: American GIs marching through Paris on Sunday, August 27.

parts of Paris, jeeploads of US troops pushed their way through crowds of young women, who plied them with champagne and smothered them with kisses. Elsewhere, the FFI (French Forces of the Interior) were handing out summary justice, lining up suspected collaborators against walls and shooting them.

Over by Christmas?

Meanwhile, Allied armies had surged to the north-east, pursuing the fleeing and apparently broken Germans. On September 3 the British Guards Armoured Division entered Brussels, where its welcome equalled the one the Americans had received in Paris. Advancing along the coast the Canadian First Army reached Ostend a week later. Even more

THE COST OF COLLABORATION A young French woman cradles her baby as she is hounded through the streets of a liberated town. Her shaven head proclaims her guilty of sleeping with the enemy.

spectacular were the advances made by the Americans. By early September Hodges' First Army had reached Luxembourg, and the bulk of Patton's Third Army was on the Moselle. Patton had also detached a corps to link up with General Jack Devers' Seventh Army which had landed in the South of France on August 15 – it had advanced north along the Rhône against patchy German opposition in what became known as the 'Champagne campaign'.

The mood at Allied high command was euphoric. It seemed clear that the decisive battle had been the 77 day struggle for Normandy in which the Germans had suffered 400 000 casualties. Since the closing of the Falaise pocket on August 21 the Germans had lost another 200 000 troops, virtually all as prisoners. To senior Allied commanders, all veterans of the First World War, the situation seemed like the one that developed in the late summer of 1918, when German morale suddenly and unexpectedly collapsed. It was imperative to keep up the pressure.

Unfortunately, however, the advance now ground to a halt, not because of German resistance but because it had run out of petrol. British and US supply lines ran 400 miles (640 km) back to the Normandy beaches and Cherbourg. Despite the heroic efforts of the 'Red Ball Express', the Afro-American-run motor transport system, not enough supplies were reaching the half dozen armies to allow them to advance simultaneously.

A row broke out between the British, who wanted to concentrate all available logistics in support of a narrow thrust into Germany,

ARNHEM – OPERATION *MARKET GARDEN*

On September 17, 1944, 1600 transports, 500 gliders and 900 fighters flew eastwards across England. They carried the US 101st and 82nd Airborne Divisions and the British 1st Airborne, embarked on Operation *Market Garden*, the largest airborne operation of the war. Their task was to capture bridges across the canals and rivers of the southern Netherlands, and hold them long enough for the tanks of British XXX Corps to break through from northern Belgium. Shortly after 1 pm, the 101st started jumping north of Eindhoven; the 82nd jumped south of Nijmegan. Farther north the aerial armada crossed the Lower Rhine to the west of Arnhem, where British gliders skidded onto open fields, followed by men of the 1st Parachute Brigade.

Over the next few days XXX Corps advanced north-east, meeting up with the US divisions. But the advance was slow, and by the time it reached the Lower Rhine, British forces north of the river were in a desperate plight. They had landed in almost festive mood, greeted by cheering Dutch. By 7.30 pm on the 17th Lt Colonel John Frost's 2nd Battalion of the Parachute Regiment had occupied houses overlooking a road bridge in Arnhem. Less than 30 minutes later they opened up on SS armoured cars as they tried to cross; one end of the bridge was soon covered with burning vehicles. But more and more Germans kept appearing, and by the next afternoon 1st Airborne had been cut into two pockets: Frost's men at the bridge and the bulk of the division under Major General Urquhart farther west near Oosterbeek. Frost's men held out until the 21st when the Germans started overrunning their positions. On the 25th, Tiger tanks closed in on the Oosterbeek pocket. Tanks from XXX Corps were south of the river, but Urquhart's position was now hopeless; that night 2000 paras crossed the river, leaving their wounded, tended by volunteers, to be cared for by the Germans.

DROPPING IN A British para makes a spectacular arrival during the Allied landings near Arnhem. His slide down the roof of a Dutch manor house ends when his parachute gets tangled in the battlements.

'RED BALL EXPRESS' Named after railway slang for fast freight, the Allied supply line was run by black truck drivers. Between August 25 and September 6 they carried nearly 90 000 tons of supplies from Normandy to eastern France.

and the Americans, who preferred a slower but broader advance. The subtext to the dispute was the rivalry between Montgomery and Patton. Eisenhower sided with Montgomery, and the result was Operation *Market Garden*. The object of this was to drop paratroopers across the branches of the lower Rhine, creating a corridor along which the armoured divisions could advance. The operation was poorly planned and even more poorly executed; it can only be excused as an attempt to maintain pressure on an enemy perceived as being already beaten. But the Germans were not beaten and the result was the only defeat suffered by the Anglo-Americans in the north-west Europe campaign.

By the beginning of October the mood of the Allied commanders had switched to depressed resignation. The weather had closed in; it rained every day, and it was clear that the war was going to last well beyond Christmas. The British and Canadians slogged to the north-east to clear up the banks of the Scheldt so that the port of Antwerp could be opened. The US First Army fought its way east through rugged country between the Maas (Meuse) and Roer rivers. Seventy miles (110 km) south of the Ardennes, Patton's Third Army inched its way through Lorraine towards Saarbrücken and the Siegfried Line. The Ardennes themselves, heavily forested and hilly, were held by four weak US divisions. By the first week of December the weather

was atrocious, with freezing fog followed by heavy falls of snow. To many Allied soldiers, the memories of the liberation of Paris and Brussels seemed very distant.

The last blitzkrieg

Shortly before dawn on December 16 the Ardennes front erupted into life as 2000 German guns pulverised the Americans. Simultaneously, the Panthers and Tigers of eight German armoured divisions, spearheaded by SS *Leibstandarte*, poured westwards along narrow, twisting valleys. Two US divisions to the south of Ardennes were quickly overrun and surrendered. The cohesion of two more in the north was shattered, but individual units, although completely cut off, decided to fight on – particularly after *Leibstandarte*'s massacre of surrendering Americans near Malmédy convinced the others that there was no alternative. US resistance slowed, but did not stop the German advance, which seemed inexorable.

By Christmas Day there was growing consternation among Allied commanders. It was clear that Hitler intended the attack to be a repeat of the May 1940 offensive. On Boxing Day Patton confided in his diary 'We can still lose this war.' In Washington, the Army chief of staff, General Marshall, discussed the unthinkable with the secretary of war: 'If Germany beats us we will have to recast the whole war. We will have to take a defensive position along the German frontier. The people of the United States would have to decide whether they wanted to continue the war enough to raise large new armies.'

Yet another shock awaited the Allies. On January 1, 1945, 1035 fighters and fighter-bombers of the Luftwaffe took advantage of a break in the weather, and roared down on dozens of British and US airfields, as the pilots and ground crews nursed hangovers. The Allies lost 439 aircraft, mostly on the ground, while the Germans lost only 93. Among the dead, however, were 59 highly experienced Luftwaffe unit commanders. The German air force would never again be seen in such strength.

The Allied commanders were ignorant of this disaster. As far as they were concerned, the Germans seemed to have huge reserves of armour and aircraft. On January 6 Churchill radioed Stalin: 'The battle in the West is very heavy . . . I shall be grateful if you can tell me whether or not we can count on a major Russian offensive on the Vistula front, or elsewhere, during January.' By this time Patton's Third Army and Hodges' First were counterattacking furiously, and the German advance, which had run out of fuel, was being pushed back – but only very slowly. For their part, the Americans had suffered 70 000 casualties. Eisenhower's British driver and friend, Kay Summersby, wrote in her diary on January 19: 'German morale is very high right now.' In the Allied armies a bitter joke made the rounds – the war might still be over by Christmas . . . of 1950.

UNEXPECTED DEFEAT Their faces registering shock and disbelief, Americans captured in the Ardennes offensive on December 16, 1944, are marched eastwards to POW camps.

RUSSIA'S TEN VICTORIES

ONCE THE REINVIGORATED SOVIET ARMIES GOT INTO THEIR STRIDE THEIR ADVANCE PROVED REMORSELESS, VIRTUALLY UNSTOPPABLE

Following the Battle of Prokhorovka on July 12, 1943, the German high command called off its offensive into the Kursk salient. It had not been the great strategic victory the Germans had hoped for, but for a few days they consoled themselves with the thought that they had 'written down' much of the Soviet Union's armoured strength. They themselves were no longer in a position to undertake an offensive, but then neither, they believed, were the Soviets.

Then, on July 15, an immense artillery bombardment smashed into German Army Group Centre to the north of the Kursk salient, followed immediately by swarms of Soviet infantry and heavy tanks. Forty-eight hours later, the front to the south of the salient erupted into life. The Germans gave ground . . . though only grudgingly. It was not until July 26 that the Soviets began to make significant progress, and not until August 23 that they recaptured Kharkov.

Field Marshal von Manstein, commander of Army Group South, and Field Marshal von Kluge, commander of Army Group Centre, believed that the Soviets had now done their worst. Then, on August 26, they attacked again. By the beginning of September, the whole Soviet front – from Vyazma, north-west of Moscow, to the Caucasus – was on the move. Outnumbered and outgunned, the astonished Germans fell back. The Soviets retook Smolensk on September 25 and Kiev on November 6.

As winter fell, the Germans again hoped for respite, but on January 14, 1944, thousands of guns on the Leningrad front opened up. Twelve days later, columns of T-34s broke through into the city, ending a siege of 900 days. In late January two Soviet army groups in the Ukraine attacked south of the Pripet Marshes, and by April had pushed the Germans back to the Romanian frontier.

As spring returned to Russia, the Germans were reeling like punch-drunk boxers. In the

RED ELITE Troops of a Soviet Guards armoured division pose on top of a T-34 tank in 1943. The battle ensign is emblazoned with their triumphs of the previous winter.

WARSAW UPRISING

STILL FIGHTING Armed with an MG-42, a German panzergrenadier blazes away at Polish Home Army positions in Warsaw.

By late July 1944, German soldiers were streaming through Warsaw, fleeing from the Soviets. Soon there were only 2000 in the city, mainly signallers and engineers, while members of the AK (Polish Home Army) paraded openly in the streets. On July 27, the AK learned that the Soviets had reached Wolomin, 10 miles (16 km) to the east. The news was not wholly welcome. General Bor-Komorowski, AK commander in Warsaw, and others decided that they would have to seize the capital and set up an administration loyal to the London-based Polish government-in-exile, before the Soviets occupied it and established one loyal to Moscow. On August 1 they attacked the German garrisons and in 48 hours of bloody fighting established a liberated area.

By August 3, however, the Germans were recovering. Himmler had assembled 20 000 troops, including notoriously brutal units, which murdered and plundered their way through the suburbs until they went too far even for Himmler. On August 5 he ordered the city's evacuation. The Germans moved up heavy weapons, which began the systematic destruction of central Warsaw, aided by squadrons of Stukas. By mid August the AKA's situation was desperate. It was clear that the Soviets were not going to renew their offensive westwards for the time being. Nor would they allow the Anglo-Americans to parachute supplies from Soviet-controlled airfields.

The fighting continued until October 3. A battle which had begun with massacres ended with almost 18th-century chivalry. Bor negotiated the surrender of his 9000 fighters and they marched out past columns of saluting Germans. The Germans and their allies suffered 11 000 casualties but the cost to the Poles was horrific – 24 000 AK casualties, 200 000 civilian dead, and Warsaw reduced to rubble.

entire history of war there had never been an offensive of this scale and duration. The Germans again tried to convince themselves that the Soviets were a spent force; in fact, they were just getting into their stride.

The two years following the German invasion had witnessed an astonishing Soviet recovery. During that time 25 million people and 2593 major industrial plants had moved eastwards and relocated in cities of the southern Urals. As the Germans ravaged much of European Russia, this region became as productive as the Ruhr or the English Midlands, with enormous factories mass-producing T-34s and Stormoviks. The Soviet armies, meanwhile, had already proved themselves masters of defensive warfare outside Leningrad and Moscow, in the streets of Stalingrad and in the Kursk salient. They now showed that they could launch and sustain offensives on a large scale, for Stavka (Soviet high command) had rediscovered the 'deep battle' doctrine of Marshal Tuchachevskii, the father of Soviet manoeuvre operations, who had been liquidated by Stalin in 1937.

As the Germans were finding out, 'deep battle' was not like a blitzkrieg. It did not depend on achieving surprise in the hope of avoiding attritional battles. Rather, the Soviets accepted that breakthroughs were likely to be bloody. The Russian technique depended on massing artillery on breakthrough sectors, and simply ripping a corridor through the German defences. The first echelon of a Soviet attack would consist of low-grade motor rifle divisions, often conscripts from Central Asia, whose task was to absorb surviving German defensive firepower. Second, third and even fourth echelons soon followed, composed of tank armies, whose task was to probe their way up to 200 miles (320 km) into the enemy's defences, dislocating and destroying not just divisions and corps, but armies and army groups.

By summer 1943, Stavka had ample formations for carrying 'deep battle' into effect.

FROM RED MENACE TO FRIEND Although poles apart politically, this British Ministry of Information booklet stressed the importance of their Soviet ally. Bottom: The Red Army in action at Kursk, one of the decisive battles of the war.

July 1943
Soviet offensive
from Kursk salient

November 1943
Soviets retake
Kiev

June 1944
Operation
Bagration

October 1944
Warsaw Uprising
crushed

January 1945
Soviets overrun
Auschwitz-Birkenau

February 1945
Soviets reach
the Oder

MARCHING ON THE REICH Trampling the swastika flag underfoot, Soviet troops enter East Prussia in January 1945.

These included 24 tank corps with about 5500 tanks and 90 000 guns, and they were growing in strength all the time. At the same time, a new generation of skilled commanders had emerged, men whose bravery, ruthlessness and cunning had allowed them to survive both Stalin's execution squads and Hitler's onslaught. For the now numerically inferior Germans, the only way to deal with Soviet offensives was to be flexible, to give ground and to counterattack when the Soviets had exhausted their logistics. But Hitler had a fear of sacrificing territory, and was insisting that German forces stand their ground.

Operation *Bagration*

In the early summer of 1944, Germany's eastern front snaked south from the Baltic along the Belorussian-Russian border, then swung west almost to the Polish frontier, from where it ran south to the Dniester and Black Sea. No part of this line was firmly held; it seemed clear to the German commanders that their only hope was to withdraw from Belorussia and form a shorter line running from Riga due south to the Dniester. But Hitler would have none of it. Certain that a Soviet attack would come between the Pripet Marshes and the Carpathians, the Führer ordered that the towns and cities along this ancient invasion route, Lvov, Przemysl, and Lubin, be fortified and held to the last man.

The Soviet Belorussian offensive, Operation *Bagration*, began

on June 22, 1944, the third anniversary of *Barbarossa*. Three Soviet army groups numbering 1.2 million men smashed through the perimeter of Army Group Centre. From his headquarters in Minsk, Field Marshal von Busch commanded some 700 000 men, supported by 10 000 guns and more than 2000 tanks, by no means a contemptible force. Von Busch's air force, however, had been siphoned off to deal with the Anglo-American landings in Normandy; his 1400 front-line warplanes were quickly overwhelmed by nearly 6000 Soviet aircraft. With air superiority assured, the Soviet thrusts converged on Minsk, which they captured on July 3. Von Busch's army was shattered; it had lost 381 000 killed and 158 000 captured.

The destruction of Army Group Centre dwarfed any earlier German defeat. The Soviets had torn a 250 mile (400 km) gap in the German front, and there was nothing to stop them. Their armies surged westwards for 450 miles (720 km), coming to a stop on the east bank of the Vistula at the beginning of August. Then, for both logistical and political reasons, Stalin decided to halt the advance. Instead, on August 20, the Soviets

MILITARY MEDAL The Soviet Order of Victory medal was awarded to members of Stavka who had commanded successful operations. Below: Bulgarian partisans and civilians greet the Soviet Army as it enters the small town of Lovtich, September 8, 1944.

launched an offensive into Romania. Five days later Romania changed sides; overnight Germany's hold on the Balkans collapsed. On September 5 the Soviets were in Bulgaria; a week later they were driving on Hungary.

The following month Stalin struck north. Finland had already sued for peace, so Soviet army groups concentrated on the Baltic states, cutting off the remnants of Army Group North in Latvia. Between October 16 and 28 one Soviet Army Group penetrated East Prussia. A German counterattack recaptured the area on November 5 and found that the Russians had massacred the entire population of the town of Nemmersdorf, a chilling indication of what lay in store for the Reich.

In October 1944 Stavka considered plans to exploit their victories. They decided to concentrate on the Warsaw-Berlin axis, but the Germans would be sure to prepare for such an obvious eventuality, so the Soviets devoted much effort to *maskirovka*, concealing their intentions. In the autumn and early winter they kept up offensives against East Prussia and Hungary, hoping to persuade the Germans to divert forces north and south away from the central axis. The moves fooled Hitler, now obsessed with the Ardennes offensive against the Americans.

hear the tinkle of water dripping from icicles hanging from his window. A sudden thaw unfroze the Oder; within days the river was in spate, giving eastern Germany floods unequalled until the summer of 1997. It was early April before the river began to subside.

For Stalin the year from January 1944 to January 1945 had been an *annus mirabilis*. It began with the Germans everywhere on Soviet territory; it ended with the Soviets in Budapest and only 90 miles (145 km) from Berlin. The Stavka summary of the period divided it somewhat artificially into ten distinct operations; Stalin decreed that it should be known as the Year of the Ten Victories.

OVER THE ODER With water up to their ankles, Soviet gunners heave their gun across the melting ice to their bridgehead at Frankfurt an der Oder.

At 4.35 am on January 12, in the midst of a blizzard, the artillery of Marshal Konev's 1st Ukrainian Army Group opened up from a bridgehead at Sandomierz, on the west side of the Vistula. Twenty-five minutes later, the barrage lifted and Soviet assault engineers swarmed forward. The barrage started again at 10 am, destroying the headquarters of Fourth Panzer Army. By 11.30 am Soviet observers reported Germans fleeing in panic from their bunkers. Seizing the moment, Konev stopped the barrage and threw in his first attack echelon. Five hours later Soviet tanks had penetrated the German defences to a depth of 20 miles (32 km). Forty-eight hours later, as the German panzer reserve moved to plug the gap, Marshal Zhukov's 1st Belorussian Army Group erupted from a bridgehead at Magnuszew, just south of Warsaw. Caught by surprise, the German reserve was overwhelmed.

There was nothing to stop the Soviets. The winter was exceptionally cold, the rivers of Poland were frozen and the often muddy Polish plains had acquired the consistency of concrete. Nearly quarter of a million vehicles, tanks, self-propelled guns, armoured personnel carriers and trucks poured 250 miles (400 km) westwards in the largest single armoured offensive in history. By the beginning of February they had reached the Oder, only 90 miles (145 km) from Berlin. It was now that nature intervened to save the Reich for a few months. On the night of February 2, Goebbels wrote in his diary that he could

THE RUSSIANS DISCOVER NAZI DEATH CAMPS

On January 27, 1945, the Soviet Sixtieth Army overran what had been the Auschwitz-Birkenau complex. The Germans had evacuated the camps weeks earlier, and had attempted to obliterate the evidence of the mass slaughter by demolishing the gas chambers and crematoria. But much remained. The Russians found sheds packed with spectacles, false teeth and bags of human hair, then they noticed areas of grey mud behind the crematoria. On closer inspection these proved to contain fragments of charred bone. Marshal Konev received reports but decided not to visit the site. He explained later: 'The combat operations were in full swing, and to command them was such a strain that I could find neither time nor justification for abandoning myself to my own emotions.' Radio Moscow broadcast the news but it was not reported by Western agencies. Goebbels was accusing Soviet forces of atrocities in East Prussia, and British and US propagandists may have felt the reports were a Soviet attempt to justify the behaviour of some of their troops, though by then the highest echelons of the Anglo-American leadership knew what had been going on at Auschwitz.

WELCOME FOR THE LIBERATORS The Jewish inmates had been evacuated, but a handful of survivors – mostly political prisoners – were still in Auschwitz's factory complex when Soviet troops arrived.

CLOSING ON BERLIN

THE 'THOUSAND-YEAR' REICH ENDED AFTER JUST TWELVE YEARS IN A BUNKER HIDDEN BENEATH THE RUINS OF GERMANY'S RAVAGED CAPITAL

On January 27, 1945, the German high command assembled in the partly destroyed Chancellery in Berlin. Guderian, the army chief of staff, noted that Hitler looked ill; he shuffled and his right arm hung limply by his side. Guderian thought that the Führer's will might be broken. But appearances were deceptive. The conference lasted two and a half hours, most of it dominated by Hitler's sometimes hysterical raging as he gave his assessment of the current situation.

LAST RESORT A middle-aged *Volkssturm* officer instructs a woman on how to aim and fire a *Panzerfaust*. Such incidents were, in fact, rare because most Nazi leaders insisted on keeping women out of the front line.

In the west this was still good: the Allies were making little progress. In the east, according to the Führer, the disastrous situation would soon be transformed. From this time forth every city, town and village in the path of the Soviet advance was to be converted to a *Festung* – fortress. The men who would make possible the *Festung* policy were already at hand. Three months earlier, on October 18, 1944, Hitler had decreed the creation of the *Volkssturm*, from all German men aged between 16 and 60. Meanwhile, new jet aircraft, pouring off the assembly lines, would win back control of the air. V-weapons would break the morale of the British; the high casualties inflicted on the US armies in the Ardennes and Lorraine would destroy the will of the American people, and the new Walter U-boats would once again make the Atlantic a dangerous place.

A slog for the Allies

In truth, the picture for the Allies was by no means rosy. In the west, their nerves were beginning to recover from the shock of the Ardennes offensive and their armies were once more attacking. But it was a grim slog through rugged, heavily defended terrain. The weather, too, was atrocious. On January 26, the sea in the Strait of Dover froze for the first time in nearly 100 years. Then in early February, just as Eisenhower's 'broad front' offensives were getting underway, the temperature shot up to nearly 16°C (60°F). On February 8, the British Second Army launched Operation *Veritable*, fighting its way through 'an ocean of mud' to get to the Reichswald forest between the Dutch frontier and the Rhine. They reached the Rhine on March 3.

To the south, the Americans had been smashing their way through the West Wall, a reinforced and expanded Siegfried Line. Eisenhower had assigned to Patton's Third Army the 'active defence' of the right flank of the drive, which Patton interpreted as *carte blanche* to launch full-scale armoured offensives through the Eifel Hills. By the end of the first week in March his XII Corps had reached the Rhine near Coblenz.

Hodges' US First Army, too, had been slogging its way east, and early on March 7 a company of armoured infantry, commanded by Lieutenant Karl Timmermann, emerged from the Hurtigen Forest to look over the Rhine near Remagen. To his astonishment Timmermann saw that the Ludendorff railway bridge across the river was still intact. Just before 4 pm he led his company across it to seize a foothold on the east bank. Eisenhower had originally intended to concentrate on a crossing much farther north. Now, he agreed with the excited reaction of General Bradley: 'A bridge is a bridge and mighty damned good anywhere across the Rhine.' He directed the main US effort away from the north to the First Army.

When Hitler heard the news his rage knew no bounds. He ordered the execution of the officer responsible for demolishing the bridge and dismissed von Rundstedt as commander in chief, replacing him with Field Marshal Kesselring. The Germans used everything – air and artillery attack, V-2s, floating mines and frogmen – to destroy the bridge, but still it stood. When it finally collapsed on March 17, the Americans had a bridgehead 20 miles (32 km) long on the east bank, and were sustaining it with six pontoon bridges.

Meanwhile, Patton, like the Führer, had been upset by First Army's success. Convinced that the Germans had few troops on the bank opposite, he sent his 11th Infantry Regiment paddling across the river on the night of March 22/23. That afternoon, a bridgehead

UNEARTHING THE HORROR The British liberators of Belsen found 10 000 unburied corpses and 30 000 dazed survivors, most of whom were desperately ill. Despite efforts to feed and care for them thousands died.

secured, he phoned Bradley: 'Brad, for God's sake tell the world we're across! I want the world to know Third Army made it before Monty started across. I can outfight that little fart anytime.' Bradley complied. In a press release, he announced: 'Without benefit of aerial bombardments, ground smoke, artillery preparation and airborne assistance, the Third Army at 22.00 hours Thursday evening 22 March crossed the Rhine river.'

The implied criticism of Montgomery was unfair. In the north, the British Second and US Ninth armies had to approach the Rhine across a flat, clear flood plain; in addition, there were large cities along the east bank like Wesel and Düsseldorf. Monty approached the crossing with typical thoroughness. Since March 14 smoke generators had been pumping out an impenetrable fog which now lay along 20 miles (32 km) of the river. Behind it nearly a million men, 7500 guns and thousands of tanks moved into position.

At 6 pm on March 23 the guns opened up. Three hours later the first assault wave of the 51st (Highland) Division, supported by DD 'swimming' tanks and Crocodile flamethrower tanks, landed on the east bank. At 10.30 pm more than 200 Lancasters and Mosquitos dropped 1000 tons of bombs on Wesel. A little over two hours later, Simpson's Ninth US Army prepared to cross near Düsseldorf. By mid morning on March 24, the British and Americans had established five bridgeheads across the Rhine. Over the next three hours, transport aircraft and gliders dropped more than 21 000 paratroopers into or near the pockets. An ecstatic Montgomery fired off a message to the CIGS, General Sir Alan Brooke: 'My main goal is to drive hard for the line of the Elbe . . . then via the autobahn to Berlin, I hope.' He was to be disappointed.

In a visit to Montgomery's HQ the following day, Eisenhower agreed that 'Berlin is the main prize'. On March 27, however, he told newsmen that he thought the Russians would get to Berlin before the Anglo-Americans. He transferred Simpson's Ninth Army from Montgomery to Hodges, setting the US armies' objectives in southern Germany, while the British 21st Army Group was to advance north-east towards the Baltic.

The Anglo-American armies tore across Germany. On April 1, the tanks of the US

ACROSS THE RHINE Vehicles of the US Ninth Army cross a pontoon bridge into the German heartland. Above: Relieved to be occupied by the Americans, not the Soviets, Germans festoon their towns with white flags.

Ninth and First Armies, encircling the Ruhr from north and south, met at Lippstadt. The 350 000 defenders held out until April 19, when their commander, the fanatical Field Marshal Walther Model, shot himself. Meanwhile, on April 11, the British Second Army had reached the Bergen-Belsen death camp, where they found some 30 000 survivors. On

YOU ARE NOW CROSSING THE RHINE RIVER THROUGH COURTESY OF 'E' CO. 17 ARMD. ENGR. BN. AND 'C' CO. 202 ENGR. C. BN.

the same day Simpson's Ninth Army reached the Elbe at Magdeberg, 60 miles (95 km) from Berlin. Simpson pleaded with Eisenhower to be allowed to continue east, but the supreme commander was adamant. The Elbe was as far as the Western allies were to go.

In Berlin, meanwhile, Hitler had confided on March 25 to a visiting Gauleiter that he felt for the first time that the war was lost. Two weeks earlier he had issued an order for the destruction of all industry and buildings in the path of the advancing Allies. He now decreed that all captured Allied airmen were to be executed. Summary executions were to be carried out, too, by 'Flying Courts Martial' on any German soldiers accused of cowardice or suspected of desertion. Thanks to Speer's intervention the 'scorched earth' decree was only partly implemented, and the Luftwaffe simply refused point blank to murder British and US air crew. But the advancing Allies found the lampposts of German villages and towns festooned with corpses, the victims of the SS's latest efforts to sustain the fighting spirit of the *Volkssturm* and the Wehrmacht. For all that, the collapse in the west was general. Patton's Third Army was held up not by German resistance but by the sheer number of Germans who were surrendering.

More bad news came from Italy, where General von Vietinghoff's Army Group C held a strong front along the crest of the Apennines. On April 9 the British Eighth Army opened an offensive to the east, followed by the US Fifth Army in the west. The German defences were little more than a crust; a week later the Allies entered Bologna, and on April 22 took Modena and Ferrara.

The orders of Ehrenberg

The Russian poet Ilya Ehrenberg had written a manifesto for the Soviet forces: 'Kill! Kill! None of the Germans are innocent, neither the living nor those yet born! Follow the advice of Comrade Stalin and wipe

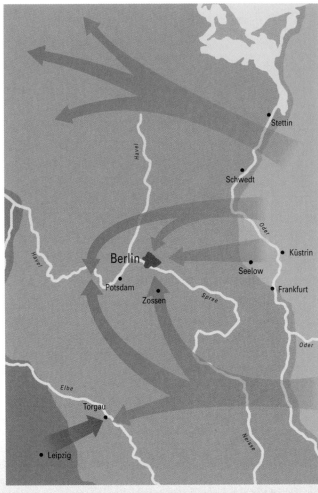

Russian advance
Anglo-American advance

INTO BERLIN Zhukov's tanks reach Berlin's suburbs (left). Soviet troops celebrate victory over the ruins of a bunker.

SOVIET BEAR HUG With Zhukov's forces attacking from the north-east and Konev's from the south-east, the Soviets fought their way through determined resistance to envelop the city on April 24.

PARTY TIME Two days after their encounter at Torgau on April 25, Soviet and US officers dance with Red Army girls.

out the Fascist Beast in his lair for ever!' In February and March, as Soviet troops smashed through Pomerania and East Prussia towards the Baltic, they set out to repay the atrocities of the Germans in an orgy of rape and murder.

Millions of German women and children now experienced the terror which their own armies had inflicted on much of Europe, as long columns of refugees choked the roads back to the Oder, desperate to escape before the Soviets reached the coast and cut them off. The Soviets reached Kolberg on the Baltic on March 18 and swinging east closed on Danzig (Gdansk), which fell on March 30. They then smashed their way into Königsberg. In the Danube valley, they had taken Budapest on February 11 after bitter house-to-house fighting. The 2nd Ukrainian Army Group reached Bratislava on April 4 and entered Vienna nine days later.

Despite these victories, the first two weeks of April were a worrying time for Stalin. Like Hitler, he had expected the Anglo-US armies to be held up by the Rhine defences. The speed of the crossing threw him into a panic, and he did not believe Eisenhower's assurance that Berlin was not an Anglo-US objective. On March 29 two of his key commanders, Zhukov and Konev, had flown back to Moscow for urgent consultations. Over the next 18 days the Soviets conducted a massive redeployment. By mid April they had concentrated three army groups along the Oder against

Berlin – 2.5 million men with 6250 tanks and self-propelled guns and 7500 aircraft.

Hitler, too, had decided that Berlin would be the decisive battle. He had concentrated the last of Germany's reserves along the Oder to the east of the capital. On paper they looked impressive – 60 divisions with 1 million men, 1500 tanks and 3300 aircraft – but many of the divisions had been brought up to strength by draftees from the *Volkssturm* and the aircraft were desperately short of fuel.

At 3 am on April 16 the 10 000 guns of Zhukov's 1st Belorussian Army Group opened fire on German positions on the Seelow Heights, to the north-east of Berlin. Thirty minutes later 143 searchlights, placed 200 yd (180 m) apart along the breakthrough sector, illuminated the battlefield as Soviet motor-rifle troops swarmed from the bridgehead at Kurstin towards the ridge. The technique of creating 'artificial moonlight', pioneered by the British and the Germans, depended on aiming searchlight beams at low clouds, so that a diffuse light was reflected all over the battlefield. The Soviets directed their beams straight at the Seelow Heights, which silhouetted their own troops for surviving German machine-gunners.

By dawn Zhukov was aware that something had gone badly wrong. His infantry were lying in bloody piles at the foot of the heights, unable to advance, and the fighting on April 17 was no easier; by the end of the day Zhukov had lost 30 000 dead. After nearly two years of astounding success, Zhukov had at last run into one of Germany's best defensive generals, General Gotthard

Heinrici. A veteran of the great defensive battles of the First World War, Heinrici had disobeyed Hitler's orders and thinned out his front-line positions on the crest of the heights, so that the Soviet barrage fell on empty trenches. As the Soviet infantry came forward, his men reoccupied the heights.

In a fury, Stalin decided to give priority to Konev's 1st Ukrainian Army Group, which was making better progress to the south-east of Berlin. By the evening of April 20 Konev's spearhead had reached the outskirts of the Wehrmacht headquarters at Zossen. Over the next five days Zhukov's and Konev's army groups slogged their ways to the south-west and north-west of Berlin. Finally, on April 25, Zhukov's and Konev's forces met about 10 miles (16 km) west of Potsdam, completing the encirclement of Berlin. On the same day, at Torgau on the Elbe, the Soviets met US forces; the Reich was now cut in two.

DEATH OF MUSSOLINI

On the evening of April 27, 1945, Radio Milan announced that Mussolini had been captured by Italian Communist guerrillas. In Berlin, the news plunged Hitler into brooding melancholia. Among Mussolini's other admirers – Franco in Spain, Salazar in Portugal, Perón in Argentina – it caused deep alarm. Equally anxious was Churchill, who suspected that Mussolini might be carrying details of embarrassing offers of territory he had made to the Italian dictator in the dark days of 1940. He ordered British SOE and SAS teams in Italy to locate Mussolini and dispose of the evidence.

Before British agents could get to him, however, the Communists had decided that *Il Duce* was better dead than alive. On April 28, Radio Milan carried an interview with his executioner. He had persuaded the ex-dictator and his mistress, Clara Petacci, that he had come to rescue them from the shepherd's hut where they were held. They hurried along with him, until he pointed a sten gun at them and ordered them to stand against a wall. 'Mussolini was terror-stricken. Clara Petacci threw her arms around his shoulders and screamed: "He must not die." I said: "Get back in your place if you don't want to die too." The woman jumped back. From a distance of three paces I shot five bursts into Mussolini . . . Then it was Petacci's turn. Justice had been done.' Their bodies were carried to Milan, where they were hung upside-down from rafters in the Standard Oil petrol station in Piazzale Loreto.

DEADLY KATE Soviet troops load a *Katyusha* ('Little Kate') rocket launcher. These terrifying weapons rained rocket-propelled mortars into the heart of Berlin.

On April 23 Goebbels, the Nazi propaganda chief, issued a stirring proclamation to the population of Berlin: 'I call on you to fight for your city. Fight with everything you have got, for the sake of your wives and your children, your mothers and your parents.

Your arms are defending everything we have ever held dear. . .'

Two days later the Soviet Third Shock Army, attacking Berlin from the north, crossed the Hohenzollern Canal and fought its way into the Tiergarten. Meanwhile, the Eighth Shock Army had been fighting its way westwards through the city, and by April 29 was two blocks from the Reich Chancellery. A total of 15 000 guns were now concentrated on the diminishing German perimeter. Having finally despaired, Hitler and Eva Braun committed suicide on April 30. But the fighting was not over. In the Reichstag 5000 SS, Hitler Youth and *Volkssturm* still

RED FLAG FLYING On May 1, a Soviet soldier raised the Red Flag on the Reichstag. Below him, Berlin lies in ruins.

VICTORY IN EUROPE

May 8, VE (Victory in Europe) Day, was warm and sunny and by mid afternoon large crowds had gathered in Trafalgar Square. Churchill's detective, Walter Thompson, remembered the scene as the prime minister tried to drive to the House of Commons:

'. . . the car was literally forced through the crowds. No engine power was necessary. Everyone seemed to be determined to shake him by the hand. In Parliament Square the cheering crowds closed right in. Mr Churchill came forward to stand on the front seat of the open car while mounted police cleared the way.'

Over the next two hours excitement grew as people began to pour into central London. Among the crowds was Noël Coward who recalled:

'I walked down the Mall and stood outside Buckingham Palace, which was floodlit. The crowd was stupendous. The King and Queen came out on the balcony, looking enchanting. We all roared ourselves hoarse. I suppose this is the greatest day in our history.'

DEATH IN THE BUNKER

By April 20, 1945, Hitler was a very sick man. He could not walk more than 30 paces without gripping something for support, and his bloodshot eyes were so weak that he had difficulty reading even large type. He wore spectacles most of the time, his hair was ash grey, and his breath had begun to smell. He slept only fitfully and irregularly, kept going by injections of glucose and morphine from his physician, Dr Morrell. He was leading a troglodyte existence underneath the Chancellery in the Führerbunker, really an underground village with an administrative HQ, living accommodation, barracks and a large hospital.

That evening Hitler announced his intention of staying in Berlin. 'I am going to fight in front of Berlin, fight in Berlin, and fight behind Berlin.' He wanted to turn Berlin into a Stalingrad. Almost immediately some of his closest colleagues began making excuses to leave the city. Goering led the way, requesting permission to go south to Berchtesgaden; a few days later he tried to assume authority throughout the Reich. Himmler tried to negotiate a separate peace using contacts in Sweden. But others remained loyal. Eva Braun, Hitler's mistress, had arrived in Berlin on April 15 and immediately declared her intention of never being separated from the Führer. His secretaries, too, wanted to stay and would leave only when Hitler actually ordered them out of Berlin.

Those left in the bunker were subject to violent mood swings. On April 27, Hitler became convinced that the battle was going his way. Then on April 29 news of the execution of Mussolini and Claretta Petacci in Milan seems to have pushed Hitler and Eva Braun towards suicide. The fighting was now only a few streets away. Between 1 and 3 am on April 29 they were married. That evening they said goodbye to the female staff in the Bunker complexes. The next afternoon they sat together in Hitler's study. At about 3.30 Eva bit into a cyanide capsule; seconds later Hitler also bit into a capsule, simultaneously shooting himself through the right temple with a heavy Walther pistol.

SURRENDER PASS Signed by the Allied Supreme Commander, this guarantee of decent treatment was the means by which hundreds of thousands of Germans gave up fighting in April and early May.

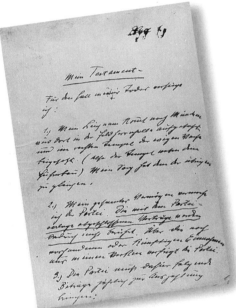

THE FÜHRER'S WILL Hitler acknowledged that he might have little to leave.

Soviets, however, a dark age every bit as dreadful as that which the Germans had visited upon Russia now descended.

Since the Soviets had first entered Germany proper in January, about 1.5 million civilians had been killed or had killed themselves. The Americans reported bodies of hundreds of women roped together with children floating down the Elbe. In the coming months possibly another 2 million were to die in massacres in Silesia, Pomerania and Czechoslovakia. Exalting racial differences and the will to power above all else, the Nazis had urged mankind to throw off the corrupting shackles of civilisation: they had succeeded beyond their wildest imaginings.

UNCONDITIONAL SURRENDER Meeting with Montgomery at Lüneberg Heath, emissaries of the Dönitz government hand over their forces in Holland, Denmark and northern Germany.

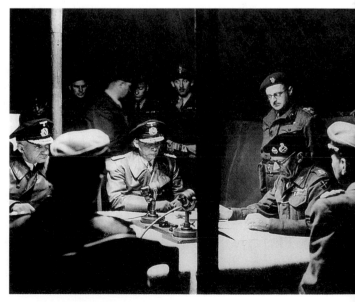

held out, fighting the Soviets room by room. When a Soviet platoon finally raised the Red Flag from its roof on May 1, the SS still held the basement and some of the lower floors, and did not surrender for another 24 hours.

The end comes

On the Anglo-American fronts fighting had been petering out in piecemeal surrenders. On April 29 Vietinghoff surrendered in Italy. Four days later a delegation met Montgomery on Lüneberg Heath and surrendered forces in north-west Germany, Holland and Denmark. By then Admiral Dönitz had become the new Führer; the man operating as his supreme commander, General Alfred Jodl, planned to keep the war going in the east in order to win time for a wholesale evacuation of the German population into areas under Anglo-American control. Eisenhower would have none of it; if Jodl did not sign a general capitulation he would close the Anglo-American front lines

to German refugees. On May 7 Jodl arrived at Eisenhower's HQ at Rheims and signed the surrender document; the next day Field Marshal Keitel signed another surrender in Berlin in the presence of Zhukov and Konev. German pockets in Czechoslovakia and Yugoslavia held out for another week.

Central Europe was in chaos. In the area occupied by British and US forces, the military strove to deal with 8 million foreign and slave workers, 9 million German refugees from the east and more than 5 million prisoners of war. The coming months were going to see widespread hunger, malnutrition and disease, and it says a great deal for Anglo-American administration that deaths were registered in thousands rather than in millions. In the area occupied by the

THE END IN THE EAST

NOT EVEN THE JAPANESE COULD HOLD OUT AGAINST THE OVERWHELMING MIGHT AND TECHNOLOGICAL SUPERIORITY OF THE USA

The fall of Saipan in July 1944 provoked a crisis in Tokyo. Cabals of plotters formed in the Japanese armed forces, preparing to assassinate Prime Minister Tojo and his cabinet. Of these the most important was a circle around Rear Admiral Sokichi Takagi. By a fantastic coincidence, Takagi's group planned to strike on July 20, 1944, the same day that Stauffenburg's bomb detonated at Hitler's Rastenberg headquarters. But on July 19, Tojo issued a press release: 'Saipan Island has finally fallen into enemy hands. I deeply regret the anxiety this has caused to His Majesty. Our empire has entered the most difficult state in its entire history.' It was followed a few hours later by the

announcement of the Tojo government's resignation. Takagi cancelled the assassination attempt; the new premier was an old friend, Admiral Kantaro Suzuki, who promised the Japanese that they now had 'the opportunity to smash the enemy and win the war. The time for decisive battle has arrived'.

All maritime states, from the time of the Athenian navy's victory over the Persian fleet at Salamis in 480 BC, have believed in the possibility of achieving victory through a single climactic encounter, even when all seems lost. As schoolchildren Japan's admirals had learned of the defeat of the Mongol invasion of 1281, when the Mongol armies had been cut off in Kyushu after a typhoon – known as

FACES OF DEFEAT AND VICTORY A Japanese soldier on Saipan carrying a wounded child through US marine positions. Below: A grim-faced and angry MacArthur wades ashore at Leyte after his landing craft ran aground.

the *Kamikaze* ('Divine Wind') – had destroyed much of their fleet. Japan's history contained many such incidents; indeed, as midshipmen most of the admirals had been involved in one such battle – when Admiral Togo annihilated the Russian Baltic fleet in the straits of Tsushima on May 27, 1905.

Far from being daunted by the task which they now faced, on July 21 Japan's military leaders began preparing the *Sho* (Victory) Plans, all of which were designed to impose a Tsushima-type defeat on the Americans. It seemed obvious to Tokyo that the USA's next objective would be the Philippines. *Sho 1*, a plan to convert these islands into a huge trap, was put into immediate effect, and reinforcements soon poured into Manila. By autumn Japan's new commander in the Philippines, Lt General Yamashita, commanded 350 000 troops and 2500 aircraft. When the Americans struck, the 70 major warships of the Japanese Combined Fleet, based in an enormous arc stretching from Singapore to Nagasaki, were to converge on the islands, annihilating the Americans as they struggled ashore.

A-Day

On the night of October 19/20, 1944, the largest fleet yet assembled in the Pacific approached the island of Leyte, a central point in the Philippine archipelago. The fleet consisted of 738 transports and escorts carrying the 203 000 troops of General Walter Kreuger's US Sixth Army, supported by the 18 aircraft carriers and 100 other major warships of Admiral Halsey's Third Fleet. General MacArthur had designated the day of landing A-Day; he refused to employ the more customary D-Day because this had already been used by the man who only five years earlier had been his aide, the one-time Major Dwight D. Eisenhower.

At dawn warships and aircraft started a devastating bombardment of the north-east coast of Leyte, just south of the town of Tacloban. At 10 am the bombardment lifted and four divisions began to land. Resistance was negligible. At 1.30 pm a landing craft carrying MacArthur and other senior officers grounded off the beach.

Over the next three days the Americans expanded their beachhead against little opposition. In fact, the trap had been sprung and three task forces of the Combined Fleet, the northern, central and the southern, were converging on Leyte. The Northern Force, a fleet

KAMIKAZE: FIGHTERS OF THE 'DIVINE WIND'

When Vice Admiral Onishi arrived in Manila in early October 1944, he learned he had fewer than 100 operational aircraft with which to stem the expected US onslaught. Onishi assembled his air crew, and explained that the only hope of victory was for pilots to volunteer to crash their bomb-laden aircraft directly into the US ships. He said they would be like the typhoons which wrecked Mongol invasion fleets in 1274 and 1281, the so-called 'divine winds' or *kamikazes*. The idea of self-sacrifice was deeply ingrained in the Japanese military through the Samurai code of *Bushido*, the way of the warrior. The *kamikazes* consciously adopted Samurai ritual as each tied a *hachimaki*, a white cloth emblazoned with the sun and a prayer, around his head. The first smashed into the heavy cruiser HMAS *Australia* off Leyte on October 21, 1944.

For the last nine months of the Pacific War, *kamikazes* were the greatest danger for the Allied fleets. They had most effect off Okinawa. On April 13, 1945, 185 took off from bases in Japan, accompanied by eight twin-engined bombers, each carrying a new invention, the *Ohka*, a manned rocket-powered flying bomb. The pilot could steer 1 ton of high explosives into a target. Together the *kamikazes* and *Ohkas* sank 36 ships and landing craft. The majority of the 5000 *kamikaze* pilots were young men with little flying experience. The *kamikaze* onslaught off Okinawa contributed to the American decision to use the atomic bomb.

SUICIDE BOMBER An officer on the bridge of USS *Nashville* snapped this *kamikaze* seconds before impact.

consisting of Japan's four surviving aircraft carriers, two battleships, three cruisers and eight destroyers under Admiral Ozawa, steamed south from Japan. It looked powerful but the carriers had scarcely 100 aircraft and its real role was to act as a decoy, enticing Halsey's fleet away from the beachhead. Meanwhile, a Centre Task Force under Admiral Kurita comprised the super battleships *Yamato* and *Musashi*, three other battleships, 12 cruisers and 15 destroyers. This was sailing north along the western side of Palawan from where it would turn east

through the Sibuyan Sea and San Bernadino Strait to attack the US beachhead at Leyte Gulf from the north. A Southern Task Force commanded by Admiral Nishimura was sailing east across the Sulu Sea, from where it was to pass through the Surigao Strait and strike the Leyte anchorage from the south.

Shortly after 1 pm on October 23, US submarines sighted and attacked Kurita's Centre Task Force. By dawn Halsey's aircraft were roaring down on the Japanese battleships. Kurita pressed on through the blue waters of the Sibuyan Sea, his ships taking

July 1944
Fall of Tojo
government

October 1944
Naval Battle of
Leyte Gulf

February 1945
US landings on
Iwo Jima

March 1945
Fire bombing
of Tokyo

April 1945
US landings
on Okinawa

August 1945
Hiroshima and Nagasaki;
Japanese surrender

hit upon hit. On October 24 *Musashi* began to lose speed, and Halsey's airmen gave the stricken battleship their undivided attention; at 5 pm she rolled over and sank. By this time Kurita had reversed course, taking his ships back towards the South China Sea. Meanwhile, Halsey had made contact with Ozawa's Northern Force. Convinced that Kurita's battleships had been decoys, Halsey sped off north, thinking that he was about to destroy the heart of the Combined Fleet.

Well to the south, Nishimura's warships had also been spotted by US reconnaissance. The Seventh Fleet's commander, Admiral Kinkaid, had sent Rear Admiral Jessie B.

BATTLE FOR THE PHILIPPINES A Filipino guerrilla fighting in Manila. Below: A Sherman tank smashes through the gate of Port Santiago, the Japanese HQ in the city of Intramuros.

Oldendorf and virtually all Seventh Fleet's major warships steaming south at full speed. They were to lay an ambush in the Surigao Straits. Shortly after midnight on October 25, Nishimura's warships ploughed into Oldendorf's battle line. As US motor torpedo (PT) boats and destroyers launched successive spreads of torpedoes, Oldendorf's battleships opened up at virtually point-blank range. The torpedoes and shells ripped into the Japanese destroyers, sending three to the bottom, and then hit the Japanese battleships. The *Fuso* exploded and Nishimura's flagship *Yamashiro*, also badly hit, began to settle. The remnants of the Southern Task Force put about, but as they did so the cruisers *Mogami* and *Nachi* collided. The *Mogami* was so badly damaged she was abandoned to the Americans.

As dawn broke over the Surigao Straits Oldendorf knew he had won a great victory. But a very different situation was developing off the beachhead, 200 miles (320 km) to the north. During the night the four battleships, six heavy cruisers and ten destroyers of Kurita's Central Task Force had reversed course, passed through the San Bernadino Strait and were heading at full speed for the US transports. With Halsey's Third Fleet pursuing Ozawa far to the north, the only US warships between the beachhead and Kurita were Rear Admiral Clifton T. Sprague's seven destroyers and six slow, unarmoured, escort carriers, which fled south, pursued by the Japanese.

Still more than 20 miles (32 km) distant, Kurita mistook Sprague's escort carriers for the heavy fleet carriers of Halsey's Third Fleet, and believed that the decisive battle was about to be fought. *Yamato* opened up at 35 000 yd (32 000 m), her 18.1 in (46 cm) shells obliterating the escort carrier *Gambier Bay*. Soon after, kamikazes swept in and plunged into the flight decks of the escort carriers *Santee*, *Suwannee*, *St Lo* and *Kalinin Bay*, all of which were soon ablaze. Off the beachhead there was panic as ships attempted to get up enough steam to flee south to the relative safety of Kinkaid's fleet, still in the Surigao Strait. Kurita had a major victory within his grasp, but at 9.23 am he ordered his fleet to put about and head back for the San Bernadino Strait. He believed that he had engaged and severely damaged Halsey's Third Fleet, and that therefore his mission was accomplished.

Meanwhile, Halsey had caught up with Ozawa. At about 8 am, 180 aircraft from Rear Admiral Mitscher's fast carrier Task Force 38 located and sank the light carrier *Chitose*; later strikes from Task Force 34 hit

IWO JIMA Within weeks of the publication of Joe Rosenthal's photo of US marines raising the flag on Mount Suribachi, the event was celebrated on US postage stamps.

the carriers *Choyoda*, *Zuikaku* and *Zuiho*. During these actions Halsey had received urgent requests from Kinkaid to send his carrier task forces back to Leyte, requests Halsey had ignored. A message now arrived from Nimitz, insisting that Halsey put about and ending with the question, 'Where is Task Force 34, the world wonders?' Halsey later recalled it was 'as if I had been struck in the face'. He slammed his cap onto the deck, but he obeyed the order. Unfortunately, by the time Task Force 34 came within range of the San Bernadino Strait, Kurita was long gone.

The Battle of Leyte Gulf was the largest and most complex naval battle in history. Japan had lost four aircraft carriers, three battleships, ten cruisers and eleven destroyers, and virtually every other ship had been damaged, some very seriously. These were grievous losses, but the surviving Japanese admirals consoled themselves that they had sunk at least six of Halsey's fleet carriers, thereby imposing a serious delay on American operations. The sudden disappearance of US carrier aircraft from the skies over Leyte – Halsey had withdrawn his carriers for re-fuelling – convinced even the sceptical Japanese Army that the Combined Fleet had, indeed, won a victory.

Persuaded that the decisive land battle could now be fought on Leyte, Yamashita poured reinforcements into the island. An attritional struggle developed, fought for ridges which the Americans named 'Breakneck' and 'Shoestring'. On November 27 a Japanese counterattack was pulverised by US firepower. Thereafter the Americans began to crush the Japanese through sheer weight of numbers. By mid December, 203 000 Americans were closing on fewer than a third that number of Japanese. Organised resistance collapsed on Christmas Day; Japanese losses totalled 75 000, about 10 000 of whom had been lost to US aircraft and submarines while on transit to the island.

MacArthur's next major objective was Luzon. Between January 2 and 9, an assault force covering 500 sq miles (1300 km²) of ocean fought its way through kamikazes and suicide motorboats packed with explosives from Leyte to the west coast of Luzon. The week-long battle cost the Americans 91 ships sunk or damaged and 3000 casualties, including 1230 dead. On January 9, 200 000 troops of Sixth Army began landing on the shores of Lingayan Gulf, the only large protected anchorage on the shores of Luzon, with the exception of heavily defended Manila Bay. Opposition was surprisingly light. Rather than expose his men to pulverising US naval gunfire, Yamashita had decided to abandon all coastal positions and pull back to the mountains east and north-east of Manila, where he would be able to prolong resistance.

The 'liberation' of Manila

When he first heard reports that the Japanese were evacuating Manila, MacArthur had one thought; he must get to the city and re-establish his headquarters in the same buildings from which the Japanese had ejected him more than three years earlier. Flying columns of the 1st Cavalry Division dashed south and reached the northern suburbs of Manila on February 3, liberating more than 4000 civilian prisoners held at the campus of Santo Tomás University. MacArthur then announced to the Press that Manila was liberated, news that Roosevelt conveyed to Churchill and Stalin as they met for the first day of the Yalta Conference.

But the triumph was short lived. A force of some 20 000 Japanese, mainly naval troops, had refused Yamashita's order to evacuate the city. Their commander, Rear Admiral Sanji Iwabuchi, was determined to avenge what was now known to have been the crushing defeat of the Imperial Japanese Navy in the Battle of Leyte Gulf. For the next month Iwabuchi's troops fought three US divisions in the streets of central Manila, contesting every steel and concrete building, before making their final stand in the old walled city of Intramuros. MacArthur, desperate to preserve the city, had at first prohibited the use of air strikes and artillery, but as American casualties mounted he relented. By early March it was possible to see from one side of the city to the other, because nothing remained standing; in the smoking ruins lay the bodies of 20 000 Japanese, 1200 Americans and more than 100 000 Filipinos.

The battle for Manila was still raging when Nimitz's fleet sailed into the Bonins, an island group only 700 miles (1130 km) south-east of Japan, to secure advanced bases for an invasion of its home islands. On February 17 two Marine divisions stormed ashore on the 8 sq mile (21 km²) cinder and ash volcanic island of Iwo Jima, and took five

GONE TO GROUND US troops clearing Japanese-occupied caves by lobbing explosive packs into the entrance. Others wait, ready to gun down any Japanese who try to escape.

weeks and 26 000 casualties to exterminate the 25 000 strong Japanese garrison. The marines captured the highest point of Iwo Jima, the volcanic cone of Mount Suribachi, on February 23. Associated Press photographer Joe Rosenthal snapped the moment five marines raised the Stars and Stripes on top of the mountain, an image which was later used as the basis for the Marine Corps monument in Washington.

In the last week of March the largest armada ever assembled in the Pacific – 1450 ships including the carriers and battleships of the newly formed British Pacific Fleet – sailed for Okinawa in the Ryukyu Islands, only 360 miles (580 km) south of Kyushu. Tokyo was determined to hold it at all costs: a 130 000-man garrison and hundreds of kamikaze and conventional squadrons defended the island. During the next eight weeks Japanese air strikes – kamikaze and conventional – sank 36 and damaged 368 Allied ships, destroying 800 aircraft and inflicting nearly 10 000 casualties. This, the most sustained aerial offensive ever mounted against a fleet, cost the Japanese a staggering total of 8000 aircraft. In the midst of the aerial attacks the Imperial Navy dispatched the battleship *Yamato* on its own kamikaze mission against the Allied fleet, but swarms of US aircraft sank her well to the north of Okinawa. Ashore the fighting was the bloodiest of the Pacific War. The 300 000 troops who landed in the first days of April took 11 weeks and 39 000 casualties to kill 137 000 enemy troops and 100 000 Japanese civilians – a grim foretaste of the likely cost of an invasion of the home islands.

ROAD TO MANDALAY British mortar teams near Pagoda Hill firing on Japanese positions in Fort Dufferin.

In Burma

As catastrophe after catastrophe overwhelmed Japan in the islands of the Pacific and the East Asian littoral, the Imperial Army had taken an almost perverse satisfaction in the fact that the emperor was being dishonoured by the navy not by the army. By the spring of 1945, however, theatres controlled by the army were also reporting disasters. The most serious was in Burma. Here General Kimura had withdrawn his substantially reinforced Burma Area Army south of the mile-wide Irrawaddy, from where he intended to counterattack the British XIV Army when it crossed. Kimura looked forward to this action, which he referred to as the 'Battle of the Irrawaddy Shore'; it was to be yet another 'decisive' battle, in which Japan would snatch victory from the jaws of defeat.

Thanks to excellent signals intelligence, XIV Army's commander, Lt General Sir

BRAVING BULLETS From the relative safety of a foxhole, an American photographer captures the moment when a marine dashes forward to a new position.

William Slim (he had been knighted after the Imphal-Kohima battles), quickly learned of Kimura's plans. While his 19th Indian Division headed towards Mandalay, Slim sent his IV Corps, entirely sustained by US transport aircraft, more than 200 miles (320 km) south through the savannah country of central Burma and around Kimura's left flank. Engineers made a road as they went, unrolling lengths of 'Bithess', hessian soaked in bitumen, which provided an all-weather surface. One Japanese reconnaissance aircraft did manage to penetrate the dense British fighter screen, but his report of long columns of British tanks 100 miles (160 km) behind Japanese lines was attributed to too much saki. IV Corps crossed the Irrawaddy on February 13, and dashed for Kimura's main ordnance base at Meiktila, 100 miles south of Mandalay. Kimura's positions along the southern bank of the Irrawaddy were suddenly untenable. He made a desperate effort to retake Meiktila, and then attempted an orderly withdrawal towards Rangoon. But XIV Army pursued closely, and by early April Kimura's retreat had turned into a rout.

Slim's plans were almost thrown into disarray by the Americans, when they withdrew their transport aircraft to China at a crucial point in the operation. Japan still based more

B-29s OVER TOKYO

On March 10, 1945, a gigantic firestorm swept through the closely packed wooden houses of south-eastern Tokyo. A military rescue unit, headed by Dr Kubota Shigenori, reached the Ryogoku bridge across the Sumida River before dawn. He later wrote:

'In the black river countless bodies were floating, clothed bodies, naked bodies, all as black as charcoal. It was unreal. These were dead people, but you couldn't tell whether they were men or women. You couldn't tell if the objects floating by were arms and legs or pieces of burnt wood.'

Dr Kubota commanded just nine doctors and eleven nurses. In their emergency headquarters in the Honjo national school, they tried to help the injured. Most were suffering from various forms of oxygen deficiency. One man gasped, 'It hurts so much I'd like to cut open my chest and let some clean air in.'

TOKYO CALLING B-29 ground crew based in Tinian hear of the latest successful US raid in a broadcast by 'Tokyo Rose' – an American-born Japanese working for the Japanese Broadcasting Corporation – who denounces the 'insane and criminal' firebombing of Tokyo.

than 25 per cent of its army in China, and it could still launch successful offensives there, driving the Chinese from their rice paddies just before harvest, so that the crop could feed the Japanese. But the offensive which began between the Yellow and Yangtze rivers in March 1945 had an additional objective. On March 26 the Japanese overran the vast

COLLAPSE IN BURMA In scenes unimaginable only a few months earlier, demoralised Japanese soldiers began to surrender to the British in late July 1945.

USAAF base at Laohokow, from which the US long-range strategic bombers, the B-29s, had been operating. Success was short-lived; soon Japanese troops were being transferred in ever-larger numbers from central China to Manchuria, because on April 10 Moscow had announced that it would not be renewing the Soviet-Japanese non-aggression treaty. Laohokow was soon in operation again but it was hardly needed, because now most B-29s flew from the Marianas.

Fire bombs on Tokyo

The first B-29s had hit Japan in the summer of 1944, but flying at altitudes of more than 30 000 ft (9000 m) in the violent jet streams in the stratosphere over East Asia, the results had been negligible. On the night of March 9/10, 1945, however, 334 B-29s attacked Tokyo using low-level tactics; their new commander, General Curtis LeMay, had first tested these over China the previous December. The result was a firestorm; 15 sq miles (40 km^2) of the city were destroyed, more than 83 000 killed and an additional 100 000 injured. Over the next three months B-29 fire raids destroyed nearly 40 per cent of Japan's five major cities, Tokyo-Yokohama, Kawasaki, Osaka, Kobe and Nagoya. Japanese industrial production plummeted, as workers and their families fled the cities and coalesced into roaming mobs which scoured the countryside, foraging for food.

Beginning in 1942 the submarines of the US Navy had been taking an increasingly heavy toll on Japanese merchant shipping. Unlike the British, the Japanese were unable to institute an effective system of convoys and maritime reconnaissance, while the Americans developed 'wolf pack' techniques similar to those employed by the U-boats of the Kriegsmarine. US shipyards built 200 large, long-range submarines between 1942 and 1944, and by 1945 these had sunk more than 1100 merchant ships amounting to 4.8 million tons – around 56 per cent of the total lost to Japan. This, too, had had an effect on Japanese industry. In addition, by the spring of 1945 the import of food was badly disrupted, leading to widespread malnutrition and in some areas actual starvation.

By July 1945 the Allies planned a series of operations to take place over the following year. In September the British were to land in Malaya (Operation *Zipper*), while at about the same time Soviet armies were to invade Manchuria. In November the Americans were to land on Kyushu (Operation *Olympic*) and in the following spring three huge Allied armies were scheduled to land on Honshu, to the north of Tokyo. The US Marine Corps was promising its men 'Golden Gate by 48'; it was not unreasonable to anticipate at least another three years of war, before the survivors of the battles for the Japanese home islands sailed back into San Fransisco Bay. The US War Department reckoned on at least a million Allied casualties, the vast majority of whom would be Americans.

Some historians have argued on the basis of peace feelers from Japan's foreign ministry

THE MANHATTAN PROJECT

In the summer of 1940 with Britain facing invasion, Churchill ordered the formation of a committee to investigate the feasibility of an atomic bomb. Codenamed MAUD, this quickly discovered that developments in physics in the 1920s and 30s had made atomic fission a possibility. Jewish refugee scientists from Germany, working at the University of Birmingham, had concluded that a device could be constructed of Uranium-235 (U-235) isotopes which would have an explosive power equivalent to 'several thousand tons of dynamite'. The MAUD committee concluded that 'a uranium bomb was practicable and likely to lead to decisive results

HIROSHIMA AFTER THE BOMB Exploding into a fireball 1885 ft (575 m) above the ground, 'Little Boy' reduced an area of 5 sq mile (13 km²) to ash. A year later, the death toll was put at 120 000.

in the war'. But there was a problem. U-235 did not occur naturally in isolation. It would have to be separated from other uranium isotopes in sufficient quantities to produce a bomb, and this would require resources beyond the capacity of beleaguered Britain. Refugee scientists in the USA had long been convinced that Germany was on the point of developing a bomb, and in 1939 had persuaded Albert Einstein to write to Roosevelt urging that the United States begin its own research. Nothing much happened until Pearl Harbor, but by early 1942 an ultra secret bomb-making project, codenamed *Manhattan*, was under way.

The Manhattan Project was weapon development on a scale never before seen. Lt General Leslie R. Groves was placed in charge. He had a work force which in time grew to more than 600 000, including more than half the physicists working in the English-speaking world, and European refugees from Hitler. By 1944 the project was being pursued in dozens of sites, chiefly Oak Ridge in Tennessee and Los Alamos in New Mexico. The final bill was over $2 billion. It was an enormous gamble. There was no guarantee that the bomb would work, and there was a possibility that it might work too well, and set off, say, a chain reaction in the atoms of the atmosphere. On the night of July 15/16, 1945, hundreds of young men and women, physicists, laboratory assistants, technicians, sat with hampers and crates of beer on the hillsides overlooking the test site. Shortly before dawn a gigantic fireball, brighter than the sun, erupted across the desert. The world knows that one of the chief scientists, Robert Oppenheimer, was moved to recite a Hindu prayer: 'I am become death.' But on the hillsides the young scientists cheered, drank beer and made love.

that Tokyo was on the point of surrendering in July 1945. Yet the government of Admiral Suzuki rejected the Allied demand for an unconditional surrender made at Potsdam on July 27. It is clear that whereas some civilian elements wished to capitulate, the Japanese military were still full of fight. They planned to meet the Allied invasion fleet with 8000 carefully husbanded aircraft (many of them kamikazes) and hundreds of explosive-packed suicide boats and human torpedoes. Ashore, 2 million regular soldiers and a vast home guard would dispose of even more invaders.

At 8 am on August 6, 1945, a single B-29 dropped an atomic bomb on Hiroshima, destroying the city and killing 80 000 instantaneously. When the Suzuki cabinet met on August 8, the majority still wished to fight on. On the morning of August 9, Japan reeled under two new shocks: a second atomic bomb devastated Nagasaki and the USSR declared war – within the hour, 1.5 million Soviet troops and 5000 tanks were advancing into Manchuria. Now at war with two superpowers, its cities being systematically destroyed by incendiary raids and a new and terrifying bomb, its industrial production at only one-third of prewar levels and many of its population starving, Japan's cabinet on August 10 accepted the Potsdam declaration, asking only that the emperor should remain sovereign. The Americans readily acceded and on August 15 Hirohito broadcast Japan's capitulation.

IMPERIAL SEAL Not in their worst nightmares could the Japanese have imagined this – the insignia of Emperor Hirohito affixed to the instrument of surrender.

WORLD WAR TO COLD WAR

AFTER THE FIGHTING CAME THE RECKONING – JUDGMENT FOR THE WAR CRIMINALS AND NEW ALLIANCES FOR A NEW BALANCE OF POWER

In the summer of 1945 statisticians began trying to calculate the cost of the previous six years. One obvious measure was the number of dead, but there were so many it took more than 50 years to arrive at a figure.

At first, the Soviet Union thought that it had lost 13 million but this was soon revised up to 20 million, and then revised again to 27 million. Soviet statisticians eventually found a more chilling means of expressing their loss; only 3 per cent of male babies born between 1920 and 1925 could be found in the census for 1946. For more than 20 years after the war, Western visitors to the Soviet Union would remark on the large numbers of middle-aged women working on construction sites. Exactly the same imbalance of the sexes was observable in the ruins of the Reich. Germany's losses, initially put at about 3 million, were eventually revised upwards to 7 million, a figure which included about 1 million ethnic Germans massacred in Poland and Czechoslovakia. In the Far East, China had suffered the largest loss of life, though officials could arrive only at rough estimates. Eventually a consensus emerged – about 20 million had died as a direct and indirect consequence of what Japan still called the 'China Incident'.

While these three nations lost more than any others in absolute terms, smaller nations lost more in proportional terms. The Polish Census Bureau found that Poland's population had shrunk from 30 million in 1939 to 24 million in 1946; among those missing were virtually all of Poland's prewar Jewish population. The losses in some countries were distributed very unevenly. In Yugoslavia, for example, most of the 1.7 million dead came from Serbia, Montenegro and Bosnia rather than Croatia and Slovenia. Some populations had disappeared altogether; the Indian population of Burma, about 1 million in January 1942, had been massacred to a man by the Burmese during the Japanese invasion.

In the end, the human cost of the war worldwide proved impossible to calculate and rough estimates had to suffice – certainly more than 75 million and rather less than 100 million – perhaps about one in twenty of the population of the planet.

United Nations

As early as 1942 Allied officials had begun discussing the need to replace the League of Nations with an international organisation able to prevent another war. In December 1943 the Soviets had agreed; the result was an international conference in San Francisco in April 1945 from which the United Nations Organisation was to emerge. There was much

THE BIG THREE AT YALTA In February 1945, an ailing Roosevelt – he died two months later – sits between Churchill and Stalin, allies whose marriage of convenience is by now almost at an end.

genuine idealism involved; at the same time, the surviving powers all refused to be tied by the resolutions of the General Assembly if these conflicted with their national interests. Despite the carnage, realpolitik still governed relations among nations.

The mood in September 1945 was very different from that of November 1918 when the League of Nations had been born; no one in 1945 believed that they had just fought the 'war to end wars'. As early as spring 1943 there had been widespread discussion in both Allied and Axis media of a Third World War. Some German analysts argued that it had already begun. One, Giselher Wirsing, wrote in *Signal*: 'For months past we have been emphasising in this periodical that the subterranean war within the war being fought out on the one side between the British Empire and the United States and, on the other side, between those powers and the Soviet Union, is no less important than the open war being waged by those three powers against Germany, Italy, Japan and their allies.'

Even between the British and Americans there were stresses. During the war the leadership of both nations had stressed the extraordinary degree of cooperation between them. But unknown to the public, bitter battles had been fought about strategy. In the Far East and Pacific, for example, it was difficult to mask the fact that the British and Americans were fighting different wars with different objectives. The commander in chief of the US Navy, Admiral Ernest J. King, did everything in his power to prevent the British

April 1945 Death of Roosevelt	June 1945 San Francisco Conference completes United Nations charter	July 1945 Churchill ousted in general election	July-August 1945 Potsdam Conference	November 1945 Start of Nuremberg trial

from deploying a large fleet in the Pacific in January 1945, because he suspected that its primary objective would be to re-establish European colonial rule throughout South-east Asia. Once the fleet had arrived the Americans did their best to limit its mobility by severely restricting its supplies of oil. Washington wanted the defeat of Japan, but wanted it to be a US, not an Allied, victory.

The summer of 1945 saw an increase in tension. Roosevelt was dead, Churchill voted out of office, and neither President Truman nor the new British prime minister,

Clement Attlee, had the personality or time to develop a close relationship. Just 13 days after Hirohito's broadcast of Japan's surrender, Truman ordered the cancellation of all further Lend-Lease shipments, which had kept the British economy afloat since the spring of 1941. Anglo-American tension was thus very real; on the other hand, the mere fact that the United States and the British Empire were so unequal in strength limited its significance. The disharmony between them was the inevitable grinding of gears as an old empire left the world stage to make way for a federation of its former colonies, now a superpower.

By contrast, the relations of both countries with the Soviet Union were problematic and produced some strange contortions. As secretary for war after 1918, Churchill had done his best to strangle the infant

SWEETNESS OF VICTORY **Clearly intent on having a good time, a line of WAAFs parade down the Strand on VE Day, May 8, 1945. Below: In Piccadilly, every face in the crowd is smiling with relief.**

USSR at birth, yet during the war he welcomed Britain's cobelligerent (he did not, at first, extend the term 'ally' to the Soviet Union) with the words '. . . if Hitler were to march on hell I should attempt a few favourable references to Satan in the House of Commons'. In Hollywood, Warner Brothers transformed US Ambassador Joseph E. Davies' apologia for Stalinist terror, *Mission to Moscow*, into a film with Walter Huston playing the diplomat, and Mannart Kippen an avuncular Soviet dictator.

The first extensive meeting between the US and Soviet leadership took place at Tehran in November 1943, when Roosevelt and Stalin began to develop a personal relationship which excluded Churchill. This alarmed the British who became concerned about a US-Soviet alliance, in which 'naive and idealistic Americans' would be manipulated by the 'sophisticated and ruthless Soviets'. For its part, Britain landed forces in Greece, for example, as the Germans retreated from the Balkans in November 1944, and began to help pro-monarchist forces to crush their former allies in the Communist resistance.

Meeting at Yalta in February 1945, the Western Allies and the Soviets agreed on zones of influence in Europe. Churchill felt that the Americans were conceding too much, but the Americans argued that they needed Soviet participation in the war against Japan in order to minimise US casualties. Five months later the Allies met again at Potsdam and confirmed the division of Europe into Soviet and Western spheres.

An iron curtain

The problem in late 1945 was that the Americans were withdrawing from Europe as fast as they could. By itself Britain had neither the military nor the economic weight to balance the USSR. Worse still, much of Europe was in ruins, with economic activity running at less than one-third of prewar levels and some 20 million refugees to repatriate or resettle. Powerful Communist parties had emerged in France and Italy. And large Soviet armies remained intact along the eastern banks of the Elbe.

Britain's new foreign secretary, Ernest Bevin, was desperately worried, as was his old friend, now leader of the opposition, Winston Churchill. In an attempt to galvanise opinion in the United States, on March 5, 1946, at Fulton, Missouri, Churchill declared that Stalin had lowered an 'iron curtain . . . from Stettin in the Baltic to Trieste in the Adriatic' and went on to warn that the USSR was aiming for 'the infinite expansion of its power and doctrines'. In retrospect, the speech marked the beginning of the Cold War, but it was not seen as such at the time. The USSR was still cooperating closely with the USA and Britain in the 'denazification' of Germany. On both sides of the Atlantic Churchill's speech was denounced as warmongering.

A year later opinion was beginning to turn. On March 12, 1947, Truman asked Congress for $400 million to give aid to Turkey and

HOME TO MOTHER RUSSIA Although this greeting was posed for propaganda purposes, there was nothing feigned in the delight of the women at seeing the men return.

ODESSA

Organisation der ehemaligen SS Angehörigen (ODESSA) was a network of Nazis and Nazi sympathisers who ran escape routes from the Tirol via Rome to South America or the Middle East. It centred on right-wing members of the Vatican's Curia, who provided clothes, passports and money. Both Eichmann and Mengele used the route. How much Pope Pius XII knew about it is a point of controversy. Accusers point out that he did not condemn National Socialism until June 1945; defenders point out that the Vatican helped many more Jews and escaped Allied POWs than it did fleeing SS officers.

Greece, and proposed extending military and economic aid to other nations threatened by Soviet power. The Press immediately dubbed this the 'Truman Doctrine', a policy to contain the Soviet Union. Three months later General Marshall, now US secretary of state, gave a speech at Harvard suggesting US economic assistance to help Europe to recover. By April 1948 the Marshall Plan was in operation.

US public opinion was still, however, very hostile to 'entangling foreign alliances' – until the Soviets helped to change its mind.

In February 1948 a Communist coup in Czechoslovakia was followed by the Soviet closure of land routes across Soviet-occupied East Germany into the Western-occupied sector of Berlin, a clear attempt to starve British, US and French forces out of the city. The Americans and British responded with

NUREMBERG – THE NAZIS ON TRIAL

FACING JUDGMENT Worried but alert, ex-Reichmarshal Goering confers with his lawyer.

The scene was without precedent in modern times. On October 1, 1946, 21 of the surviving leaders of the Nazi state sat in the dock of a Nuremberg courtroom and heard a judge pronounce sentence – three were acquitted, seven (including a now deranged Rudolf Hess) received long periods of imprisonment and eleven were sentenced to hang. Among the last group were Herman Goering, senior SS men, and men who considered themselves honourable soldiers like Field Marshal Wilhelm Keitel. Two weeks later ten went to the gallows – Goering had managed to take cyanide a few hours before the time of the execution. Over the next few years many lesser functionaries were brought to trial, a process which continues to this day.

At the end of the 20th century the world has become used to the idea of bringing to justice the perpetrators of war crimes. In 1945 this notion was novel. Implicit in Churchill's rhetoric as early as 1940 was the idea that there would be retribution after the war; by late 1943 the British, Americans and Soviets foresaw an International Military Tribunal to prosecute the Nazi leadership on charges that they had 'conspired to wage war' and committed 'crimes against humanity'. It began work in October 1945. Goering, who had lost weight and had been weaned off morphine, was mentally more alert than he had been for years. Displaying the skills of a first-rate barrister, he often had the prosecution on the defensive, particularly on issues like aerial bombardment of cities, in which the Allies were as guilty as the Germans. Had the trial been solely concerned with the methods of waging war, it is difficult to see how the defendants could have been found more guilty than their enemies. But the evidence for more general crimes against humanity was overwhelming.

Nuremberg has been dismissed by some historians as 'victor's justice'. There is some truth in this, yet it did expose extraordinary horrors, and thus probably prevented the development of cults around the Nazi leaders.

an airlift; between June 1948 and May 1949, the USAF and RAF lifted 2.35 million tons of food and coal into Berlin. On July 21, 1949, the US Senate ratified the North Atlantic Treaty, committing the United States to the defence of Western Europe. Thus it was that as the tenth anniversary of Hitler's invasion of Poland approached, two hostile alliances faced each other in Europe.

A Cold War had also emerged in the Far East. Here, the USA had aligned itself with anticolonial forces – including, at first, the Viet Minh, the Communist-dominated liberation movement in French Indochina. The lynchpin of the US policy was an alliance with a strong Nationalist China, but in January 1947 General Marshall had reported after a fact-finding mission that Mao Zedong and his Communist People's Liberation Army were almost certain to win the civil war which had exploded back into life after Japan's surrender.

Eighteen months later Marshall's prognostication proved correct. The United States faced Communist regimes in China and North Korea, which it assumed were little more than stooges for Moscow. Over the next quarter of a century it either waged or assisted in 'hot' wars in Korea (1950-3) and Indochina (1959-75); these cost it more than 100 000 dead and ended ignominiously in April 1975, when it had to evacuate its personnel by helicopter just before a triumphant North Vietnamese Army arrived in Saigon. With hindsight, it seems clear that the fall of Saigon brought to an end an era of Asian conflict which had begun with Japan's invasion of China in 1937, a war of Asian independence which lasted for 38 years, four of which – 1941-5 – coincided with the Second Great European War of the 20th century.

ON THE TOWN US sailors and marines celebrate VP (Victory in the Pacific) night, August 15, 1945, in New York's Times Square.

TIMECHART

1939

JANUARY

26 In the Spanish Civil War **Barcelona** falls to General Franco's forces.

30 In a speech to the **Reichstag** Hitler warns that another war will see 'the annihilation of the Jewish race in Europe'.

FEBRUARY

27 Britain and France recognise **Franco**'s government in Spain.

MARCH

15 German forces occupy the rump of **Czechoslovakia**.

21 Hitler demands that Poland relinquish the port of **Danzig** (Gdansk) and the corridor of former German territory that gave Poland access to the Baltic. Lithuania is forced to give up **Memel and Memelland** to the Germans.

31 Britain and France guarantee support for **Poland** if it is attacked by Germany. They subsequently offer guarantees to Romania and Greece (April 13).

APRIL

7 Italy invades **Albania**.

AUGUST

23 The German-Soviet **non-aggression** treaty clears the way for a combined attack on Poland.

SEPTEMBER

1 Germany invades **Poland**.

2 Bloody Sunday: Poles massacre about 13 000 ethnic Germans, mainly in Silesia.

3 At the expiry of ultimatums sent to Berlin some hours earlier, Britain and France **declare war** on Germany. Chamberlain forms a war cabinet, with Winston Churchill as First Lord of the Admiralty. The German submarine, U-30, torpedoes the British liner,

OVERCONFIDENT Flanagan and Allen's Phoney War hit suggested that German fortifications were already crumbling.

Athenia. **German U-boats** score a series of spectacular successes, sinking the aircraft carrier *Courageous* (September 17) and the battleship *Royal Oak* in Scapa Flow (October 14).

5 In response to a **rapid German advance**, the Polish high command orders its forces to retreat behind the River Vistula.

17 The **USSR invades Poland** from the east.

19 Beginning of the **collapse** of the Polish army, with 100 000 surrendering to the Germans.

25 The Luftwaffe launches huge **air attacks** on the now isolated city of Warsaw.

27 Warsaw surrenders.

OCTOBER

6 The last organised **Polish forces surrender**, but guerrilla operations have already begun. In a speech in the Reichstag **Hitler offers peace** to Britain and France.

NOVEMBER

30 The USSR invades **Finland**.

DECEMBER

12 Battle of **Tolvaajarvi**. The Finns bloodily repulse Russian attacks north of Lake Ladoga.

13 Battle of the **River Plate**. Although they are all damaged in the exchange, two British cruisers and a New Zealand-manned cruiser trap the German pocket battleship *Admiral Graf Spee* in Montevideo harbour.

15 Battle of **Suomussalmi**. In their greatest victory of the war, the Finns destroy two Soviet divisions.

17 *Admiral Graf Spee* is **scuttled** in the estuary of the River Plate.

DANZIG GREETS ITS FÜHRER Hitler acknowledges the cheers of Germans delighted to be reunited with the Reich (left). Within days of the Battle of the River Plate, Hamleys was selling a new board game (above), in which the object was to hunt the *Graf Spee*.

1940

JANUARY

10 Mechelen Incident: Bad weather forces a German aircraft to land at Mechelen in Belgium. On board is an officer with the plans for Hitler's projected spring offensive in the West. The Belgians pass copies to the French high command. This leads Hitler and von Manstein to develop the alternative *Sichelschnitt* plan (February 24).

27 Fearful that Britain and France will use the Russo-Finnish war as an excuse to occupy Norway and thereby cut off Germany's supplies of iron ore, Hitler begins planning a pre-emptive **invasion of Scandinavia**.

SPITFIRES FROM SCRAP Following an appeal for aluminium in summer 1940, a young boy carries the family bath tub to a collection point in London.

FEBRUARY

1 Soviet forces, heavily reinforced and reorganised, begin a massive **offensive** against Finnish defences.

16 The British destroyer *Cossack* violates Norway's neutrality by sailing into Jossing Fiord, near Stavanger, to rescue British prisoners from the German transport **Altmark**.

MARCH

12 Short of munitions and having suffered nearly 70 000 casualties since the beginning of the war, **Finland capitulates**.

APRIL

8-10 As German invasion convoys approach the **Norwegian coast**, they clash violently with British naval forces. The Germans lose two cruisers and many warships are damaged, but the convoys land their troops.

9 German forces occupy **Denmark**.

15-18 British and French troops begin to land in **Norway**, well after German troops have established a foothold.

19 The Luftwaffe destroys the town of **Namsos**, the main Allied base in central Norway.

MAY

1-2 Unable to counter German air attacks, the Allies **evacuate** southern Norway.

7-10 Following attacks in the House of Commons on the failure of the Norwegian campaign (May 7), **Neville Chamberlain resigns** as prime minister and is replaced by Winston Churchill (May 10).

10 The German **onslaught in the west** begins. Von Bock's Army Group B strikes into Belgium and the Netherlands, triggering an Anglo-French advance into Belgium. Meanwhile, von Rundstedt's Army Group A advances through the supposedly impassable Ardennes around the right flank of powerful French and British forces.

13 Army Group A reaches the **Meuse** and begins to cross.

DUNKIRK: THE ITALIAN VERSION A Turin paper showed bombers sinking British ships and pulverising panicking British soldiers on the evacuation beach.

14-15 Following the **bombing of Rotterdam**, Holland capitulates.

15 French counterattacks against German **bridgeheads** on the west side of the Meuse are all destroyed by rapidly advancing German armour.

19 Amidst increasing panic, French Commander in Chief General Gamelin is replaced by General **Weygand**.

20 Spearheads of Army Group A reach the coast near the mouth of the Somme, thereby **splitting the Allied armies** in two.

21 The British succeed in decrypting Luftwaffe **Enigma** transmissions.

23-25 Scarcely able to believe the scale of the German success and fearing a trap, Hitler orders his **panzers to stop**. The advance resumes on May 25.

25 King Leopold of Belgium informs the British and French that he is going to **surrender** the Belgian Army.

26 Until June 4: Over 300 000 British and French troops trapped around **Dunkirk** in north-eastern France are evacuated to England.

JUNE

5 Reinforced and regrouped, the Germans **strike south-west** into France, against considerably weakened French forces.

9 Following the evacuation of Anglo-French forces from their last foothold

in the north (Narvik on June 8), **Norway capitulates**.

10 Italy **declares war** on France and Britain.

13 Churchill flies to Tours for **crisis talks** with French premier Paul Reynaud.

14 The Germans enter **Paris**.

15 Reynaud appeals unsuccessfully to Roosevelt for immediate US intervention.

15-17 USSR occupies **Estonia**, **Latvia** and **Lithuania**.

16 Reynaud resigns as premier and is replaced by Marshal Henri **Pétain**.

17 The MAUD Committee is set up in Britain to investigate the possibility of an **atomic bomb**.

18 Prime Minister Churchill makes his **'finest hour'** speech in the House of Commons, hurling defiance at Hitler and Germany.

21 British scientist **R.V. Jones** begins work to 'bend' the German *Knickebein* radio navigation beam.

PARIS: THE GERMAN VERSION The Wehrmacht's magazine, *Signal*, announces the fall of Paris with a picture of Me110s circling the Eiffel Tower.

22 Pétain concludes an **armistice** with Germany, dividing France into an occupied zone and a rump French state with its capital at Vichy. In Washington, the US Congress votes massive increases in **defence**

virtually undefended provincial city of **Coventry**.

DECEMBER

10 Operation *Compass*. Two British divisions attack and defeat much larger Italian forces at **Sidi Barrani** in western Egypt.

AIR RAID PRECAUTIONS Playing cards (above) urged people to observe basic ARP drill. Background: Women joined the work force in Britain's expanded aircraft factories.

THEIR FINEST HOUR A grim-faced Churchill walks through the ruins of Battersea after a Luftwaffe raid on London in September 1940.

expenditure, raising the national debt to $49 billion.

23 Determined to continue the war, General de Gaulle forms the **French National Committee** in London.

25 Japan occupies the northern provinces of French **Indochina**.

28 The USSR occupies the eastern Romanian province of **Bessarabia**.

JULY

3 The British Navy attacks and sinks or disables the French fleet at **Mers El Kébir** in Algeria.

6 A **triumphal parade in Berlin** celebrates the fall of France and the expulsion of British forces from the Continent.

10 The Luftwaffe begins widespread **air attacks** on Channel shipping and on southern England.

16 Hitler orders preparations for a seaborne **invasion of England**, Operation *Sea Lion*.

19 Hitler offers Britain peace in his **'Last Appeal to Reason'** speech in the Reichstag. The text of the speech is subsequently dropped by the Luftwaffe over Britain.

22 Britain **rejects** Hitler's peace offer.

AUGUST

1 Hitler sets September 15 as provisional date for **Operation *Sea Lion***.

3 Italian forces from Ethiopia **invade British Somaliland**, which Britain evacuates on August 14.

13 *'Adler Tag'* marks the beginning of massive Luftwaffe **daylight attacks** on RAF Fighter Command bases over southern England.

24-25 Responding to accidental Luftwaffe bombing of London, the **RAF bombs Berlin**. British cities are now increasingly the Luftwaffe's objective.

SEPTEMBER

3 With the German U-boat campaign sinking more and more British merchant shipping, Churchill trades British bases in the Western Hemisphere for 50 old **US destroyers**.

13 The Italian Army in Libya invades **Egypt**.

15 Battle of Britain Day. RAF fighters **smash major Luftwaffe attacks** on London, shooting down 56 enemy aircraft.

17 Hitler **postpones** Operation *Sea Lion*.

23 A British and Free French attempt to take **Dakar** is vigorously resisted by Vichy French forces.

OCTOBER

28 Italian forces in Albania **invade Greece**. The Greek Army later launches a successful counterattack (November 14).

NOVEMBER

10 Advancing from the Sudan and Kenya, British forces begin an offensive against Italian forces in **Ethiopia**.

11 British torpedo-bombers from HMS *Illustrious* sink or damage three Italian battleships in **Taranto** harbour. The raid is soon being closely studied by Japanese naval attachés in Europe.

14 Operation *Mondlicht Sonate*: 440 German bombers destroy the

18 Hitler orders preparations for Operation *Barbarossa*, the **invasion of Russia**, scheduled for May 1941.

29 Regular Luftwaffe attacks on London since September 7 culminate in an **incendiary attack on the City**, which results in the second Great Fire of London.

1941

JANUARY

5 In a continuation of Operation *Compass*, Australian forces capture the Italian fortress town of **Bardia** in Libya, taking 45 000 prisoners. The Australians then take **Tobruk** (January 22) and **Derna** (January 30).

FEBRUARY

5 British and Australian forces encircle the Italian Army at **Beda Fomm** in Libya, completing the annihilation of the forces that had invaded Egypt five months earlier.

MARCH

11 Roosevelt signs the **Lease-Lend Bill**, which allows the USA to supply all Britain's arms requirements.

24 General **Erwin Rommel**'s newly arrived German forces launch a counterattack against the British in eastern Libya.

28-29 Battle of **Cape Matapan**. The British Mediterranean fleet intercepts an Italian task force attempting to attack British troop convoys to Greece. It sinks three Italian cruisers and two destroyers, and damages the battleship *Vittorio Veneto*.

ATHENIAN SPLENDOUR Following their blitzkrieg through the Pindhos mountains, senior Wehrmacht officers pose before the Parthenon.

APRIL

5 South African troops capture the Ethiopian capital, **Addis Ababa**, from the Italians.

6 Germany invades **Yugoslavia** and **Greece**.

13 After a lightning dash from Beda Fomm, Rommel's advance is brought to a stop by **Tobruk**'s Australian garrison. Rommel is forced to besiege the town, which will hold out until relieved at the end of 1941.

17 The Yugoslav Army **capitulates**.

20-22 Large numbers of **Greek forces** in Albania and northern Greece surrender.

24 British and Greek forces fail to hold the German advance at **Thermopylae**.

27 As the Germans enter Athens, **British forces evacuate** to Crete and Egypt.

MAY

9 'Habforce', a brigade-sized British flying column, advances into Iraq from Palestine, and drives Raschid Ali and pro-Axis Iraqi forces from Baghdad (May 30).

10 Rudolf **Hess**, Hitler's deputy, flies to Scotland, on a bizarre peace mission.

15 Operation *Brevity*, a limited British offensive, captures the

Halfaya Pass on the Egyptian-Libyan frontier.

16 The **Blitz**, which had been under way since the previous summer, finally comes to an end with major raids on Birmingham and the West Midlands.

20 German paratroops and glider forces begin landing on **Crete**.

24 Breaking out into the Atlantic through the Denmark Strait, the German battleship *Bismarck* **sinks the British battlecruiser** *Hood* and damages the *Prince of Wales*, Britain's most modern battleship.

27 After an epic sea chase the **Bismarck is cornered and sunk** by the battleships *King George V* and *Rodney*.

28 Until June 1: Under constant German air attack, British, New Zealand and Australian troops **evacuate Crete**.

BISMARCK CORNERED Ablaze from stem to stern, the German battleship begins the plunge that will take 2200 of her crew to the bottom.

JUNE

1 In Britain, **clothes rationing** is introduced.

8 British, Commonwealth and Free French forces invade Vichy French-controlled **Syria and Lebanon**. The Free French occupy Damascus on June 21.

15-17 The British launch Operation *Battleaxe*, a major **armoured offensive into Libya**, which *Afrika Korps* counterattacks quickly defeat.

22 Operation **Barbarossa**. In the largest land offensive in history, 120 German divisions cut through

BUDDING RESISTANCE
In France, Resistance was emerging. A poster shows a fighter linked to an international alliance, symbolised by de Gaulle, Stalin, Roosevelt and Churchill.

Soviet forward defences, and encircle large numbers of Soviet troops.

JULY

2 No longer fearing an attack by the USSR, Japanese forces land in **southern Indochina**.

3 Recovering from a nervous collapse, **Stalin broadcasts** to the Soviet people, announcing that the Russians will scorch the earth before the German invader.

15 After an astonishing advance of nearly 300 miles (480 km), the Germans **encircle large Soviet forces** in a pocket around Smolensk.

27 Responding to **Japan's southward expansion**, Roosevelt orders the freezing of all Japanese assets in the USA, in effect cutting off Japan's oil supplies. Britain and the Netherlands government-in-exile soon follow suit. At the same time, the USA begins reinforcing its Pacific fleet at Pearl Harbor and sending the new B-17 bombers to the Philippines.

AUGUST

5 The Germans overrun the **Smolensk pocket**, taking 310 000 Soviet prisoners.

10-12 Churchill and Roosevelt meet at Placentia Bay on the coast of Newfoundland and sign the **Atlantic Charter**.

12 Hitler postpones the direct advance on Moscow, deciding instead to divert the bulk of his panzer forces south and to **encircle Kiev**.

21-31 The first British convoy heads for Russia via Norway's **North Cape**.

SEPTEMBER

8 Having reached the shore of Lake Ladoga, the Germans now lay **siege to Leningrad**.

26 The Germans finally crush the **Kiev pocket**, taking 665 000 Soviet prisoners.

30 SS *Einsatzgruppen* murder more than 30 000 Jews at **Babi Yar** outside Kiev.

OCTOBER

1 Hitler now orders the **advance on Moscow**, codenamed Operation *Typhoon*, to be resumed.

16 With German forces at Mozhaisk, only 80 miles (130 km) to the west, **panic grips Moscow** and thousands flee.

17 Unable to persuade the US Government to resume normal economic relations the Japanese Government resigns, and is replaced by a **military-dominated administration** under General Hideki Tojo.

18 Steadily worsening autumn weather compounds German logistic difficulties and brings their Russian advance to a **virtual standstill**.

NOVEMBER

15 Snow and frost having frozen the mud of autumn, the **Germans**

ISOLATION TICKET Charles Lindbergh was the main attraction at this America First rally, held just five weeks before Pearl Harbor.

resume their advance on Moscow, but the Soviets now have more than 80 divisions defending the city.

18 A British offensive in the **Western Desert**, Operation *Crusader*, pushes Rommel back and relieves pressure on Tobruk (November 24).

20 While their envoys continue to negotiate in Washington, the Japanese high command issues orders for **naval and land attacks** to be launched simultaneously against US, British and Dutch forces throughout the Pacific and the Far East.

26 Japan's **Pearl Harbor strike force** leaves its anchorage in the Kurile Islands and sails east into the North Pacific, bound for Hawaii.

28 Until December 7: On the Egyptian-Libyan border Rommel counterattacks, comes close to destroying the British, but is forced back to **Gazala**, west of Tobruk.

DECEMBER

5 Having reached the north-western suburbs of Moscow, a combination of sub-zero temperatures, logistic difficulties and **resolute Russian resistance** brings the German advance to a halt.

5-6 To the astonishment of the Germans (and everyone else), the **Soviets launch major offensives** along 300 miles (480 km) of front before Moscow.

7-8 Day of Infamy: **Japan launches surprise attacks** across one-quarter of the planet, sinking eight American battleships in Pearl Harbor, destroying the B-17 strike force at Clark Field in the Philippines, and landing troops on the west coasts of Thailand and Malaya.

8 Experimenting to find more effective ways of solving the 'Jewish problem', the SS begin killing Jews at the rate of more than 2000 per day in gas vans parked in a clearing near **Chelmno** in western Poland.

10 Returning from an abortive foray against Japanese beachheads, the British battleships *Prince of Wales* and *Repulse* are sunk off the west coast of Malaya by Japanese aircraft.

11 Honouring the Axis agreement, Germany and Italy **declare war** on the USA.

17 With German commanders beginning to withdraw in the face of the Soviet offensive, **Hitler takes over direct operational control** of the Wehrmacht and issues a halt order. Commanders who fail to comply are summarily dismissed.

19 Advancing down the west coast of Malaya, the Japanese take **Penang**.

22 The **Japanese land** in Lingayen Gulf and Lamon Bay on Luzon, the main island of the Philippines, and advance towards Manila from the north and south. Until January 13, 1942: the Anglo-American **Arcadia Conference** decides on a 'Germany First' policy.

DEATH TRAIN In December German Jews board a train at Bielefeld to be sent for 'resettlement' in the east.

24 In a continuation of Operation *Crusader*, the British retake **Benghazi**.

25 The British garrison in **Hong Kong** surrenders to Japanese.

26 The US army commander in the Far East, General Douglas MacArthur, withdraws his forces to the **Bataan Peninsula**, and declares Manila an open city.

27 The first major British Commando attack is launched against the **Lofoten Islands** off Norway.

HAPPY CHRISTMAS? Following the British surrender, the Japanese hold a victory parade through Hong Kong.

1942

JANUARY

2 The Japanese occupy **Manila**.

11 Beginning of Operation *Drumbeat*: Coordinated **U-boat attacks** on shipping off the east coast of North America. In Malaya, the Japanese take **Kuala Lumpur** and Japanese paratroopers land at Menado in the Celebes in the Dutch East Indies.

20 At the **Wannsee Conference** in Berlin, Reinhard Heydrich outlines plans for the *Endlosung* – the Final Solution to the 'Jewish problem'.

SS GATHERING Himmler (third from left) and Heydrich (third from right) pose with other senior SS personnel outside the Interpol HQ at Wannsee.

21 Until February 4: In North Africa, **Rommel launches an offensive** from his positions near El Agheila, and in the next two weeks pushes the British back to Gazala.

FEBRUARY

8 After their lightning 70 day advance down the Malayan peninsula, the **Japanese cross the Johore Strait** and put Singapore's 80 000 defenders to flight. Some 90 000 German soldiers are cut off by the Soviets in a **pocket around Demyansk**, and have to be supplied by air.

11-12 In one of the most embarrassing incidents in British naval history, the German battlecruisers *Scharnhorst* and *Gneisenau* and the heavy cruiser *Prinz Eugen* leave Brest and, in the face of ineffective British resistance, **dash up the Channel** to the relative safety of Wilhelmshaven.

15 The British commander in Malaya, General Arthur Percival, **surrenders Singapore**.

19 Japanese bombers devastate the port of **Darwin** in northern Australia, sinking or damaging 16 ships.

27 The construction of gas chambers and five crematoria begins at **Auschwitz**. Until March 1: British, Dutch, American and Australian warships make repeated attempts to prevent a Japanese landing on Java, but are defeated with heavy losses in the **Battle of the Java Sea**.

MARCH

8 Having driven British and Indian forces from successive defence lines, the **Japanese occupy Rangoon**.

9 Allied forces on **Java** surrender.

19 Logistic difficulties and stiffening German resistance finally bring the **Soviet winter offensive** to a halt. Since December 6, the Soviets have pushed back the Germans more than 100 miles (160 km) from Moscow.

20 Having escaped by torpedo boat and B-17 bomber from the Philippines to Australia, General Douglas MacArthur promises **'I shall return'**.

21 More than 100 000 **Japanese-Americans** are deported from California to camps in Oklahoma.

27 The first trainloads of **French Jews**, rounded up and deported from Vichy France reach the Auschwitz-Birkenau extermination camps. Laden with high explosive, the British destroyer *Campbeltown* rams and destroys the dock gates at **Saint-Nazaire**.

28 In the first attempt at **area bombing**, 190 British aircraft carry out an incendiary raid against the largely wooden medieval city of **Lübeck**, with spectacular results. Hitler orders reprisals against historic British cities, the so-called **Baedeker raids**.

APRIL

5 Japanese carrier aircraft **attack Colombo** and sink two British cruisers off the coast of Ceylon (Sri Lanka).

GEORGE CROSS ISLAND Bombed-out women and children in Valetta survey the damage after yet another air raid.

9 Emaciated and diseased, US and Filipino forces on the **Bataan Peninsula** surrender to the Japanese.

16 In recognition of the bravery of the **Maltese** in holding out against months of devastating Axis aerial bombardment, King George VI awards the island the **George Cross**.

18 Sixteen B-25 bombers fly from the carrier *Hornet*, 800 miles (1300 km) from the Japanese coast, and **bomb Tokyo**.

MAY

1 Advancing through Burma, the Japanese take **Mandalay**.

4-8 Without warships ever making visual contact, Japanese and US carrier aircraft clash in the **Battle of the Coral Sea**, sinking one Japanese and one US carrier.

5 Fearing a Japanese landing, **British forces invade Madagascar** and are resisted vigorously by the Vichy French garrison.

6 In the Philippines, the American General Wainwright **surrenders** the fortress island of **Corregidor**.

12-29 A large-scale Soviet offensive in the Ukraine is trapped by skilful German manoeuvres (May 18). The **Soviets surrender**, losing more than 200 000 men.

26 Until June 21: Displaying tactical brilliance **Rommel outmanoeuvres** larger British forces at Gazala (May 28), and in a series of rapid offensive moves surges east to take Tobruk (June 21).

30-31 RAF Bomber Command launches its first **'millennium' raid** (with 1000 bombers) against Cologne. Japanese midget submarines attack shipping in **Sydney Harbour**.

JUNE

4-7 The **Battle of Midway**. In a devastating blow to the Japanese Navy, a US carrier task force surprises and sinks four Japanese carriers to the north of the island of Midway. Only one US carrier is sunk.

6-7 The Japanese occupy Kiska and Attu in the **Aleutian Islands**.

10 In retaliation for the shooting of Heydrich on May 27, the German 'Protector' of Bohemia-Moravia, the Germans destroy the Czech village of **Lidice**.

18 Until June 30: Ignoring orders to stop, **Rommel invades Egypt**, pushing the British back as far as El Alamein, only 70 miles (110 km) from Alexandria.

LIDICE'S LOST CHILDREN After the massacre of their fathers and the deportation of their mothers, most of Lidice's 98 children were classified as *Untermenschen* and murdered.

28 Until July 7: Operation *Blau*. The **German summer offensive** begins with two army groups advancing into the Donets Basin in the eastern Ukraine against apparently diminishing Soviet resistance.

JULY

1 **'Ash Wednesday'** in Cairo, so called because of the pall of smoke from burning paper which shrouds the city as British administrative HQs destroy their documents, in expectation of Rommel's arrival.

1-27 First Battle of El Alamein. His logistics overstretched and his men exhausted, Rommel attacks but is beaten back by stubborn British resistance.

4 German U-boat and air attack destroys the Murmansk-bound convoy, **PQ17**.

16 Foreign Jews in Paris are rounded up by René Bousquet's police and **deported to Auschwitz**.

21-22 The Japanese land on the northern coast of Papua-New Guinea and begin to advance south along **Kokoda Trail** towards Port Moresby.

27 A mass demonstration (with more than 60 000 people) takes place in Trafalgar Square, demanding the immediate establishment of a **Second Front** to remove pressure on the USSR.

29 The Japanese take the village of **Kokoda** in Papua-New Guinea.

31 In Oxford the Oxford Committee for Famine Relief, later called **Oxfam**, is founded.

AUGUST

3 Visiting the Middle East on his way to Moscow, **Churchill dismisses Auchinleck** as C in C. Until September 5: Mass arrests are made of **IRA suspects** in Belfast, following the discovery of plans to attack British and US troops in Northern Ireland.

7 US marines land on **Tulagi** and **Guadalcanal** in the Solomon Islands.

8 The Indian Congress Party calls on Britain 'to **quit India** immediately', a demand followed by widespread and prolonged civil disorder.

9 A Japanese naval task force sinks four Allied heavy cruisers in the **Battle of Savo Island**, off the northern coast of Guadalcanal.

12-15 Churchill and Stalin meet in **Moscow**.

13 General **Bernard Montgomery** is appointed to command Eighth Army.

15 After fighting off heavy Axis air and submarine attacks, the battered remnants of the **Pedestal Convoy** reach Malta, saving the island from starvation and surrender.

17 The US Eighth Air Force conducts its **first bombing mission** over Europe, an attack on rail communications at Rouen.

RAF IN TRAINING   Despite its apparent eccentricity, this was a cheap and effective method of imparting the basics of formation flying.

19 A British and Canadian **raid against Dieppe** is repulsed with very heavy casualties.

21 At Tenaru river on **Guadalcanal** US marines repulse a Japanese attack on their beachhead.

21-23 The German advance in Russia **reaches the Volga** north of Stalingrad and Mount Elbrus in the Caucasus Mountains.

22-25 In the **Battle of the Eastern Solomons**, US and Japanese carrier forces inflict severe damage on each other.

26 Until September 6: In their first major defeat on land, a Japanese invasion force is driven back into the sea by the Australians at **Milne Bay** in Papua-New Guinea.

31 The Germans reach the **outskirts of Stalingrad**. Until September 2: Rommel tries to outflank British positions at El Alamein but is driven back in a battle for the **Alam Halfa Ridge**.

SEPTEMBER

12-14 US marines fight off successive Japanese attempts to destroy their **Guadalcanal beachhead**.

16 After outflanking and overrunning successive Australian positions, the Japanese reach **Ioribaiwa Ridge**, only 32 miles (51 km) from Port Moresby.

21 British and Indian troops advance into the **Arakan** in Burma.

OCTOBER

3 The first successful launch of an experimental **V-2 rocket** from Peenemunde. British Commandos land on **Sark in the Channel Islands**, and kill three German engineers.

11-13 A US task force sinks or damages four Japanese cruisers and destroyers in the **Battle of Cape Esperance**, off Guadalcanal.

18 Hitler issues the **Commando Order**, which states that all British Commandos taken prisoner will be executed.

23 Until November 4: Montgomery's Eighth Army breaks through Rommel's defences in the **Second Battle of El Alamein**.

26-27 US and Japanese carriers clash in the **Battle of the Santa Cruz Islands** in the Solomons. The Americans lose one carrier.

NOVEMBER

5 Axis forces in North Africa are **in full retreat** after the battle at El Alamein.

8 Operation **Torch**. British and US forces land in Morocco and Algeria. Hitler announces the fall of 'virtually all' of **Stalingrad**.

11 Germans troops **occupy Vichy France**.

12-15 The **naval Battle of Guadalcanal** in which US battleships sink two Japanese battleships in point-blank gun duels.

19-23 A **Soviet offensive** north and south of Stalingrad cuts off General Paulus' Sixth Army in the city.

29 The British and US advance from Algeria to Tunis is halted by Germans in the **Battle of Tebourba-Djedeida**.

30 Off **Tassafaronga** in the Solomon Islands, a Japanese task force sinks or damages four American cruisers.

DECEMBER

2 The **Beveridge Report**, outlining plans for a postwar 'Welfare State', is published in Britain.

9 The Australians take **Gona** on the northern coast of Papua-New Guinea.

12-23 The Germans **fail to break through** to the Sixth Army, trapped in Stalingrad.

21 The Eighth Army retakes **Benghazi**.

24 The Vichy French commander in North Africa, **Admiral Darlan**, is assassinated.

WARFARE TO WELFARE   Sir William Beveridge's report promised Britain a future free from poverty and deprivation.

31 In a naval action in the **Barents Sea**, a powerful German cruiser force bungles a chance to destroy a British convoy. This leads Hitler to order the scrapping of the German surface fleet.

Background: The *Gneisenau*, one of the most successful of all Germany's large warships presents her sinister yet beautiful profile.

1943

JANUARY

2 Australian and US forces take **Buna** on the northern coast of Papua-New Guinea.

10 Soviet armies begin **advancing** into the Stalingrad pocket.

13 The Soviets cross the River Don to begin a **major offensive westwards**.

14-24 Meeting at **Casablanca**, Churchill and Roosevelt demand the **unconditional surrender** of the Axis.

22 The Australians and Americans crush the remnants of the **Japanese beachhead** in Papua-New Guinea.

23 The British Eighth Army takes **Tripoli**, capital of Libya.

FEBRUARY

1-8 The Japanese evacuate **Guadalcanal**.

2 The last German forces in **Stalingrad surrender**.

3 The British and Indian **advance into Arakan** is brought to a stop by Japanese resistance at Rathedaung.

4 The British Eighth Army reaches the **Mareth Line** on the Tunisian-Libyan border.

8-20 The Soviet offensive **surges west into the Ukraine**, retaking Kursk, Rostov, Kharkov, Pavlogrod and Krasnograd.

BEHIND ENEMY LINES   The Chindits pose during an expedition that took them 200 miles (320 km) behind Japanese lines in Burma.

13 The **Chindits**, a British long-range raiding force, cross the Chindwin into Burma.

14-25 The US advance into Tunisia is defeated by Rommel's surprise attack through the **Kasserine Pass**.

18 In a speech to Nazi officials in Berlin, Goebbels declares that Germany will now wage **total war**.

20 Until March 18: Von Manstein launches a **German counteroffensive**, cutting off and destroying Soviet armies, and retaking Kharkov and Belgorod.

MARCH

1-4 Allied air attacks destroy a Japanese convoy bound for Lae on the north coast of New Guinea in the **Battle of the Bismarck Sea**.

6 The British Eighth Army repulses an Axis attack at **Medenine** in southern Tunisia.

13-17 British and Indian forces are driven from the **Arakan** by Japanese counterattacks.

15-19 In the climax of the **Battle of the Atlantic**, U-boats sink 21 ships, effectively destroying two convoys.

20-27 The British Eighth Army breaks through the Axis-held Mareth Line **into Tunisia**.

31 Opening night of the musical *Oklahoma* at the St James Theatre in New York.

APRIL

7 The British Eighth Army and US forces **link up** in Tunisia.

13 The Germans announce the discovery of

mass graves at Katyn, near Smolensk.

18 Japan's naval commander, **Admiral Yamamoto**, is shot down and killed by US fighters on his way to an inspection tour of the Solomons.

19 Until May 16: An **uprising of Jews** in the Warsaw ghetto.

MAY

3 In Britain **work conscription** is introduced for all women aged between 18 and 45.

4-6 The **Battle of Convoy ONS5**. Escorts and aircraft sink seven U-boats for the loss of only 12 merchant ships.

11-30 US troops **land on Attu** and in bitter fighting wipe out the Japanese garrison.

12 The **surrender of Axis forces** in North Africa.

13-25 Roosevelt and Churchill meet for the **Trident Conference** in

JOIN UP   The women of Britain's Land Army contributed significantly to agricultural production.

24 Having lost 40 U-boats in the preceding three weeks, Dönitz **withdraws his submarines** from the North Atlantic.

JUNE

1 British actor **Leslie Howard** is killed when German fighters shoot down his airliner over the Bay of Biscay, en route from Portugal to Britain.

MORNING AFTER   Water floods through the breach in the wall of the Möhne Dam after the 'bouncing bomb' attack.

Washington and agree on May 1944 as the date for the invasion of Europe.

16 The RAF's **'Dambuster'** raid destroys two dams in the Ruhr.

22 Successful test flight of German **Me262 jet fighter**.

15 The Luftwaffe tests the **Arado 234 jet bomber**.

20 The beginning of **race riots in Detroit**, which leave 34 dead and many hundreds injured.

JULY

1 Until August 25: **New Georgia** in the Solomons falls to the Americans after prolonged Japanese resistance.

VOICES OF BRITAIN Blunt northerner J.B. Priestley (left) and urbane southerner Leslie Howard (right) complemented each other perfectly in regular BBC broadcasts.

4 Until July 13: Operation *Citadel*. The Germans launch attacks against the heavily defended **Kursk salient**, and are fought to a standstill in the **Battle of Prokhorovka**, the biggest tank battle in history (July 12).

10 The Allies **land on Sicily**.

15-17 The **Soviets launch offensives** against German Army Groups Centre and South.

24-25 A large **bombing raid on Hamburg** disrupts water and power supplies.

25 Mussolini is overthrown and arrested.

27-28 Round-the-clock bombing of Hamburg produces a **firestorm**.

AUGUST

1 The American fast patrol boat *PT-109*, commanded by Lt **John F. Kennedy**, is rammed and sunk by a Japanese destroyer in the Solomons.

3 In Sicily, General Patton **slaps a battle-shocked American soldier** in a field hospital.

5 The Soviets liberate **Belgorod** and **Orel**.

12 Clark Gable, now a captain in the US Eighth Air Force, flies his first mission over the Ruhr.

14-24 Roosevelt and Churchill meet in Quebec for the **Quadrant Conference**.

17 The US Eighth Air Force suffers heavy casualties during daylight raids on **Schweinfurt** and **Regensburg**.

23 The Soviets liberate **Kharkov**.

SEPTEMBER

3 British Eighth Army lands in **Calabria**.

4 Australian and US troops land east of Lae on the **north coast of New Guinea**. Stalin **reopens churches** and seminaries, and re-establishes the Orthodox Church.

8 After Eisenhower broadcasts the news of the secretly negotiated Italian surrender, the Germans speed up their **occupation of Italy**.

9 Allied forces land at **Salerno**.

12 A German raid led by Otto Skorzeny **rescues Mussolini** from imprisonment on Gran Sasso.

14 A **German counterattack** threatens to drive the Salerno landing into sea, but the Allied forces hold on.

15 Mussolini proclaims a new **Italian Social Republic**, with its capital at Salò.

21-22 The German battleship *Tirpitz* **is damaged** by British midget submarines in Alta Fiord in Norway.

22 Australians land at **Finschhafen** on the northern coast of New Guinea.

25 Advancing on a 400 mile (640 km) front, Soviet forces liberate **Smolensk** and **cross the Dneiper**.

OCTOBER

1 US forces, advancing north from Salerno, **enter Naples**.

9 In Russia, the Germans complete the **evacuation of their forces** from the Taman Peninsula to the Crimea.

13 The **new Italian Government**, with its capital at Brindisi, declares war on Germany.

14 Heavy US Eighth Air Force losses in a raid on **Schweinfurt** lead to the temporary suspension of daylight bombing.

19-30 Allied foreign ministers meet in Moscow and agree to establish an international organisation to replace the League of Nations. This will become the **United Nations**.

28 Until November 1: More than half a million US coal miners are **on strike**.

NOVEMBER

1 US marines **land on Bougainville** in Solomon Islands.

6 The Soviets liberate **Kiev**.

9 The Allied nations establish the **United Nations Relief and Rehabilitation Administration** (UNRRA).

20-23 At a cost of 3500 casualties, US marines take tiny **Tarawa Atoll** in the Gilbert Islands in the Central Pacific.

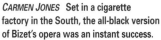

CARMEN JONES Set in a cigarette factory in the South, the all-black version of Bizet's opera was an instant success.

23-27 Roosevelt, Churchill and Chiang Kai-shek **meet in Cairo** and agree measures for the defeat of Japan.

28 Until December 1: Roosevelt, Churchill and Stalin **meet at Tehran** to devise a strategy for 1944.

DECEMBER

2 The all-black musical, ***Carmen Jones***, opens on Broadway.

15 US forces land on the southern coast of **New Britain**, the largest island in the Bismarck Archipelago.

26 British battleships **sink** the German battlecruiser **Scharnhorst** off Norway's North Cape.

27 The slow Allied advance up the Italian peninsula comes to a complete stop before **Monte Cassino**, key to the German Gustav Line defences.

CLOSING THE TRAP US marines landing on New Britain complete the isolation of the Japanese base at Rabaul.

1944

JANUARY

22 In Italy the British and Americans land north of the Gustav Line at **Anzio**.

27 A Soviet offensive breaks the German **siege of Leningrad**.

FEBRUARY

1 Until March 19: **Coal miners** in South Wales go on strike.

3-12 The Anglo-American forces resist a German **counterattack at Anzio**.

4-24 Supplied entirely by air, British and Indian forces in **the Arakan** fight off and defeat besieging Japanese forces.

ANCIENT AND MODERN   As a bullock cart wends its way across the airfield, RAF mechanics prepare a Hurricane for strikes against the Japanese in Burma.

15 A massive Allied bombing attack destroys the **monastery of Monte Cassino**.

19-26 The Luftwaffe launches heavy **attacks on London**.

MARCH

4 The first US Eighth Air Force **daylight raid on Berlin**.

4-17 The Soviet offensive in the Ukraine **reaches the River Dniester**.

5 Until May 25: A large airborne operation lands the **Chindits** on the Japanese lines of communication in central Burma.

30-31 In a raid on Nuremberg, the RAF loses 96 out of 795 aircraft, its **most costly operation** of the war.

APRIL

3 British carrier aircraft attack the **Tirpitz** in Altenfiord.

5 Advancing from Burma into the Indian state of Manipur, the Japanese besiege the British bases of **Imphal** and **Kohima**.

22 US forces land at **Hollandia** on the north coast of west New Guinea.

MAY

5 After heavy fighting, the Soviets **clear the Germans** from the Crimean peninsula.

7 The start of six months of **Japanese offensive operations** in China, designed to capture airfields from which the Americans can bomb Japan.

18 The **Poles take** Monte Cassino.

25 Tito flees to the British-held island of Vis, off the Yugoslav coast, after narrowly escaping an SS paratrooper assault on his HQ at Drvar.

27 US forces land on **Biak Island**, off New Guinea.

JUNE

5 The US Fifth Army **enters Rome**.

6 D-Day, start of Operation *Overlord*. Seven Allied divisions, two airborne, land on the Normandy coast.

D-DAY   Their landing craft pitching in heavy seas, GIs of the US 29th Division head for *Omaha* Beach.

13 The **first V-1s** are fired against England.

15 B-29 Superfortresses **raid Japan** for the first time from bases in India via refuelling stops in China.

17 US marines land on **Saipan**.

19-20 In the Battle of the Philippine Sea, Japanese carrier aircraft are shot out of the sky in 'the **Great Marianas Turkey Shoot**'.

19-22 Violent **storms in the Channel** severely disrupt the Allied Normandy build-up.

22 The Soviet **Bagration offensive** is launched on a 300 mile (480 km) front. British and Indian forces **break through to Imphal**, ending a siege of 88 days.

26-30 Operation *Epsom*. The British attempt to break out of the Normandy beachhead west of Caen is **pushed back** by German counterattacks.

27 The Americans take the port of **Cherbourg** on Normandy's Cotentin peninsula.

JULY

4 The Soviets **liberate Minsk** and destroy an entire German army group.

8-11 In Operation *Charnwood*, British heavy bombers **destroy much of Caen**, killing 6000 French civilians.

13 The Soviets take **Vilnus** in Lithuania.

17 Rommel is wounded by British fighter-bomber attack while inspecting defences in Normandy.

18 Operation *Goodwood*, the British attempt to break out east of Caen, is defeated with heavy casualties. **General Tojo resigns** as Japanese prime minister.

20 The Soviets **reach the River Bug** near Warsaw. The **attempt to assassinate Hitler** at his Rastenburg HQ in East Prussia fails.

21 US marines land on **Guam**.

22 The Soviets create the **'Polish Committee for National Liberation'**.

23 The Soviets reach **Maidenek** in eastern Poland, the first of the **extermination camps** to be liberated.

24 US marines land on **Tinian**.

25 In Operation *Cobra* on the west side of the Normandy beachhead, the Americans succeed in **breaking through German defences**.

26 Meeting in Hawaii, MacArthur persuades Roosevelt and Nimitz to concentrate US Pacific forces on the liberation of **the Philippines**.

Background: With a 1260 horsepower engine, the Yak 9D could produce a speed of more than 360 mph (580 km/h). It was the first Soviet fighter to take on a German Me109 or Fw190 on equal terms.

31 The Soviets **halt their advance** 8 miles (13 km) short of Warsaw.

AUGUST

1 The **Polish Home Army** in Warsaw rises up against the Germans. Patton's US Third Army breaks out of Normandy at **Avranches**.

3 US and Chinese troops under General Stilwell **capture Myitkyina** in northern Burma.

7-16 In Operation *Totalise*, the Canadian First Army strikes south and **takes Falaise**.

8 US Third Army liberates **Le Mans**.

12 Swinging north, Patton takes **Argentan,** just to south of Falaise, creating a 'pocket' in which German forces are almost trapped.

13-22 Allied troops take the **Falaise Pocket**.

15 Operation *Anvil-Dragoon*. Allied forces **land in the south of France** and advance up the Rhône.

19 Uprising in Paris by the French Resistance.

20 Soviets attack into **Romania**.

21-29 Dumbarton Oaks Conference: ideas for a **United Nations Organisation** are discussed by US, British, Soviet and Chinese delegates.

23 Hitler orders **General Choltitz**, governor of Paris, to destroy the city. Choltitz disobeys.

SETTING PARIS FREE Soldiers of the Resistance engage in street fighting with German and Vichyite snipers.

23-31 Following the capitulation of Romania (August 23), Soviet forces **occupy Bucharest**.

25 US and Free French forces **enter Paris**. Romania **declares war** on Germany. Finland seeks **an armistice** with the USSR.

29 Until December 29: The British Eighth Army slogs up the **east coast of Italy**, taking four months to advance 50 miles (80 km).

SEPTEMBER

1 Patton's Third Army reaches the **Moselle river**.

3 The British Second Army liberates **Brussels**.

8 The **first V-2** rocket hits London. Bulgaria **changes sides** and declares war on Germany.

11 The spearhead of the US First Army crosses the Luxembourg border **into Germany**.

12 Allied forces liberate **Florence**.

12-16 The Octagon Conference in **Quebec**: The Allies agree to start work on a permanent United Nations organisation.

15 Until October 14: US forces **take Peleliu**, after prolonged Japanese resistance.

17-26 Operation *Market Garden*. An Allied airborne army allows an advance **into southern Holland**, but the British spearhead is destroyed in heavy fighting at Arnhem.

OCTOBER

1 Until November 1: Canadian and British forces **clear the River Scheldt**.

2 The last elements of the Polish Home Army **surrender in Warsaw**.

4 The British land in **Greece**.

6 Until November 29: The US First Army begins a long, bitter battle for the **Hürtgen Forest** near Aachen.

10 The Soviets **reach the Baltic**, cutting off German forces in Courland.

13 The Soviet Baltic offensive **reaches Riga** in Latvia.

14 Rommel commits **suicide**.

18 Germany creates the *Volkssturm*, a national militia in which all males between the ages of 16 to 60 will serve.

20 Following the German evacuation, Tito's Partisans **liberate Belgrade**.

20-22 US forces **land on Leyte** in the Philippines.

23-26 Battle of Leyte Gulf. In the largest and most complicated naval battle ever fought, the US Navy sinks four Japanese aircraft carriers, three battleships and ten cruisers.

NOVEMBER

12 British Lancaster bombers **sink the Tirpitz**.

19 Until December 3: The British cross the Chindwin and **advance into central Burma**.

24 The first US B-29 Superfortress **raid on Tokyo** from bases on Saipan and Tinian.

DECEMBER

3 Britain stands down the **Home Guard**.

MAJOR BAND LEADER Glen Miller's music became the 'sound' of the 1940s.

4 Civil war breaks out in Greece between Communists and Royalists.

16 In the **Ardennes**, three German armies launch a **massive offensive** which catches the Allies completely by surprise. The US band leader **Glen Miller** disappears, presumed killed in an air crash.

17 In the Ardennes offensive, SS *Kampfgruppe Peiper* **massacres US prisoners**.

18 A low-level B-29 raid destroys Japanese-held **Hankow** in China.

26 The Soviets besiege **Budapest**.

26 After an advance of 50 miles (80 km), the German Ardennes offensive **grinds to a halt**.

IN THE ARDENNES A US soldier trudges cautiously through heavy snow, which grounded Allied aircraft but also slowed the German advance.

1945

JANUARY

1 Operation *Bodenplatte*. The Luftwaffe launches **large-scale attacks** against Allied air bases.

6 Worried by the situation in the west, **Churchill asks Stalin** to accelerate Soviet offensive plans.

9 US forces land in **Lingayen Gulf** on the west coast of Luzon, the main island of the Philippines.

12-14 The Soviets open a massive offensive **across the Vistula**.

14-16 British and Indian forces **cross the Irrawaddy** north-west of Mandalay.

17 Soviet forces enter the **ruins of Warsaw**.

22 After an astonishing advance, Soviet forces **reach the Oder**, only 90 miles (145 km) from Berlin.

28 In the Ardennes, the Germans are **finally pushed back** to the positions they held on December 16.

30 The German liner *Wilhelm Gustloff* is torpedoed by a Soviet submarine in the Baltic; 7000 die in the **worst maritime disaster** in history.

FEBRUARY

3 Until March 3: MacArthur's forces **liberate Manila** from the Japanese, destroying much of the city.

8 Until March 4: The British and Canadians engage in a bitter battle to **clear the Reichswald** between the west bank of the Rhine and Dutch-German border.

13 **Budapest** falls to the Soviets.

13-14 British and American **bombers destroy Dresden** in a devastating firestorm.

16 US paratroopers recapture the **fortress island of Corregidor** in Manila Bay.

AFTER THE BATTLE Scene of the SS's last stand in Berlin, the shattered Reichstag bears witness to the intensity of the fighting.

19 Until March 14: US Marines take **Iwo Jima** in a long and bloody battle.

22 Until March 3: Taking the Japanese completely by surprise, **British and Indian forces** cross the Irrawaddy west of Mandalay and overrun an enemy logistic base at **Meiktila**.

MARCH

2 After hard fighting in the Rhineland, the US First Army **reaches the Rhine** opposite Düsseldorf.

5-15 Operation *Spring Awakening*. The Germans launch an offensive in Hungary to **recapture its oil fields**.

7 The Americans seize the still-intact Ludendorff railway bridge across the **Rhine at Remagen**.

9-10 The first major B-29 **incendiary raid on Tokyo** destroys 16 sq miles (41 km^2) of the city.

22 Elements of the US Third Army **cross the Rhine** at Nierstein and surprise the Germans.

23-24 Main Allied **crossings of the Rhine**, from Wesel in the north to Mannheim in the south.

27 The **last V-2** lands on Britain.

28 The British and Americans attack out of their **Rhine bridgeheads**.

29 The **last V-1** attack on Britain.

30 The Soviets capture **Danzig**. Slim's **XIV Army** pursues the retreating Japanese south of Meiktila.

APRIL

1 US forces complete the **encirclement of the Ruhr**. Until June 22: In the battle for **Okinawa**, both Americans and Japanese suffer huge casualties.

6-13 The Soviets take **Vienna**.

7 On a suicide mission to Okinawa, the Japanese battleship **Yamato is sunk** by US aircraft.

9 Opening of the **Allied offensive in Italy**.

12 President **Roosevelt dies** at Warm Springs, Georgia, and is succeeded by Vice-President Harry Truman.

MOMENT OF LIBERATION Russian prisoners (below) rush to greet their US liberators at the gates of Stalag 326 near Hamel. Zyklon B (left) was IG Farben's trade name for a commercial pesticide derived from prussic acid, which was also used to murder people at Auschwitz.

15 British spearheads reach the concentration camp of **Bergen-Belsen**.

16 The Soviets begin the **Berlin offensive**.

16-18 The German defence of the **Seelow Heights** delays Zhukov's advance.

18 US forces overcome German resistance in the **Ruhr pocket**.

19 US forces take **Leipzig**. The musical *Carousel* opens at the Majestic Theatre in New York.

20 Hitler makes **his last appearance** outside the *Führerbunker*.

21 In Italy, Allied forces capture **Bologna**.

22 The British Eighth Army **reaches the River Po** in northern Italy.

25 US and Russian forces **meet at Torgau** on the Elbe. Until May 2: The **Battle of Berlin**.

28 Mussolini and his mistress, **Clara Petacci**, are shot dead and their bodies hung upside down from a Milan petrol station.

29 The German commander in Italy **surrenders unconditionally** to the Allies.

30 Hitler commits **suicide**.

MAY

3 The British Second Army captures the **ruins of Hamburg**. The British take **Rangoon**.

9 Hostilities in Europe **officially cease** but diehard SS units keep fighting for about another week in Czechoslovakia, Austria and Croatia.

JUNE

18 The beginning of a **mass deportation** of Germans from Czechoslovakia.

JULY

1 Australians land at **Balikpapan** in Borneo.

A JOB WELL DONE In transit through London, a Pacific-bound GI learns of the German surrender.

3 Western Allied troops **enter Berlin**.

15/16 The first **atomic bomb** is tested at Alamogordo in New Mexico.

17 Until August 2: The Potsdam Conference reaffirms the demand for Japan to **surrender unconditionally**.

23 The Vichy French leader **Pétain goes on trial** in Paris.

26 In the British General Election the Conservatives are defeated and **Attlee replaces Churchill** as prime minister.

AUGUST

6 A B-29 drops the atomic bomb on **Hiroshima**.

9 As the Americans drop the second atomic bomb on **Nagasaki**, Soviet troops invade Manchuria.

10 At a meeting of the Imperial Council, the Emperor Hirohito decrees that **Japan must surrender**.

14 An **attempted coup in Tokyo**, by dissident officers trying to prevent Japan's surrender, is bloodily suppressed.

15 Emperor Hirohito **broadcasts** the surrender of Japan.

17 The **last U-boat at large**, *U-977*, arrives at Mar del Plata in Argentina and surrenders.

22 Japanese forces in Manchuria cease resistance and **surrender** to the Soviets.

23 British, US and French troops **arrive in Vienna** to take up their occupation zones.

24 President Truman orders the cessation of **Lend-Lease**.

SEPTEMBER

2 The **official surrender** of the Japanese aboard the battleship USS *Missouri* in Tokyo Bay.

7 The Allied **victory parade** in Berlin.

NOVEMBER

20 The trial of major German **war criminals** begins in Nuremburg.

TIME TO CELEBRATE A banner (below) welcomes returning British servicemen. Background: In New York a British sailor does his bit for Anglo-American relations on the day of Japan's surrender.

It's grand to see you HOME again

INDEX

ACKNOWLEDGMENTS

Abbreviations:
T=Top; M=Middle; B=Bottom;
R=Right; L=Left

3 Novosti, L; Imperial War Museum, LM; Mary Evans Picture Library, RM; Topham Picturepoint, R. 6 AKG. 7 Getty Images, TL; Topham Picturepoint, TM; Harlingue-Viollet/Roger-Viollet, BL; Suddeutscher Verlag Bilderdienst, BR. 8 Getty Images. 8-9 Imperial War Museum. 9 Imperial War Museum. 10 Getty Images, TM, MR; Topham Picturepoint, BL. 11 Ronald Grant Archive, ML; Topham Picturepoint, B. 12 Imperial War Museum, TL; Suddeutscher Verlag Bilderdienst,B. 13 Imperial War Museum, TR, MR. 14 Popperfoto, T; Imperial War Museum, B. 15 Getty Images, background; Jean-Loup Charmet, L; AKG, M; Imperial War Museum/Norman Brand, R. 16 Topham Picturepoint, TR; Getty Images, BL. 17 Getty Images. 18 Map by Advanced Illustration; Suddeutscher Verlag Bilderdienst, ML; Imperial War Museum/Norman Brand, MR; Ullstein Bilderdienst, BR. 19 Ullstein Bilderdienst. 20 LAPI-Viollet/Roger-Viollet, TL; Topham Picturepoint, MR; Getty Images, B. 21 Getty Images. 22 Imperial War Museum/Norman Brand, ML; Getty Images, R; Popperfoto, BM. 23 Topham Picturepoint, TL; AKG, BR. 24 Getty Images, L, MR. 25 Illustration by Martin Woodward; Suddeutscher Verlag Bilderdienst, B. 26 Corbis-Bettmann, TR; Suddeutscher Verlag Bilderdienst, M; Imperial War Museum/Norman Brand, MR; Imperial War Museum, BL. 27 Getty Images. 28 Imperial War Museum. 29 Imperial War Museum, TL; Jean-Loup Charmet, MR; Map by Advanced Illustration. 30 Mary Evans Picture Library, TL; Ullstein Bilderdienst, MR. 30-31 Imperial War Museum. 31 Ullstein Bilderdienst. 32 Jean-Loup Charmet, ML; Mary Evans Picture Library/Alexander Meledin Collection, MR. 32-33 Ullstein Bilderdienst. 33 Getty Images; background Topham Picturepoint; Montage by Roy Williams, TR. 34 Ullstein Bilderdienst, TL, B; Collection Viollet/Roger-Viollet, BR. 35 Map by Advanced Illustration; Ullstein Bilderdienst, BR. 36 Mary Evans Picture Library/Alexander Meledin Collection, TR; Ullstein Bilderdienst, ML, BR. 37 AKG, background; from left to right: Imperial War Museum; Getty Images; AKG; Harlingue-Viollet/Roger-Viollet; Topham Picturepoint. 38 Harlingue-Viollet/Roger-Viollet, BL; Topham Picturepoint, BM. 39 Suddeutscher Verlag Bilderdienst, L; Imperial War Museum, MR. 40 Ullstein Bilderdienst, TL; Mary Evans Picture Library, RM; Corbis-Bettmann, BR. 41 Ullstein Bilderdienst, TL; Brown Brothers, BR. 42 Topham Picturepoint, BL; LAPI-Viollet/Roger-Viollet, BR. 43 Topham Picturepoint, TL; AKG, BM; Corbis-Bettmann, BR. 44 Suddeutscher Verlag Bilderdienst. 44-45 Corbis-Bettmann. 45 Map by Roy Williams. 46 Popperfoto, ML; Mary

Evans Picture Library, M; Imperial War Museum/Norman Brand, B. 47 Illustration by Graham White; AKG, BR. 48 Mary Evans Picture Library, TL; Corbis-Bettmann, TR; Topham Picturepoint, BL. 49 AKG, M, BR. 50 AKG, TR; Mary Evans Picture Library, M; Popperfoto, BL. 51 Corbis-Bettmann, TM; Illustration by Martin Woodward. 52 Suddeutscher Verlag Bilderdienst, BM, BL. 53 Corbis-Bettmann. 54 Mary Evans Picture Library, TL; Corbis-Bettmann, ML. 54-55 Illustration by Graham White. 55 Corbis-Bettmann, TR; AKG, M. 56 Popperfoto, TR; Culver Pictures, B. 57 Getty Images, TL; Topham Picturepoint, BR. 58 Mary Evans Picture Library. 58-59 Topham Picturepoint. 59 Imperial War Museum, MR; Popperfoto, BR. 60 Jean-Loup Charmet, TL; Mary Evans Picture Library, TM; Map by Advanced Illustration. 61 Popperfoto, TR, ML, B. 62 Ullstein Bilderdienst, ML; Corbis-Bettmann, B. 63 Collection-Viollet/Roger-Viollet, MR; Corbis-Bettmann, BR. 64 Ullstein Bilderdienst. 64-65 AKG. 65 Collection-Viollet/Roger-Viollet, TL; Mary Evans Picture Library, RM. 66 Map by Roy Williams; Ullstein Bilderdienst, MR; Mary Evans Picture Library, B. 67 Popperfoto, TL; Ullstein Bilderdienst, BR. 68 Map by Roy Williams; AKG, BL. 69 Suddeutscher Verlag Bilderdienst, TR; Topham Picturepoint, B. 70 AKG, TR; Drawing by Leo Rawlings, BL. 71 Map by Roy Williams; Imperial War Museum, BM; Getty Images, BR. 72 Getty Images. 72-73 Collection-Viollet/Roger-Viollet. 73 AKG, TL; Corbis-Bettmann, MR. 74 Popperfoto 74-75 Ian Kerr-Jarrett/Norman Brand. 75 Popperfoto, M; Ian Kerr-Jarrett/Norman Brand, ML. 76 Getty Images, L; AKG, BR. 77 Illustration by Martin Woodward; Ullstein Bilderdienst, TR; Brown Brothers, B. 78 Topham Picturepoint, TR; Ullstein Bilderdienst, B. 79 Ullstein Bilderdienst, TR; Popperfoto, BL. 80 Ullstein Bilderdienst, TR; Topham Picturepoint, background; Getty Images, BL, BM. Montage by Roy Williams. 81 Getty Images, background; Novosti, L; Topham Picturepoint, LM; Getty Images, RM; AKG, R. 82 Mary Evans Picture Library, ML; Popperfoto, B. 82-83, Topham Picturepoint. 83 Imperial War Museum, TL; Getty Images, BR. 84 Topham Picturepoint, TR; Robert Opie Collection, B. 85 AKG, TL; Getty Images, BR. 86 Getty Images, TL, MR, B. 87 The Kobal Collection, MR, B. 88 Imperial War Museum/Norman Brand, TL; Getty Images, TR; Topham Picturepoint, BL. 89 Imperial War Museum/Norman Brand, T; Getty Images, L. 90 AKG, TR; Ullstein Bilderdienst, BL. 91 AKG, TM, BR. 92 Topham Picturepoint, M; Suddeutscher Verlag Bilderdienst, L. 93 Mary Evans Picture Library, TL; Ullstein Bilderdienst, BR, BL. 94 Jean-Loup Charmet, MR; Suddeutscher Verlag Bilderdienst, BL. 95 Getty Images, TR; AKG, TM; Suddeutscher Verlag Bilderdienst, TL; Montage by

Roy Williams; Ullstein Bilderdienst, BR. 96 Culver Pictures, TR; Suddeutscher Verlag Bilderdienst, BL. 97 Getty Images, L; Brown Brothers, MR; Topham Picturepoint, BM. 98 Ullstein Bilderdienst, T, BL; AKG, BR. 99 Culver Pictures, BR. 100 Ullstein Bilderdienst, TL; Popperfoto, ML; Topham Picturepoint, MR; AKG, BL. 101 AKG, BL. 102 Novosti, L; Suddeutscher Verlag Bilderdienst, M; Roger-Viollet, B. 103 Suddeutscher Verlag Bilderdienst, TL; Topham Picturepoint, TM; Montage by Roy Williams; Erich Lessing/AKG, BR. 104 Ullstein Bilderdienst, LM; AKG, M. 105 Ullstein Bilderdienst, background; David King Collection, L; Collection-Viollet/Roger-Viollet, LM; Imperial War Museum, RM; Popperfoto, R. 106 Topham Picturepoint. 107 Topham Picturepoint, TR; Ullstein Bilderdienst, ML, B. 108 AKG, R; Collection-Viollet/Roger-Viollet, BL. 109 Roger-Viollet, TL; AKG, MR; Popperfoto, BR. 110 Popperfoto, TL. 110-11 Topham Picturepoint. 111 Robert Capa/Magnum. 112 AKG, TL; Jean-Loup Charmet, TR. 112-13 Popperfoto. 113 Topham Picturepoint. 114 Map by Roy Williams; Culver Pictures, BR. 115 Topham Picturepoint, TL; Robert Capa/Magnum, BR. 116 Ullstein Bilderdienst, MR; AKG, B. 117 Map by Roy Williams; Popperfoto, TR; Suddeutscher Verlag Bilderdienst, BL. 118 Corbis-Bettmann. 118-19 Brown Brothers. 119 Getty Images, M; Topham Picturepoint, MR. 120 Getty Images, TL; Ullstein Bilderdienst, BR. 121 Ullstein Bilderdienst, TL; Suddeutscher Verlag Bilderdienst, BR. 122 Ullstein Bilderdienst, TR; David King Collection, BL. 123 Novosti, TL, B; David King Collection, MR. 124 David King Collection, TL; Novosti, MR; AKG, BR. 125 AKG, TL; Ullstein Bilderdienst, BR. 126 Ullstein Bilderdienst. 126-7 Topham Picturepoint. 127 Imperial War Museum, TL; Collection-Viollet/Roger-Viollet, MR. 128 Map by Roy Williams; AKG, ML; Meledin Collection/Mary Evans Picture Library, B. 129 Suddeutscher Verlag Bilderdienst. 130 Meledin Collection/Mary Evans Picture Library, TL; Jewgeni Chaldej/AKG, B. 131 Brown Brothers, TR; Topham Picturepoint, ML; Popperfoto, BR. 132 Imperial War Museum, TR; Collection-Viollet/Roger-Viollet, B. 133 Imperial War Museum. 134 Imperial War Museum, M, BL. 135 United States Postal Service, TL; Imperial War Museum, BR. 136 Imperial War Museum, TR, BL. 137 Imperial War Museum, TR, L. 138 Getty Images, L; Imperial War Museum, BR. 139 AKG. 140 Popperfoto, ML; Getty Images, B. 141 David King Collection. 142 Getty Images, TL; Corbis-Bettmann, B. 143 John Frost Historical Newspaper Service, TM; Imperial War Museum, BL; Robert Opie Collection, BR. 144 Jean-Loup Charmet, TM; Imperial War Museum, BL; AKG, MR. 145 Image Library of New South Wales, background; Topham Picturepoint, TL;

Roy Williams; Ullstein Bilderdienst, BR. 146 Mary Evans Picture Library, TR; Ullstein Bilderdienst, MR; AKG, BL. 147 AKG, TR; Culver Pictures, BL; Suddeutscher Verlag Bilderdienst, BR. 148 Topham Picturepoint, TM; Suddeutscher Verlag Bilderdienst, ML; Ullstein Bilderdienst, MR. 148-9 Suddeutscher Verlag Bilderdienst, background. 149 Getty Images, TM; Popperfoto, MR. 150 Robert Opie Collection, TR; Ullstein Bilderdienst, MR; Topham Picturepoint, BL. 151 Imperial War Museum, TL; Culver Pictures, TR; AKG, BR. 152 Topham Picturepoint, TR; Popperfoto, ML. 152-3 AKG, background. 153 AKG, TR, BR; Topham Picturepoint, BL. 154 Black Star, TM; Getty Images, MR; Brown Brothers, BR. 155 Corbis-Bettmann, background; Getty Images, TL; Robert Opie Collection, BR.

Front Cover:
Collection-Viollet/Roger-Viollet, background top; Suddeutscher Verlag Bilderdienst, background bottom; United States Postal Service, L; Imperial War Museum, LM; Robert Opie Collection, RM; Getty Images, R.

Back Cover:
Collection-Viollet/Roger-Viollet, background top; Suddeutscher Verlag Bilderdienst, background bottom; Mary Evans Picture Library, TL; Suddeutscher Verlag Bilderdienst, TR; Getty Images, BL; AKG, BR.

Endpapers: all supplied by John Frost Historical Newspaper Service.

The editors are grateful to the following individuals and publishers for their kind permission to quote passages from the publications listed below:

Chatto & Windus, from The Past is Myself, by Christabel Bielenburg, 1975.
Hamish Hamilton, from Berlin Diary: The Journal of a Foreign Correspondent, 1934-1941, by William L. Shirer, 1942.
HarperCollins, from The Day the War Ended, by Martin Gilbert, 1995.
Harrap, from December 7, 1941: The Day the Japanese Attacked Pearl Harbor, by Gordon W. Prange, 1988
W.W. Norton and Co., New York, from Valley of Darkness: The Japanese People and World War Two, by Thomas R.H. Havens, 1978.
University Press of Kentucky, from Under the Bombs: The German Home Front, 1942-1945, by Earl R. Beck, 1986.
Virago Press, from Winter in the Morning: A Young Girl's Life in the Warsaw Ghetto and Beyond, by Janina Bauman, 1986.